Judith Martens
Doing Things Together

Epistemic Studies

Philosophy of Science, Cognition and Mind

Edited by
Michael Esfeld, Stephan Hartmann, Albert Newen

Editorial Advisory Board:
Katalin Balog, Claus Beisbart, Craig Callender, Tim Crane, Katja Crone,
Ophelia Deroy, Mauro Dorato, Alison Fernandes, Jens Harbecke,
Vera Hoffmann-Kolss, Max Kistler, Beate Krickel, Anna Marmodoro, Alyssa Ney,
Hans Rott, Wolfgang Spohn, Gottfried Vosgerau

Volume 41

Judith Martens
Doing Things Together

A Theory of Skillful Joint Action

DE GRUYTER

ISBN 978-3-11-067017-2
e-ISBN (PDF) 978-3-11-067131-5
e-ISBN (EPUB) 978-3-11-067133-9
ISSN 2512-5168

Library of Congress Control Number: 2020935438

Bibliographic information published by the Deutsche Nationalbibliothek
The Deutsche Nationalbibliothek lists this publication in the Deutsche Nationalbibliografie;
detailed bibliographic data are available on the Internet at http://dnb.dnb.de.

© 2020 Walter de Gruyter GmbH, Berlin/Boston
Typesetting: Integra Software Services Pvt. Ltd.
Printing and binding: CPI books GmbH, Leck

www.degruyter.com

To Bas, Wil & Erna

Contents

1		**Introduction: A Multidimensional Understanding of Acting Together** —— 1
1.1		Doing Things Together —— 1
1.2		A Short Overview of the Collective Intentionality Debate —— 7
1.3		Dancing Together —— 9
1.4		Comparing Examples of Doing Things Together —— 14
1.5		Three Aspects of Joint Action —— 15
1.5.1		Control —— 15
1.5.2		Coordination —— 17
1.5.3		Jointness —— 18
1.6		Overview of the Chapters —— 20
2		**The Automatic/Non-Automatic Divide** —— 21
2.1		Dual-Process Theories —— 23
2.1.1		The Four Features of Automaticity —— 24
2.1.2		Theoretical Development and Gradual Distinctions —— 26
2.2		Separating Non-Automatic and Controlled —— 29
3		**Control and Intentions in Individuals** —— 33
3.1		Control and Mere Activity —— 35
3.1.1		Habitual and Skillful Actions —— 37
3.1.2		Mere Activity —— 38
3.2		Autonomous Agency and Self-Control —— 41
3.3		Diachronicity and Control —— 46
3.4		Synchronic and Diachronic Self-Control —— 47
4		**Motor Control and Skillful Action** —— 51
4.1		Motor Control —— 51
4.1.1		Hierarchical Division of Labor —— 52
4.1.2		Skill Acquisition —— 54
4.2		Skillful Action —— 57
4.2.1		Reasons for Less Automation – Stepping away from the Dichotomy —— 57
4.2.2		Three Levels of Control —— 58
4.3		Degrees of Freedom —— 62
4.3.1		Degrees of Freedom and Skill Acquisition —— 64
4.3.2		Degrees of Freedom in Joint Action —— 65
4.4		Conclusion —— 66

5 Planning Agency and Shared Agency —— 69
- 5.1 Introduction —— 69
- 5.2 Planning Agency —— 75
- 5.2.1 The Methodology of Creature Construction —— 75
- 5.2.2 Eight Steps to Planning Agency – A Creature Construction —— 78
- 5.2.3 Creature Construction of Social and Shared Agency —— 82
- 5.3 Shared Agency —— 85
- 5.3.1 Sufficiency Conditions of Shared Cooperative Activity —— 87
- 5.3.2 I Intend That We J —— 89
- 5.3.3 Two Problems Concerning "I Intend That We J" —— 90
- 5.4 Diachronic and Synchronic Coherence —— 92
- 5.4.1 Synchronic Coherence and Guiding Desires —— 94
- 5.4.2 Coherence through Planning. Too Demanding? —— 95
- 5.5 Policies and Shared Policies —— 97
- 5.5.1 Policies in Planning Agency —— 97
- 5.5.2 Shared Policies —— 99
- 5.6 Cognitive Limitations and Purposive Agency —— 103
- 5.6.1 Bounded Rationality and Planning Agency —— 104
- 5.6.2 Purposive Shared Action —— 107
- 5.7 Control, Autonomy and Agentic Purpose —— 109
- 5.7.1 Agential Direction and Agential Control —— 112
- 5.7.2 Intend That and Intend To —— 115
- 5.8 Conclusion —— 117

6 Joint Action and Interaction —— 121
- 6.1 Emergent Coordination —— 122
- 6.1.1 Mechanisms of Emergent Coordination —— 124
- 6.1.2 Conclusion —— 128
- 6.2 Minimal Architecture Model of Joint Action —— 128
- 6.2.1 Four Modules for Joint Action —— 129
- 6.2.2 Conclusion —— 132
- 6.3 Enactivism, Joint Action, and Control —— 133
- 6.3.1 Autopoiesis —— 134
- 6.3.2 Autopoietic Interaction —— 136
- 6.3.3 An Enactive Approach to Dancing Together —— 141
- 6.3.4 Conclusion —— 145
- 6.4 A Sense of Control and a Sense of Agency in Joint Action —— 146
- 6.4.1 Phenomenological Exploration of the Sense of Us —— 149

6.4.2	The Psychology of the Sense of Agency and the Sense of Us —— 153
6.4.3	Conclusion —— 157

7	**Skillful Joint Action —— 161**
7.1	Introduction —— 161
7.2	Stepping Away from Binary Distinctions —— 162
7.2.1	The Orthodox Binary Distinction —— 163
7.2.2	Mapping the Different Types of Coordination —— 166
7.3	Three Levels of Control and Coordination —— 170
7.3.1	Control —— 170
7.3.2	Three Levels of Coordination and Control —— 173
7.3.3	Expanding Beyond Fast-Paced Skillful Action: NDM and Heuristics —— 176
7.4	Diachronicity, Jointness and the Difference Between Parallel Action and Joint Action —— 179
7.4.1	Diachronicity —— 180
7.4.2	Jointness —— 181
7.4.3	Parallel Action and Joint Action —— 183

References —— 185

Subject Index —— 199

Index of Names —— 205

1 Introduction: A Multidimensional Understanding of Acting Together

1.1 Doing Things Together

In everyday contexts we do numerous things together. We walk together, we cook, eat, and drink together, do chores together, and engage in more complex activities such as building complex machines, work in highly structured organizations, and play in bands and orchestras together. Whether we cycled to work together or by sheer coincidence cycled to work almost at the same time and only a few meters apart, makes a difference in the way we prepare for the cycling, do the cycling, and experience the cycling. What this difference between parallel and joint action consists in is hotly debated. This debate on joint action is shaped by both philosophers and psychologists. Their traditions give them different starting points and different worries, leading to different theories. In recent scholarship, there is a tendency to distinguish between emergent coordination and planned coordination. I will argue that this pushes us to a position of dualism, a strict division between two kinds of joint action, which I deem problematic. Such a push towards two processes or conceptualizations through which to understand joint action has several consequences. For example, certain phenomena become understudied because they do not fit nicely with the distinction. The transition and relation between the "two" kinds of joint action become harder to conceptualize because we formulate the conceptualization of the one in contrast to the other.

The tendency to introduce and use binary distinctions, so I will argue, is not unique to the study of joint action. In fact, in this book I will point at several different binary distinctions, which are all intuitively appealing but fail to give us the tool to conceptualize many everyday phenomena. I will also argue that these binary distinctions relate to one another. The four binary distinctions that I will focus on are:
1. Automatic versus controlled processes
2. Mere bodily movements versus full-blown intentional actions
3. Emergent coordination versus planned coordination
4. Joint action versus parallel action.

These binary distinctions stand in complex relations to one another. Take, for example, distinction 2. The distinction between mere bodily movements and (full-blown) intentional action has a strong relation to whether the process can be controlled by the agent or happens to the agent. Reflexes have often been understood as mere bodily movements. Mere bodily movements are thought to occur automatically and therefore to be out of reach for the agent to control. I will argue, however, that 'automatic' and 'controlled' should not be understood as two opposites: there are processes that can be described as both controlled and automatic. This has an impact on the distinction between mere bodily movements and intentional actions. A similar relation also exists between distinctions 1 and 3, which makes it harder to conceptualize the space between emergent coordination and planned coordination. In all of these cases I will argue that it is a mistake to think about the distinctions as clear-cut dichotomous distinctions. Instead, the two opposites should be understood as ends of spectrums. In the case of the binary distinction between automatic processes and controlled processes, I will also argue that two distinctions are mixed up, namely the spectrum from automatic to non-automatic processes, and that from controlled to not-controlled processes.

A better understanding of the reason why I want to move away from a binary distinction between joint action and parallel action becomes available once we have gone through the first three binary distinctions and their problems. By moving towards more gradual distinctions and multiple factors that weigh into the success of a joint action, we also open up the intermediate space that lies between joint action and parallel action.

I develop two claims: (1) There are several functions that help human agents coordinate, which entails that joint action can be best understood by understanding the differences but also the interrelatedness of these different types of coordination. (2) In order to understand the different forms of coordination and their contribution to join action we need a multidimensional conceptual space. This multidimensional space will allow us to understand the jointness of an action in a more encompassing way.

The notion of control and how it relates to the dichotomy between automatic and non-automatic processes will be central in the book. I argue that the concept of control offers us a possibility to a better, more gradual, understanding of emergent coordination and planned coordination and a richer and more varied understanding of the jointness of our actions. This allows me to step away from the dichotomy between joint action and parallel action. I will use a provisional three-way distinction of levels of control that we find in skillful action (Fridland, 2014; Christensen, Sutton, & McIlwain, 2016; Christensen, Sutton, & Bicknell, 2019).[1]

---

[1] It should already be noted that these levels should not be understood too literally as three highly distinct levels with completely different functionality, or as each level only consisting of one specific capacity. The authors are not committed to such a claim, and neither am I.

These three levels of control provide an understanding of different ways in which we can coordinate our actions, leading to different ways of acting together. Control and coordination are two core elements that I will explore in detail in the second part of the book. A third element, relating to "what it feels like to act together", will also be explored. This element of togetherness or sense of togetherness, I argue, can arise from the different forms of coordination, as well as from situational and historical factors.

When we ask what we mean when we say that a behavior is automatic or a process is automatic, the answer will be different depending on the specific capacity we are interested in. For example: decision-making, language processing, or social cognition. Traditionally, four features were assumed to coincide when a process was said to be automatic (see also chapter two).

Table 1: Following Bargh's (1994) "four horsemen of automaticity".

Automatic	Non-automatic
Absence of (conscious) intention	Intentional
Absence of conscious awareness	Conscious
Uncontrolled (inability to disrupt)	Controlled (ability to disrupt)
Efficient operation (fast and not/hardly needing working memory capacity)	Time consuming and using cognitive resources (slow and consuming working memory capacity)

The four features were thought of as a package deal in which you always get all four together. When a process was said to be automatic this implied, for example, that it also was unintentional and effortless. Studies have shown, however, that the four different features can be dissociated, creating problems for the traditional view (Bargh, 1994; Moors & De Houwer, 2006, 2007). Some processes can be characterized as efficient and intentional, and that would mean they are both automatic *and* non-automatic. This requires us to be more specific when we talk about whether, and in what sense, something is automatic. A process that is said to be automatic could be further described as either efficient, unconscious, non-intentional, uncontrolled, or any combination of these features. Moreover, when studying these four features, it seems that at least some of them are better understood as polar oppositions rather than as exclusive dichotomies. Take for example the feature "awareness": it might be that we are aware to some extent without all of our attention focusing on a certain process, or we might become aware of something we are doing after some time. The dissociation of the different features of the package deal and the gradual understanding of some of the individual features render inadequate the traditional, dichotomous model (automatic/non-automatic) for covering many phenomena we encounter on a day to day basis. The perniciousness of this model can only be explained by its intuitive appeal. Chapter two will give an overview of the different features that we typically associate with automatic processes, providing reasons to adopt a model where the distinction between automaticity and non-automaticity is understood through a multidimensional space with several features. Secondly, it will lead us to a model where these features of automaticity are partly understood as gradual. Overall, this will allow us to move away from a strong form of dualism and create room for phenomena that combine automatic and non-automatic processes or are best described as in-between either categorization.

Of the four features of (non-)automaticity I will focus specifically on intentions and control (chapter three). Philosophers of action and joint action have tried to conceptualize the (joint) action through an understanding of the intention(s) involved. There is an important distinction to be made between control as a more biological notion and control as a normative, agentic notion. The latter is often thought to have an intimate relation with intentions, whereas this is not necessarily true for the first. After arguing that the binary distinction between automatic and non-automatic causes a gap in our conceptual tools for analyzing the middle ground, I will turn to current developments in the debate of skill acquisition and skillful action. Our understanding of the notion of control has implications for the way we can think about joint action (chapters five and six). At the same time, the way in which emergent coordination is spelled out in psychology also bears implications for our philosophical discussion of control and agency.

Chapter three will briefly report on the distinction between intentional and unintentional bodily movement. This distinction appears at first to be a dichotomy. I will point at a discussion where "intermediate" phenomena are said to cause problems for this dichotomy and review some proposals to conceptualize this intermediate category. The result will be a first conceptualization of the space in between, which can later be used to define such a space for cases of joint action. *If* such an intermediate category makes sense, or if we should think about intentional/unintentional as a gradual distinction, then we most likely also act together on such "intermediate actions" and we need an adequate theory on how this could work and what consequences this has for our theories. The idea of an intermediate space will be further developed in chapter four, where I focus on recently developed accounts of skillful action. Current views in the debate in skill acquisition and skillful action might give us an understanding of the intermediate level, as well as a way to integrate the different levels. Moving from being a novice to an expert was long thought to reflect a move from reflective action to automatic action. This is much in line with the discussion on automaticity, following the idea that a process is either automatic or non-automatic. We now have data that suggests that this picture is inaccurate. Several recent proposals distinguish three "levels" of control, with different degrees of automation (Pacherie, 2008; Fridland, 2014; Christensen, Sutton, & McIlwain, 2016; Christensen, Sutton, & Bicknell, 2019). In order to see the richness of this proposal, I will first discuss current proposals that are (but should not be, as I argue) conceptualized as two distinct ways of understanding how we can act jointly.

In my review of Bratman's influential theory of planned coordination (chapter five) and the four most developed current theories of emergent coordination (chapter six), I will stick, at first, to this binary picture, although I will also point at parts in these proposals that actually show the openness and the need for a richer spectrum. I do so by linking the discussion on three levels of control and the proposal of functions that allow us to act jointly, also proposing a threefold distinction of coordination.

With all this material in hand, we will be well equipped to discuss the overarching binary distinction between parallel and joint action. Philosophers of collective intentionality have wondered how we can distinguish parallel cases from cases where we act together. Often their theories argue in favor of *one* characteristic, feature, or process that differentiates the two. An often-found methodology in the debate in collective intentionality is the use of examples as a way of specifying the subject, where we use sets of contrasting cases that point at distinctions.[2] The examples in collective intentionality debates distinguish parallel actions from joint action. Consider the following key examples (Table 2):

Table 2: Archetypical examples of collective intentionality.

Walking together versus walking in parallel	Margaret Gilbert
Painting a house together versus painting in parallel	Michael Bratman
A corps de ballet that runs to a shelter together versus some people in a park that run to the shelter (in parallel) as it starts to rain	John Searle

---

2 I thank Stephen Butterfill for bringing this to my attention.

One of the problems with contrasting cases, is that it is unclear how we should generalize from such examples. Another problem is the potential dualism lurking in the background, enticing us to see the distinction as a hard distinction.

Take the example of someone walking down a crowded street. On her way she passes several others. Most of them she passes without much difficulty, their paths are not crossing and there is no need for any sort of coordination. With others she might need some coordination, some interaction, to prevent a collision. One question that arises here is whether we would want to call this type of coordination joint action. Consider what happens when a collision seems imminent and, while figuring out how to pass each other they sway left and right several times, exactly mirroring each other, making it impossible to pass one another. They have a quick laugh, exchange a few words and finally coordinate to get past each other. Is this coordination while acting in parallel or coordination in joint action? Where do we draw the boundary between the two? In cases like this, it might not make sense to make such a strong distinction. And it seems to me many situations are like this.

There are many elements that we can point to that might play a role while we act with others. Take for example collective goals, coordination, cooperation, contralateral commitments, experience, and interdependence. Many of these elements can be brought about in several ways. Rather than presenting two instances of an activity, once joint and once in parallel, I propose to consider many versions of the same phenomenon, which give us a further understanding of the phenomena in the space of joint action. I will do this with the example of dancing together. I plea in favor of a richer understanding of "doing things together", in which several (gradual) features relate to multiple dimensions of the joint action. This will help in understanding the richness of different forms of coordination and create room to understand their relation. Dancing together illustrates such a complex case of joint action.

Bratman, Searle, and Gilbert all introduce a way to conceptualize the joint case. They do so by specifying something (X), such as a joint commitment (Gilbert), a we-intention (Searle), or the meshing of individual intentions (Bratman). This X then distinguishes the joint case from the parallel case. But with this X many other things are also given or need to be spelled out. For example, Searle's *corps de ballet* does not form its we-intention on the spot but rather presupposes a whole set of other thoughts, beliefs, and situational factors that allow them to do so. Bratman's example of a pair painting a house also requires many background conditions in place and is thought to be a team that exists over time. And the pedestrians in Gilbert's example probably share a history that makes it comprehensible that they are walking together towards a shared goal. Picking out *one* thing (a shared intention) seems wrong in the sense that this one thing can *only* be understood in a wider understanding of the situation. Assuming that the rest is "given" with this intention seems to be something that at least has to be shown.

1.2 A Short Overview of the Collective Intentionality Debate

Joint action is but one form of collective intentionality. Contributions in the field of collective intentionality that try to understand what makes two or more agents act together, as distinguished from their acting parallel but isolated, are mainly developed into three general directions, all taking their inspiration from the analysis of intentionality and propositional attitudes.[3] A propositional attitude consists of a subject, a mode, and content.[4] Each of these structural elements have been used in accounts of collective intentionality in order to situate a form of collectivity.

Collective intentionality is the power of minds (or systems) to be jointly directed at objects, matters of fact, states of affairs, goals, or values. Collective intentionality comes in a variety of modes, including shared intention, joint attention, shared belief, collective acceptance, and collective emotion. The discussion about collective intentionality concerns above all collective intentions in situations of simple or modest sociality. Let me say a few words about these two restrictions. I start with the last one. Modest sociality refers by and large to acting together of only a few agents, in situations without grave inequalities (no hierarchies, corporations, etc.). The choice for these situations has methodological backgrounds: they are relatively simple to describe and argued to be the nucleus of all sociality. Whether this is really the case, and how far and by what further means concepts for these situations can be made useful for a description of more complex social phenomena, are questions that have received some attention (Baier, 1997; Stoutland, 1997; Velleman, 1997; Tollefsen, 2015). The concentration of efforts on collective intentions means that the focus of theorizing is on one form of collective intentionality. Collective intentionality also entails phenomena like collective meanings, beliefs, values, culture and rules. Why concentrate on collective intentions? Collective intentions seem to be both a central and a highly problematic category. They are seen as central, because the other kinds of collective intentionality seem to be arranged around this category that directly concerns the coordination of co-operative actions.

---

[3] Schweikard & Schmid, 2013.
[4] In the debate on collective intentionality the concepts 'object' and 'content' are often used interchangeably. I am aware of the difference, but it is of no relevance here.

Collective intention is also a contested notion, as it is doubtful that there is more than ascription of attitudes to groups, which would probably make collective intentions impossible, or requires a collective mind (which most find inacceptable). This can be captured by the idea that collective intentions are just the sum of individual intentions and nothing more. This leads to a first important distinction between summative and non-summative accounts (Gilbert, 1987; Tollefsen, 2015). A summative account holds that we can analyze group attitude ascriptions in terms of the sum of individual attitudes with the same content as that ascribed to the group (Gilbert, 1987). Non-summative accounts argue that collective intentionality is more than the sum of individual attitudes. Within the category of non-summative accounts there are three main positions, which I will briefly discuss here. They are connected to the earlier mentioned structure of propositional attitudes.

The content account that is worked out in most detail, is Bratman's account of shared agency. Bratman's theory on planning agency and meshing intentions is a content account: it is the content of the intention that makes it the case that the intention is shared (Bratman, 1999, chapters 5–8; 2014). On Bratman's account, intentions take the form "I intend that we J". His theory is one of the main theories of collective intentionality, also focusing on collective intentions (or shared intentions as he calls them). The main idea is that the intentions of multiple agents are meshing. Bratman provides an individualistic account of collective intentionality and shared agency that is highly dependent on common knowledge.

On a mode account, individuals share an intention in case they each intend a joint action collectively. Formally this can be represented as "I we-intend X", or "I we-intend that we X". Searle's theory of collective intentionality proposes a version of the mode-account of collective intentionality, where the individual subject has a we-attitude (is in a we-mode) towards the object: "I *we-intend* to X". This description differs from subject-accounts, in which the subject is understood as a collective: "*we* intend to X". It is also different from object-accounts in which the individual is directed at a collective object: "I intend *that we* X". Another version of the mode account comes from Tuomela (2007). Tuomela (2007) suggests that we distinguish between (different strengths of) I-mode and we-mode. In I-mode an individual is having an attitude "as a private person" and in we-mode the agent has it "as a group member" (cf. Tuomela, 2007, p. 46). Searle has criticized Tuomela and Miller's account (Tuomela, 1999; Tuomela & Miller, 1988) because they would reduce collective intentions to individual intentions plus beliefs (Searle, 1990). Searle, instead, is committed to a non-reductionist account. Given Searle's commitment to the possibility of a brain in a vat to have the capacity for we-intentions, his account has likewise been criticized.

The third main option is that intentionality has a subject, that is, an entity different from the individual subject(s) whose intentionality it is, and to whom it can be ascribed as its source or bearer. One influential account is Margaret Gilbert's plural subject theory (Gilbert, 1989, 2006, 2009, 1990). Gilbert analyses collective intentionality in terms of joint commitments. In her example of walking together, the activity requires that they take on what she calls a "joint commitment" to walk together. A joint commitment can only be brought about or interrupted jointly. A number of criticisms have been put forth against Gilbert's plural subject theory. A major critique lies in the potential circularity. It seems that the formation of a joint commitment already presupposes the sort of joint action by a plural subject it is meant to bring about.

Of these different positions Bratman's content account of collective intentionality will be the main focus in this book. Not only is Bratman's theory of shared agency one of the main and most developed theories in the debate, it is also grounded in a fully developed theory of individual agency. The problems in the debate on joint action that this book analyses are dependent on the understanding of individual agency and shared agency. Bratman's theory, which discusses both extensively, is therefore a good candidate for analysis.

The following section will look at dancing together as an example of acting together. The example, which is alluded to in Bratman's theory (and many others, e.g., Searle, 1990; Vesper, Butterfill, Knoblich, & Sebanz, 2010; Knoblich, Butterfill, & Sebanz, 2011; Tollefsen & Dale, 2012), illustrates the purpose of my project well.

1.3 Dancing Together

I discuss ballroom dancing for two reasons. First of all, it already is a beloved example that has been used in the debate about joint action (i.e., Bratman, 2014; Gilbert, 2006, 2009; Vesper, Butterfill, Knoblich, & Sebanz, 2010; Tollefsen & Dale, 2012). Dancing together is an excellent example because it contains so many different aspects of human cognition and action. Secondly, having been a performing ballroom dancer and teacher myself, I can draw on experience to elucidate my theoretical account of joint action. Ballroom dancing shows that we cannot dance together based only on either only emergent coordination or planned coordination alone.[5] Furthermore, it shows that we sometimes have to

---

5 This would imply that Bratman's sufficient conditions for shared agency are insufficient.

make decisions on the spot, decisions that are not adequately described by theories such as Bratman's theory of planning agency and shared agency.

In the end, I will get back to the three main concepts based on the dancing example: What can we say about *togetherness*? How does the dancing couple *coordinate*? And what does this tell us about *control*?

At first glance it seems that dancing together can be done in two ways: through improvisation and by following a choreography. As we will see, such pure cases hardly ever exist. When a couple is improvising they will most likely depend on certain standard combinations, which could be understood as vocabulary, but also as mini-choreographies. Performing such mini-choreographies will be more likely after some problems arise. A basic, predictable, step in between can stabilize the connection and hold, creating room for more complex variations. Were a couple to follow a choreography, there are moments where they find themselves in need to (slightly) adjust their steps, stop dancing or improvise because another couple is blocking the floor. Furthermore, sometimes the couple might use the choreography, but in a slightly different direction, with a slight delay, or with smaller steps. Even if all goes well, and no other couple stands in the way to a glorious finish of the planned choreography, the dancers might find that the music might alter this particular waltz performance from the last one while the couple tries to keep everything the same. A dance couple has to communicate a lot and often needs to act shortly after or during such communication. As these examples make clear, it might be hard to draw a clear distinction between improvisation and following a choreography. A point that complements the idea that it might be hard to act merely on emergent coordination or planned coordination.

Ballroom dancing comes with technique and with rules that allow partners to communicate, or interactively determine, what they will do (Moore, 2002). The leader will signal the speed, length, and direction of the steps, but the follower will respond to this and will indicate whether it matches her possibilities, ideas, and the perspective she has onto the floor.[6] The length, direction, and speed of a step, the sway of the body, and so on will be communicated by the direction of the feet, the bending of the knees, torsion of specific body parts, etc. In principle, the leader communicates, or starts, the direction of the steps. Together with the amount of lowering (how much one bends the knees) the leader can indicate the length and speed of the movements. While the leader is lowering

---

[6] In the basic, hold both stand opposite one another and look to their left, which means that their visual fields will be different.

the follower will also lower simultaneously, the direct mirroring[7] or changes in mirroring will tell the leader what the follower is intending to do.[8] Together the couple determines how much they bend their knees and with that how large the following step will be. By reacting to, and adjusting what the leader suggests, the follower is responsible for the direction, speed, and length of the steps too.

In the ordinary case of two people dancing together there seems to be an interesting combination of pre-designed choreographies, a backdrop of rules and norms, on the spot corrections and improvisation based on the local situation or due to (previous) mistakes. The choreography could be understood as a top-down structure, however embodied it is understood, where the improvisation will be partly dependent on the current situation and the possibilities and limitations that arise from it. To sum up: Even when we accept that dancing is preceded by a planning process, and that this planning has a tremendous impact on the actions that the couple performs, this cannot explain the entire sequence of (the coordination of the) actions. For Bratman, the elements of the execution are rather categorized as enabling conditions. I argue that – at least in some cases – they are part of the sufficiency conditions.

It also cannot be merely emergent coordination that allows a couple to dance together.[9] The specific situation will be too open to specify what will happen merely based on coupling, synchrony and alignment.[10] Even emergent

---

[7] I am using mirroring in a pre-theoretical sense here, although it certainly has links to mirroring in paradigms of emergent coordination, including synchrony and alignment.
[8] As stated before, this analysis is mainly focused on ballroom dancing. There seems to be an interesting difference between ballroom dancing and other forms of dancing with a partner regarding the amount of predetermination of the steps and roles (follower, leader). Presumably contact improvisation being the freest form, with the least rules and less strict ideas about esthetics. However, also in contact improvisation these are certain rules that are followed. For example, the dancers always remain in contact. Another rule the dancers seem to follow, that seems important in dancing in general, is to not repeat the same movements endlessly. It is both boring for the dancers and for a potential audience. Thirdly, contact improvisers will often lean on or support the other dancer. As soon as the first partner is leaning in the second dancer has to provide some push back, or stability. Hence, although the clear leader/follower roles are not necessarily present, there are still roles to follow. However, this does not seem to pose a problem. If anything, these cases would be even cleaner cases of co-determining and joint action, but given my experience with ballroom dancing I will have that as the main example.
[9] Emergent coordination will be discussed in more detail in section 6.1.
[10] As I pointed out before, another big chunk of the literature on joint action in psychology and cognitive science is focused on emergent coordination, which typically focuses on mimicking and synchronizing through alignment, entrainment, and joint affordances. I will discuss these approaches in more detail in chapter six.

coordination constrained by the rules of ballroom dancing will not give the leader and follower the steps. Leaders often have to make a number of on the spot decisions that are not dictated by the situation and the coordination that emerges from the situation.

I argue that – even combined – planned coordination and emergent coordination still seem to be unable to provide a full account of joint action, partially because (combined) they do not always provide the couple with a final decision regarding their course of action, especially in cases of (non-choreographed) complementary actions and on the spot decisions.[11]

In those cases where the leader bends the knees and the follower bends them just as much we might be able to talk about alignment and entrainment. The same goes for the torsion that is applied to the bodies. Most of the time the leader and follower will have the same amount of torsion, thereby ensuring that both will make a step in the same direction. It is not merely the case that the leader decides, and the follower follows. The leader will closely monitor the direct responsiveness of the follower as the action develops over time. If either follower or leader slows down or stops the movement, this will directly impact the movement that they are currently making. In this way the couple can ensure that they bend their knees simultaneously and similarly. There is *mutual* adjustment and *mutual* alignment. They allow them to determine interactively how much they bend their knees. Hence, it is not the case that one person decides and the other merely follows. Furthermore, there are also moments where a dancer is required to make a complementary movement. For example, when the leader makes room for the follower to change her bodily position (going from a standard position to a promenade position, or to a line figure, see Figure 1) the actions are complementary, and not mimicked. These are often-occurring movements in ballroom dancing, also in the case of improvisation. The distinction between mimicking the amount of torsion and reacting by a complementary action are dependent on further situational factors and interpretation on both sides.

To illustrate "on the spot" decision-making it is helpful to consider the moment when another couple is in the way and the two dancers have to improvise. They will have to deviate from their choreography. Will they perform the steps, but with smaller movement? Or will they stop for a moment? Or change direction and improvise? As it will turn out, emergent coordination will not be sufficient to

---

[11] I use the concept of making a decision quite loosely here. It implies a certain amount of flexibility, rather than deliberation.

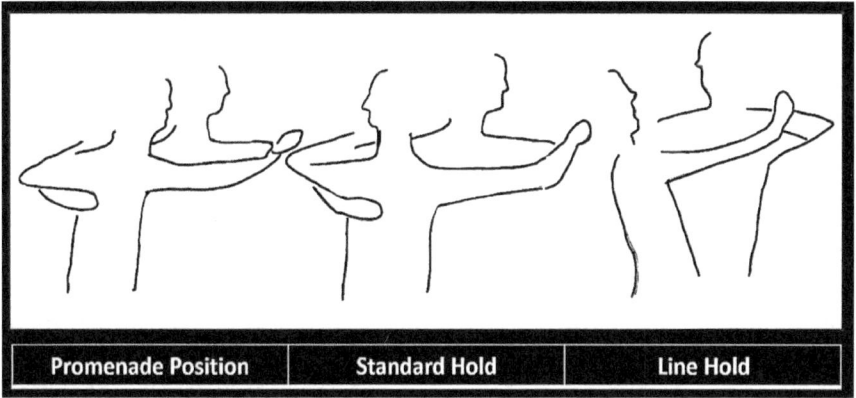

Figure 1: Dancing positions (drawing by me).

solve the puzzle of what to do next. In itself it does not give sufficient coordination for a couple to decide what to do next. A decision[12] has to be made about what the two dancers will do as a couple. Professional ballroom dancers will have hours of training, where they will also practice the skill of diverting from the choreography. There are several situational factors that are important for such improvisation that a couple will take into consideration when deciding what will be done next. Some of them are: (1) What directions (space) can they go? Is there a place between the other couples? (2) What directions does our current body position(s) allow us to go? (3) What moment in the music do we find ourselves in? (4) What is our position on the dance floor? (5) How and where can we pick up the choreography again? (6) What did we just dance? We do not want to be too repetitive.

To conclude, there seem to be (at least) three organizing structures of dancing together; (1) the (planned) choreography, (2) the (heuristic, skillful) ad-hoc improvisation, and (3) the emergent coordination as we perform the choreography/improvisation (on this specific floor, with this specific music, the couple we just met on the floor and (therefore) the last movement turned out slightly different than planned). Both the choreography and the improvisation will be dependent on the situational specificities and the awareness of such specificities by one or both of the dancers (the floor size and quality), the position of other couples, the strength and quality of the couples hold (and probably more). This goes against the idea that dancing together can be captured by one

---

12 At this point I am still very non-committal regarding the notion of a decision.

single function or interrelated intention. While dancing, a sense of jointness seems to be partly present due to the intention to dance together. Such an intention can be assumed to be formed before the couple dances. But the sense of us doing something together will be influenced by the actual performance, the smoothness of the coordination and the moves based on the bodily communication during the dance.

Regarding the relation between being in control of one's action and the fact that two people seem to be in control I would like to point at a distinction that I will further discuss in chapter three. regarding the difference between taking the initiative and being in control. Velleman (1997) noted that there seem to be "too many chiefs and too few Indians" in most accounts of collective intentionality. His remark draws on a distinction by Baier (1997) between intentionally starting something and intentionally continuing something. Especially in the joint case it seems that the latter option, where one continues something intentionally, might help us understand how we can both be in control while not necessarily have the traditional causal structure of intentional action in place.

1.4 Comparing Examples of Doing Things Together

As should have become clear, the example of dancing together is too complex to capture with "just one relation" or one type of coordination between the agents. I want to emphasize two points before I conclude the introduction with an overview of the three aspects of joint action that I will study in greater detail.

First of all, I do not think that my example should be understood differently from the examples by Gilbert, Bratman, or Searle. If we spell out all the details of the situations they describe, we will soon find that there are many factors that are not captured by their characterization of joint action. In the same way that a dancing couple cannot dance without music, we usually also follow a path when we are walking together.

Secondly, it seems that apart from the situation many more factors have to be in place. Take Bratman's example of painting a house together. The example only functions because there are many situational factors that help the agents structure their joint action. Maybe the example that Bratman uses can be described equally rich indeed. The same kind of adaptations that we find in the dancing couple seem to happen in painting a house. Imagine a couple of house painters, who are working for years together. There will be skilled professionalism between the two. Maybe the agents need *planned agency* for quite a while to let "the bodies take over", to grow the joint coordination on multiple levels.

But in such a case the two agents that are painting a house together are also doing this in a way that looks more like habitual or skillful cooperation. And in the case of Searle's *corps the ballet* that is running towards shelter, there is not only a we-intention, but the members of a group that know themselves to be members of this specific group, and they all have had a very specific training and have knowledge about the other group members to have access to similar information. One way to explain the difference between Bratman's proposal and my proposal would be to argue that his theory emphasizes *occasional* joint actions, whereas I focus on ingrained "joint skills and habits", or skillful joint action. Bratman's planning agency would then describe the earlier stages of two agents working together. And in those cases, it will still be an incomplete approach at that. I take it that many of our joint actions are more like joint skills and habits, and that we would therefore gain important conceptual tools with my approach. My approach is not merely a combination of emergent coordination and planned coordination. Emergent coordination seems too weak, local and fragile to serve for this kind of "joint skill and habit".

1.5 Three Aspects of Joint Action

In this last subsection of the introduction I will continue to spell out the three most important elements for this project: control, coordination, and togetherness. Together they will allow us to better understand the entire playfield of joint action, or so I will argue.

1.5.1 Control

In our daily lives we rely heavily on our capacity to control and rule our behavior. We make decisions and act on these decisions. Our capacity to control our behavior is intrinsically linked with the idea of responsibility for our failures and successes. Such an understanding is particularly needed against the background of recent developments in the behavioral-, cognitive-, and neurosciences that suggest that there is no such thing as behavioral control and that desires, beliefs, or intentions have no impact on what people do (Horstkötter, 2015). Instead, it is suggested, human behavior is often – if not always – caused outside of people's awareness and is the result of diverse and complex unconscious and automatic processes which are generated by various features of people's environment. Anything people do is the result of diverse and complex unconscious and automatic processes generated by various features in people's environments

(Bargh & Chartrand, 1999; Hassin, Uleman, & Bargh, 2005; Wegner, 2004; Wegner & Wheatley, 1999). I will follow Horstkötter (2015) and Fujita and colleagues (2014) in their suggestion that the facts about automatic behavior that are studied by social psychologists do not rule out controlled forms of behavior.

The idea that automaticity and control are mutually exclusive depends on the assumption that they are opposites. Phenomenologically, this opposition may seem natural, but upon closer inspection it becomes clear that this conceptualization leads to many problems. By dissolving this opposition, we create space for the possibility of automatic yet controlled actions.

This book uses literature from different disciplines. In some cases this leads to confusion for the simple reason that the vocabulary that is used overlaps, while sometimes the concepts diverge. First of all, I think it is important to note that when philosophers talk about action, their conception of it is intrinsically linked with the concept of intention. These intentions can be understood within a more or less rationalistic framework, and in both cases the two go together. When psychologists study joint action they are often focused on coordination between two (or more) agents and the mechanisms or functions that allow agents to coordinate. These mechanisms are often sub-personal, highly automatic, and not introspectable. The target phenomenon, however, is joint *action*. From a philosophical perspective, such coordination might fall onto the spectrum of bodily movement, with no commitment to whether these movements should be considered actions or mere bodily movements.

The distinction between the interests of philosophers and psychologists is reflected in the tendency to talk about collective intentionality in philosophy and about joint action in psychology. Yet this shared interest often leads to confusion, since most philosophers have rich conceptions of action that are not often shared by psychologists.

This potential for confusion repeats when philosophers and psychologists are conceptualizing the notion of control in action and joint action. When psychologists conceptualize control 1) this is coupled to the notion of automaticity or even seen as the opposite of automaticity, and 2) in the joint action debate they mainly look for structuring or coordinating factors, which may be fully subpersonal and non-introspectable. When philosophers mention control, they usually think about *self*-control. Such a notion is more intricately linked to agency and normativity (e.g., Bratman, 1987, 2000, 2007; Frankfurt, 1988; Horstkötter, 2015; Velleman, 2000). The notion, as we find it in a major part of the current philosophical debate, will be further discussed in chapter three, where I will also compare it to the notion as found in psychology.

A closer look at the relation between intentions and control, based on literature from psychology with a focus on dual-process theories and skillful actions, can help us look at different ways in which human agents react, respond, and take control. In chapter four I will review recent literature on skill acquisition and skillful action. Recent accounts of skillful action introduce three levels of control. I will argue in chapter seven that this distinction can be usefully applied to cases of joint action and that it can be translated to three "levels" of joint coordination. This will help us step away from the dualism that I will describe in chapters two and three.

1.5.2 Coordination

Experimental studies of joint action focus on various kinds of synchrony amongst actors such as whether two people who have just met will walk "in step" with each other (Knoblich, Butterfill, & Sebanz, 2011; Miles, Nind, & Macrae, 2009; Oullier, Guzman, Jantzen, Lagarde, & Kelso, 2008; Schmidt & O'Brien, 1997; Shockley, Baker, Richardson, & Fowler, 2007; Tollefsen & Dale, 2012; Wiltermuth & Heath, 2009). There is evidence both that joint motives enhance certain kinds of bodily synchrony and that bodily synchrony promotes the achievement of jointly held goals. In general, this is assumed to increase coordination.

The lower-level processes that allow for this type of coordination are those that are not immediately, easily or perhaps ever possible to be introspected. They include gestural, bodily, and movement-based forms of information-sharing and cueing. Often these processes are described as implicit and non-deliberative. Empirical research into synchronization and alignment has shown that people are influenced by, imitate and align with others in social interaction. This happens on many levels, such as eye movements, speech patterns, and bodily movement. On all these levels such influences are hardly, if at all, noticeable and almost impossible to avoid.

Philosophical theories of joint action, on the other hand, focus on intentions, plans, commitments, and common knowledge. It is assumed that agents can at least in principle be aware of these attitudes. Often the emergent coordination is seen as "filling in the details" (Bratman, 2014) or delivering enabling conditions (Zahavi, 2015), rather than as an essential part of the interpersonal coordination and jointness of the action.

Some of the processes that fall under the description of emergent coordination do offer us means to control and influence the interaction. They might not be full-blown intentional actions, but certainly not mere automatic responses either. I want to argue that separating the different phenomena into two strictly independent fields, following the distinction between automatic and controlled that I introduce prior to the discussion of coordination, causes a hole in our conceptual framework, making it impossible to capture the intermediate type of coordination, which for now I will preliminary classify as highly automatic yet intentional.

Apart from this dualistic thinking that traps us into a limited understanding of joint action, there is one further issue. Although psychologists seem more open to the idea that there is a multiplicity of ways to act jointly, philosophers are more concerned with specifying *one* aspect or one set of necessary or sufficient conditions that makes actions joint. By setting up the debate as such, philosophers fail to recognize the interdependence of the different levels of coordination. Based on the three levels of control I will introduce three levels of coordination, understanding them in a highly integrated way. The three integrated levels of coordination allow us skillful joint actions.

1.5.3 Jointness

The last feature, the jointness or togetherness that the involved agents experience, connects to the three levels of coordination, but is more encompassing than that.

People do things together, but there are different layers of "together"-ness. Sometimes people work together based on an explicit shared intention; sometimes they operate as members of an organization with explicit rules for determining collective policies. But both of these are demanding to establish and maintain, and much of social life is not really covered by either model. On the other hand, sometimes people "do things together" simply in the sense that the individual things they do add up to a total effect, without anybody intending this. In the former cases ("joint action" and "group action") it makes sense to speak of collective agency; in the latter case ("aggregate action") the individual actions add up in a non-agential way.

But there is also an intermediate layer, where people's actions seem to coordinate and interlock without an explicit plan, but with something like an implicit goal (Martens & Roelofs, 2018). This sort of case (which I call "implicit coordination") is not well-covered by the existing literature: it is not quite joint action (as discussed by, e.g., Bratman, 1993, 2014; Gilbert, 1990), and not quite group action (as discussed by List & Pettit, 2011); but it is more agential than merely aggregate action (Chant, 2007). Moreover, although there has been discussion of "emergent coordination" and other sorts of less-explicit coordination (Knoblich, Butterfill, & Sebanz, 2011; Lakin, Jefferis, Cheng, & Chartrand, 2003; Pacherie, 2013) such conceptualizations have focused on highly automatic mechanisms of coordination that usually operate in small-scale, face-to-face contexts, not in large-scale social phenomena. In this book I aim to take the first steps towards rectifying this deficiency.

The point I will make is twofold. First of all, it seems like there is something between "aggregate" and "joint", as well as between "parallel" and "joint", where we still want to say that the agents act together to some extent. Implicit coordination is, so I will argue, a way to understand such in-between cases. The feeling of togetherness, and the primacy of it for our understanding of joint action and collective intentionality, has a rich history in phenomenology. Recently, Schmid and Zahavi have published on the matter, relating to Searle's notion of the sense of us, a primitive notion of a feeling of togetherness (Schmid, 2014; Zahavi, 2015). Searle's seminal 1990 article "Collective Intentions and Actions", argued for the possibility of individuals having we-intentions. He introduced the sense of the other and the sense of us as conditions for we-intentions. The sense of the other and the sense of us are part of what he calls the *Background*,[13] a set of capacities that make collective intentions possible. Although both concepts play an important role in his theoretical framework, Searle has never provided a clear account of both senses and they remain notoriously vague, just as his important but under-discussed and explored notion of "the Background" (Martens, 2018; Martens & Schlicht, 2018; Schmid, 2014; Tollefsen & Dale, 2012; Zahavi, 2015).

Several authors have written about Searle's ideas on the background capacities that are presupposed for collective intentions, trying to clarify and work out parts of his background assumptions (Bacharach, 2006; Schmid, 2014; Tollefsen & Dale, 2012; Zahavi, 2015).[14] My aim is to introduce a picture of how the notion of a sense of *us* can (1) contribute to our understanding of the perception of possibilities for joint action, (2) how individuals can come to experience them as shared, even if they lack common knowledge, and (3) how this relates to control through a sense of we-agency. At least a major part of these three points function implicitly, evoking a sense of us in the agents involved. This sense of us depends on multiple factors, all feeding into the (potential) jointness of an action and shared goals, a thesis I will further defend and elaborate on in chapter five.

---

13 Searle's Background is, as I will discuss in section 6.4, a highly problematic notion.
14 These authors discuss either the sense of the other or the sense of us, and relate one of them to we-intentions, ignoring or neglecting the other sense of (x). As of yet, scholars have not focused on the relation between these two "senses" of our relatedness to one another.

1.6 Overview of the Chapters

To get to the idea of three levels of coordination and a multi-dimensional understanding of joint action I will have to start with some of the conceptions of individual agency. Chapter two discusses the intuitive, yet problematic, binary distinction between automatic and non-automatic processes. It ends with a proposal for a more gradual understanding of several of the features of automaticity and argues that we should understand the concept as describing a multidimensional space. It will further pull apart the two notions non-automatic and controlled, which have often been equated, opening up the possibility for processes that are controlled and automatic. From there I will move to the notion of control and self-control and its relation to agency in chapter three. The chapter starts with the traditional binary distinction between full-blown intentional actions and mere bodily movements. I will discuss a few proposals to understand the intermediate space that cannot be captured well with this strongly dichotomous picture and relate this to our notion of self-control, mainly following the tradition in which Bratman has been working. Chapter four will focus on motor control and theories that are closely related to findings in cognitive science. The main focus will be on skill acquisition and skillful action, looking at the way in which skillful agents control their actions. Here I will introduce three levels of control. That will conclude the chapters on individual agency.

Chapter five will discuss Bratman's theory of shared agency. However, much of Bratman's understanding of individual agents, as well as his methodology, inform his theory of shared agency. In order for my proposal to make sense, I will have to discuss some of the details of this part of his work because the proposal for three levels of coordination that I will make in the final chapter relates to the capacities of individual agents that are underexposed in Bratman's theory. Chapter six discusses four main theories in joint action that are more minimal than Bratman's proposal and which rely heavily on research in cognitive science and psychology. In choosing to discuss the material in this way, I at first also follow the binary distinction between planned coordination and emergent coordination. By the end of chapter six, however, it will be clear that this dichotomy compromises our understanding of all of these proposals. Chapter seven will sketch a threefold distinction between levels of coordination, creating room to understand the intermediate level.

2 The Automatic/Non-Automatic Divide

In this chapter the binary distinction between automatic and non-automatic processes takes central stage. Phenomenologically, the opposition of controlled and automatic behavior may seem natural: food is digested automatically, but eating involves the agent selecting food, using a spoon and fork, attending how much and what she is eating; a practiced driver changes gears and steers automatically, while a learner is attentive and thinks about every movement. Against our intuitions, however, these examples do not prove that evidence in support of automaticity rules out evidence in favor of control and self-control (Horstkötter, 2015). This intuitive appeal, so I believe, also relates to some of the conceptual work the distinction can do for us. The danger lies in forgetting that the distinction also bears some problematic aspects. Therefore, overall, it might be argued that it is better to step away from using the binary distinction, or at least be very careful and specific when using it (Moors, 2014; Moors & De Houwer, 2006, 2007). I agree with this movement away from a clear dichotomy and will discuss some of the details that have led to this change in our understanding of the distinction between automatic and non-automatic processes and behaviors. This chapter is mainly meant as a foundation of some of the points I want to make later in the book. When we step away from a clear binary distinction between automatic and non-automatic this has consequences for our theory of action and therefore also for our theory of shared agency. It opens up the space to think about the intermediate space of joint actions, allowing for skillful joint actions in particular, and a richer understanding of joint actions in general.

When looking at discussions about the distinction between automatic and non-automatic processes, main authors, such as Bargh (1994) describe the distinction as being between automatic and controlled. Horstkötter has pointed out a conceptual problem with the way self-control is treated in automaticity theory. Self-control refers to both causal processes and normative requirements, but scholars in automaticity theory overlook that their work only takes the causal dimension into account, not the normative requirements. Claims regarding the absence of control are usually directed at the causal aspects of the debate, but this cannot disprove the reality of self-control. This confusion partially comes from the distinction that philosophers make between control and self-control, with a strong relation between agency and self-control. Unlike philosophers, who are generally more interested in normative, agentic concepts of control, researchers in social psychology and cognitive science tend to be more interested in cognitive mechanisms and psychological functions. Interdisciplinary research risks resulting in increased confusion when this divergence of approaches is not spelled out clearly, as is, unfortunately, often the case. As Horstkötter has pointed out:

> Self-control is a hybrid term, referring both to causal processes and normative requirements. Claims regarding automaticity, however, are merely targeting causal processes and hence, even if true, they cannot disprove the reality and relevance of self-control in so far as this refers to normative requirements. To this end, it would be required to show that people lack self-control, rather than that they behave in an automatic fashion.
> (Horstkötter, 2015, p. 27)

On the one hand, social psychology attempts to understand human self-control and its mechanisms and conditions (Baumeister, Heatherton, & Tice, 1994; Baumeister, Tice, & Vohs, 2018; Mischel, Cantor, & Feldman, 1996). On the other hand, the very possibility and relevance of self-controlled behavior has been fundamentally challenged by social psychologists. Scholars have suggested that there is no such thing as mentally caused or consciously controlled action and that anything people do is the result of diverse and complex unconscious and automatic processes generated by various features in people's environments (Bargh & Chartrand, 1999; Hassin, Uleman, & Bargh, 2005; Wegner, 2004; Wegner & Wheatley, 1999). The research on which these claims are based, however, is often weak and fails to meet standards of replicability (Doyen, Klein, Pichon, & Cleeremans, 2012; Pashler, Coburn, & Harris, 2012). Furthermore, it has been shown that "unconscious thought", which has repeatedly been invoked to explain (automatic) behavior, is not as effective as has been argued (Waroquier, Marchiori, Klein, & Cleeremans, 2010).

Notwithstanding the lack of agreement about the question whether or not our behavior is largely induced automatically and generated independently of individual control, it often seems as if these two positions are our only options in making sense of human action. This pervasive dualism among social psychologists and cognitive scientists is tightly connected to dual-process theories. There are many reasons to be skeptical of this dualistic thinking. This chapter will give a short overview of the development of the debate, ending with two reasons to step away from the binary distinction. I will end with two suggestions. First, we should stop understanding automatic and controlled to be belonging to the same distinction, instead we should think about the distinctions between automatic and non-automatic and controlled and not-controlled (I will follow the suggestion by Fujita and colleagues, 2014, but see also Horstkötter, 2015). Second, I will argue that many of the features that are associated with this distinction between automatic and controlled are better understood as gradual distinctions. This more nuanced view enables a better categorization of phenomena that now fall between the sides of the traditional dichotomy, improving our conceptual tools with which we make sense of everyday phenomena.

2.1 Dual-Process Theories

The emergence of dual-process theories is seen as a very significant theoretical development in social psychology (Moors & deHouwer, 2007). The overarching assumption of dual-process theorizing is that the mental processes underlying many phenomena, including social phenomena, can be divided into two distinct categories depending on whether they operate in an automatic or non-automatic fashion (Gawronski, Sherman, & Trope, 2014, p. 3). In recent years, however, scholars have problematized the ease with which dual-process theorists make clear-cut distinctions. This section (2.1) offers a brief overview of the development from a very dichotomous dual mode view to a more complex but nuanced gradual view of the distinction between automatic and non-automatic processes. This gradual view will then be used to conceptualize the intermediate space that I pointed at in the introduction. A brief history of dual-process theories will help us understand the contemporary scholarly tendencies to carve the world up in dichotomies, as witnessed, for example, in the debates on joint action. Section 2.2 will focus on the connection between automatic and controlled processes, arguing that these should be understood as orthogonal categorizations.

According to the dual *mode* view, there are two modes of processing that each come with a fixed set of features (Bruner, 1957; Postman, Bruner, & McGinnies, 1948; see Moors & Houwer, 2007, for a discussion). The dual mode view is an all or nothing view, where we find the familiar list of characteristics or features that are coupled to the automatic/non-automatic distinction.[15] For clarity's sake I repeat them (Table 3).

The mode view was set up such that when something is said to be automatic this means there is an absence of (conscious) intentions, an absence of conscious awareness, the behavior is uncontrolled, and the operation is efficient.[16] Each characteristic is, at least at first, defined by the absence or presence of one feature. There is or is no intention; the process is efficient or not-efficient, etc. On

---

[15] This list is often attributed to Bargh (1994). Although this is correct, it should be noted that in the article where he discusses this list he is critical about the accuracy of it and never subscribes to the view that these features always co-occur.

[16] Note how one of the characteristics is "absence of (conscious) intention". In philosophy, as we will see in chapter three, there are many understandings of intentions and the need for awareness of them for an action to count as an action.

Table 3: Four horsemen of automaticity.

Automatic	Non-automatic
1. Absence of (conscious) intention	1. Intentional
2. Absence of conscious awareness	2. Conscious
3. Uncontrolled (inability to disrupt)	3. Controlled (ability to disrupt)
4. Efficiency of operation (fast and not (strongly) depending on working memory)	4. Time consuming & using cognitive resources

both the level of automatic/non-automatic and the level of the individual characteristics the distinction was traditionally perceived as a non-gradual one. Before I will discuss the models that have followed in the footsteps of the dual mode view I will first elaborate its four features.

2.1.1 The Four Features of Automaticity

The conceptualization of the four features, as I spell them out below, is based on the literature in social psychology. There is a rich debate on many, if not all, of the features and how they can coherently be conceptualized in philosophy of action. Some of what follows might appear rather unclear to someone trained in philosophy. Take for example the distinction between intentional and non-intentional. In social psychological literature, this is often conflated with the absence or presence of an intention, as will become evident below.[17] There are good philosophical arguments against understanding intentionality in terms of intentions (see e.g., Searle, 1983).

Awareness
In the debate on automaticity, awareness is about the occurring mental state. Bargh (1994) distinguishes three ways of testing whether a person may be unaware of an occurring mental process. These distinctions are meant to conceptualize the

---

[17] Take for example two publications by Bargh (Bargh, 1994, and Bargh & Gollwitzer, 1994). These two social psychological articles, which are commonly referred to as the starting point of debate, do not contain a clear definition of intentionality. In his 1994 article, Bargh mentions *intentionality* as one of the four "horsemen" of automaticity. In the article co-authored with Gollwitzer, they allude to *intentions*. They write: "To the extent that perceptual, judgmental, and behavioral processes are triggered by the environment and start up without intention, the environment is more in control" (Bargh & Gollwitzer, 1994, p. 41).

difference between being aware or unaware. Much of the literature focuses on the presentation of a stimulus, which is done in either a subliminal fashion or supraliminal. Then the tests are about the influence of thus presented stimuli. The three tests are:
1. A person may be unaware of the stimulus itself, as in subliminal perception.
2. A person may be unaware of the way in which that stimulus event is interpreted or categorized, as stereotypes and construct accessibility research have demonstrated.
3. A person may be unaware of the determining influences on his or her judgments or subjective feeling states [. . .] and thus may misattribute the reason to a plausible and salient possible cause of which he or she is aware. (Bargh, 1994, p. 7)

An important factor in the relation between awareness and automaticity, is whether one is aware of the potential influence of that event on subsequent experience and judgments (Nisbett & Wilson, 1977). Unawareness of the stimuli that influence our behavior and the types of thoughts they generate in the agent obstruct some forms of intentionality. It is possible to be aware of a stimulus yet not act on this awareness:

> Awareness as an aspect of automaticity is a critical issue for the intentional control of thought and behavior. (Bargh, 1994, p. 15)

When we are unaware of an influence, we cannot act intentionally on it, nor can we control the influence while it is affecting our behavior.

Intentionality
Intentionality, or intention, for Bargh (1994), is about the ability to *start* an action oneself. The ability to stop an action oneself is attributed to controllability rather than intentionality.

The trigger (cause) rather than the representation (of the action) takes central stage in understanding intentionality. The difference between intentional and unintentional then comes down to whether a person is involved with the initiation of a mental process. This is still rather obscure and unclear. One further conceptualization is spelled out by Bargh, who stipulates that:

> intentionality and controllability aspects of automaticity both have to do with how much one is in control of one's own thought and behavior. Intentionality has to do with whether one is in control over the instigation or "start up" of processes, whereas controllability has to do with one's ability to stifle or stop a process once started, or at least to override its influence if so desired. (Bargh, 1994, p. 16)

The main idea concerning intentionality in these accounts relates to the idea how a behavior was started; through internal factors or external factors.

Controllability

Control is related to our capacity to intervene on how things are going, it is our capacity to interfere with automatic processes, and our capacity to adjust intentional processes that do not run as planned.[18]

> Thus, what most researchers mean by the question of controllability is not the occurrence of the stereotype's or accessible construct's input into a judgment, but rather whether one is aware of such influences and is both motivated and able to counteract them.
>
> (Bargh, 1994, p. 28)

To exercise this control, three things must be in place. First, one must be aware of the existence of the influence and/or its subsequent automatic process. Second, one must have the capacity to effortfully override the automatic process. Third, one must have sufficient attentional resources. Control, just as intentions, require a certain level of awareness.

Efficiency

The efficiency aspect of automaticity refers to the extent to which the perceptual or judgmental process demands attentional resources, nowadays mostly understood as using working memory capacity. To the degree that a process does use working memory capacity, it may stop when attention is required elsewhere.

Usually the efficiency of a cognitive process is tested with tasks that are cognitively demanding. When we are performing such a task and can do the other task simultaneously it is assumed that this second task is done efficiently and is automatic.

2.1.2 Theoretical Development and Gradual Distinctions

It has become clear that the features of automaticity, although they are traditionally grouped as strictly related parts of automatic/non-automatic processes, in fact dissociate, and for this reason dual mode theories are increasingly seen as inadequate

---

18 In section 6.3, I will discuss the sense of us and its relation to the sense of agency. In the debate on the sense of agency one of the focus points is a *sense of* control (Pacherie, 2007). This sense of control is related to feelings of efficacy and effort and does not straight-forwardly relate to the notion of control as used in the debate on automaticity.

(Moors & De Houwer, 2007). Nevertheless, Moors & De Houwer (2007) conclude that they are still popular in various research domains, including social cognition:

> One of the reasons why the dual mode view seems so difficult to shake off is that it is strongly ingrained in the classic, computational metaphor of cognition on which most dual mode models rest. (Moors & Houwer, 2007, p. 15)

The overarching assumption of dual-process theorizing is that the mental processes underlying our decisions, understanding of others, and reasoning is often divided into two distinct categories depending on whether they operate in an *automatic* or *non-automatic* fashion (Sherman, Gawronski, & Trope, 2014). We need a more precise understanding of this distinction between automatic and non-automatic operation. This more precise characterization of the distinction then also needs to be spelled out in relation to specific fields. As Moors and De Houwer argue:

> The word automatic can be used to describe performances of effects, which are observable, or to describe the processes underlying the performance, which are not observable and hence need to be inferred. (Moors & De Houwer, 2007, p. 11)

Many further dualities have been introduced to describe the difference between two types of processes, such as a characterization and division of human thought in associative and rule-based processes (Smith & DeCoster, 2000), reflective and impulsive processing (Strack & Deutsch, 2004), reflective and reflexive processing (Lieberman, Gaunt, Gilbert, & Trope, 2002), System 1 versus System 2 processing (Evans & Stanovich, 2013; Kahneman, 2011), thinking "fast and slow" (Kahneman, 2011), and introspectable and non-introspectable processing (Frankish, 2016). All these characterizations seem problematic in some way or another (Brownstein, 2017; Moors & De Houwer, 2007). One reason is that dual-process theory has been widely applied to cover quite different phenomena. Although each phenomenon (decision-making, mathematical problem-solving, action, social cognition) might involve two types of processes that can be clearly distinguished and characterized, the types are not exactly the same across the different areas.[19] Any conceptualization will therefore fail to

---

[19] When dual-process theories started to emerge in the 1980s, their focus was mainly domain-specific. They aimed at explaining phenomena in particular areas of inquiry. Although some of these theories were based on general processing principles from cognitive psychology (e.g., Chaiken & Stangor, 1987; Trope, 1986), their applications were specific to particular content domains within social psychology. Prominent examples include dual-process theories of persuasion (e.g., Chaiken, 1987; Petty & Cacioppo, 1986), attitude-behavior relations (e.g., Fazio, 1990), dispositional attributions (e.g., Gilbert, 1989; Trope, 1986), prejudice and stereotyping

describe the distinction across all phenomena. Another reason is that the different phenomena are not exhaustively explained by two types of processes, but rather by multiple (interacting) processes.

These arguments suggest makes the distinction less valuable both as a conceptual tool and for integration in models (Fujita, 2011; Gawronski & Bodenhausen, 2014; Hassin, Bargh, Engell, & McCulloch, 2009).

> Counter to early *dual-mode conceptualizations* assuming an all-or-non relation between different features of automaticity, the available evidence indicates that there is virtually no process that is characterized by all four features of automaticity.
> (Gawronski, Sherman, & Trope, 2014, p. 5)

For example, a process may be unintentional and controllable, intentional and efficient, unintentional and resource-dependent, conscious and uncontrollable, unconscious and resource-dependent, controllable and resource-independent, and so forth. These discoveries inspired *disjunctive conceptualizations of automaticity*, according to which a process can be characterized as automatic if it meets at least one of the four criteria of automaticity.

However, even within this less clear-cut and more nuanced picture, Moors (2014) notes that:

> Most dual-process models, however, take things one step further. They choose two or more dichotomies and make a priori assumptions of overlap among them.
> (Moors, 2014, p. 20)

A way to retain the distinction automatic/non-automatic is by adopting a modest and promising approach and to see it as gradual,[20] as has been suggested by Logan (1985), Moors & De Houwer (2006), Shiffrin (1988), and Moors (2014).

Logan (1985) was the first to propose an alternative to abandoning the concept of automaticity. He introduced it as a continuum and emphasized that the automaticity of a process is determined by the amount of training. I will discuss this in more detail in section 3.3, which deals with skills. Similarly, Moors and

---

(e.g., Brewer, 1988; Fiske & Neuberg, 1990). Beginning around the year 2000, the focus of dual-process theorizing shifted toward the development of integrative theories. The central argument of Smith and DeCoster (2000) is that the multiple dualisms proposed by domain-specific theories reflect the operation of two basic processes that characterize any kind of human thought irrespective of its content: associative versus rule-based processes. But see also the earlier described possible ways to split up the two processes (Gawronski, Sherman, & Trope, 2014).

20 There are several other recent proposals, including the triple mode view, the gradual view, and a mechanisms-based approach (I refer to Moors & De Houwer, 2007, for a critical overview of these proposals).

De Houwer (2006, 2007) make a case for a gradual understanding of at least three of the four original features of the distinction between automatic and non-automatic processes: efficiency, awareness, and goal-relatedness.

If we accept that there are several gradual features that are part of the encompassing notion of automaticity, it becomes less clear how to answer the question whether a behavior is automatic. Gradual differences are less clear-cut than dichotomies. It becomes unlikely that a process is fully automatic or fully non-automatic. It is helpful to point at two ways in which the gradualness manifests itself (see also Moors, 2014):
1. A process can be automatic with regard to some but not other features.
2. Each automaticity feature can itself be consider as gradual.

To conclude, the gradual approach complicates our ability to formulate a clear-cut principle with which to determine whether a process is automatic or non-automatic. It is nevertheless an improvement because it allows for a much clearer conceptualization of different phenomena and a better understanding of their interrelatedness by pointing at the different features that are traditionally linked to the idea of automaticity. Instead of merely being able to distinguish black and white, we now have at our disposal a rich palette that allows us to differentiate between more than fifty shades of grey.[21] I now turn to a discussion of the problems with equating controlled processes and non-automatic processes as the opposite of automatic processes.

2.2 Separating Non-Automatic and Controlled

Having shown that the automatic/non-automatic dichotomy is better conceptualized as a series of gradual distinctions, I now problematize the equation of "controlled" with "non-automatic" behavior. By showing that these notions are not equivalent, I prepare the grounds for automatic, yet controlled, behaviors, such as skillful actions.

One way of understanding or describing "controlled" has been to say that it is non-automatic. Bargh (1994), for example, argues that:

> mental processes at the level of complexity studied by social psychologists are not exclusively automatic or exclusively controlled. (Bargh, 1994, p. 3)

---

[21] Another suggestion would be to specify "the sense in which (i.e., the feature according to which) one considers a process to be automatic or nonautomatic" (Moors, 2014, p. 26).

Although Bargh is critical about the cohesion of the four features of automaticity, he too conflates non-automaticity and control. Fujita, Trope, Cunningham, & Liberman (2014) note that this specific dichotomy is common among dual-process theories. This is confusing, because when conceptualized like this *controlled* is both the overall notion in the dichotomy and one of the features (of itself). Controlled processes indeed often are conceptualized as processes that are *not automatic*, the features often co-occur, but they do not necessarily co-occur. In the characterization by Bargh (1994) control is (a) the opposite of automatic, and (b) understood as the capacity to stop or interrupt an activity that the agent is engaged in.

Fujita et al. propose two distinctions: automatic versus non-automatic processes and controlled versus out-of-control processes. On their account a process is controlled when two further things are in place: *governance* and *purpose*. A second way to characterize controlled processes is by saying that they are *goal-directed*: the process helps to attain a desired goal or end. Control does not set the goal, but helps in achieving the goal.

> This sense of control refers not to some specific feature of an isolated process but rather to its relation to other processes from the perspective of the whole.
> (Fujita, Trope, Cunningham, & Liberman, 2014, p. 50)

One way to understand this is in terms of structure or (limited) forms of holism or coherence. Furthermore, by specifying it as such it becomes almost impossible to conceive of controlled processes that are not goal-orientated or teleologically understood.

A key notion for this specific understanding of control is that of structure: "the top-down organization of thoughts, feelings, and behavior to promote a given end" (Fujita, Trope, Cunningham, & Liberman, 2014, p. 50). Fujita and colleagues argue that in most dual-process theories the distinctions between non-automatic and automatic and controlled and lacking control are conflated. They suggest we should use the notion of control only when referring to goal-directed processes. Through this separation we open up the possibility to have processes that are both automatic and controlled (see also Fridland, 2017; Horstkötter, 2015). This way of putting things does not necessarily entail identifying control with intentions. This can be nicely illustrated with the example of implementation intentions. When an agent forms an implementation intention, she states a very explicit intention including a lot of situational details earlier on to heighten her chance to act accordingly later on. Such if-then plans produce automatic action control by "intentionally delegating the control of one's goal-directed thoughts, feelings, and behaviors to specific situational cues" (Gollwitzer, Bayer & McCulloch, 2005, p. 485). In this example we say the agent is in control because an implementation intention was formed. Control does not get equated with intentions in these cases, although there is an intimate link between the two. Control is a feature of *how* intentionality works, or can work, when we form an (implementation) intention. It does not become identical to the intentions. As discussed in the previous section, Bargh defines control as our capacity to adjust processes that do not run as planned. Fujita et al. remain close to this definition. Implementation intentions are set to make sure things run as planned, and the cues function to make this the case; they provide us control.

In order to be in control, it seems that we need a goal or intention. Only with the goal in place can control processes function: there is a motivation (the goal) to stop or start doing something, or to interrupt what is going on at the moment. Such goals can be flexibly understood and need not only include full-blown intentional action. Examples of less demanding understandings of goals could come from teleological approaches, skills, habits, and goals as outcomes.

Fujita and colleagues propose two key features for a better understanding of control as a goal-directed process; (1) governance and (2) direction or purpose. Only together can they provide structure, or a process that is *not* out of control.

Governance refers to:

> a set of mechanisms or principles that organize and structure thoughts, feelings, and behaviors. (Fujita, Trope, Cunningham, & Liberman, 2014, p. 51)

Various signals can pull in contradictory directions and we need rules and structure as a:

> top-down reductive process of creating coherence from more fragmented and disorganized elemental components. (Fujita, Trope, Cunningham, & Liberman, 2014, p. 52)

Independent of what it is that is being structured, in order to provide structure a perspective of a whole is needed, rather than the individual perspectives of the parts. A lack of governance would in turn render engaging in any goal-directed purpose impossible. On Fujita et al's account the two features, governance and purpose/direction, together provide structure. A psychological process can then be considered controlled "to the extent that it operates in a manner that is consistent with and sustains the larger integrated goal-directed whole" (Fujita, Trope, Cunningham, & Liberman, 2014, p. 53).

Whereas Fujita and colleagues have quite a bit to say about governance, they leave underspecified what a purpose or a direction is. Nor do they describe how purposes are selected and what kind of processes are involved during such selection. This choice can be defended by the observation that there are multiple processes that can give purpose and structure and we need not commit to any theory in particular. This openness allows us to conceptualize more biologically constrained purposes, as well as more normatively constrained purposes. I believe that insights from the philosophy of action can be of help in spelling out one way of understanding purpose. I therefore continue in the next chapter (3) with a possible interpretation that is inspired by and in line with Bratman's theory of agency, in which structure and coherence are also key ingredients. In chapter four I will say more about the integration of different types of control when discussing skillful action.

3 Control and Intentions in Individuals

Philosophy of action is an area in philosophy concerned with theories about the processes involved in willful human bodily movements of a more or less complex kind. It is the starting point of many theories of joint action and shared intentionality. Philosophy of action centers around multiple interrelated fundamental questions. Take for example questions about the ontological status of actions, and how we can individuate actions. Or questions regarding the relation between bodily movements and mental states such as beliefs, desires, and intentions. A further problem that has attracted much thought is our capacity of self-control, or lack thereof in some situations. The conceptualizations in answering the individual questions, have consequences for the answers to the other questions. In that sense these fundamental questions interlock. The same goes for their application to joint action.

Control is a central issue in the philosophy of agency. It is at the heart of rational practical agency, as well as at the heart of the relation between the bodily movement and mental states controlling these movements. Agential control is not only discussed when it comes to the nexus between mind and body in intentional action, but also when different desires pull the agent in different directions and the agent has to control multiple conflicting desires. This makes it possible that not all desire satisfaction, even when intentional, involves "perfect agential control", even when the body moves exactly as willed. For example, an agent may know that she chooses an action she will later on regret. A full discussion of the different conceptualizations of control goes well beyond us here, but in order to position the rest of this book, two issues will take center stage in this chapter. One is the relation between bodily movement and (intentional) action. The other is the relation between agency, control, and self-control.[22]

The first section focuses on concerns the relation between bodily movements and intentional bodily actions. The nature of intentional action, which involves an exercise of control by the agent, is intuitively captured by contrasting it with uncontrolled behaviors including compulsions, reflexes, and

---

[22] In this chapter my aim is to give a background on some important concepts we will return to in the upcoming chapters. The discussion of control in the context of the philosophy of action remains brief and can only cover so much of the rich debate in philosophy of action. The introduced concepts and their discussion is not comprehensive and is focused on the theories in chapters four and five.

https://doi.org/10.1515/9783110671315-003

tics. Our understanding of this distinction is influenced by the debate on automaticity and how it undermines self-control. Behavior that is categorized as mere bodily movement can often also be conceptualized as automatic and non-controlled (Fridland, 2017). Intuitively, this suggests that these conceptions – mere bodily movement, automatic, and non-controlled – are interchangeable, that they map onto one another. As was discussed in chapter two, doing this, however, is a mistake. Setting the debate between mere bodily movement and intentional action in such a dichotomous way leads to an incapacity to conceptualize some intermediate cases including habitual and skillful action. In reaction to this duality-thinking in the relation between mere bodily movement and full-blown intentional action some philosophers have introduced an intermediate category. Section 3.1 will briefly review the traditional dualism between mere bodily movements and intentional actions and some proposals by theorists that have tried to introduce an intermediate category. This conceptualization of the intermediate category is of importance for the skillful action proposal discussed in chapters four and seven. It is also relevant in the discussion of joint action, and as a backdrop to my reading of Bratman in chapter five. In line with the discussion in the previous chapter, I propose a more gradual and fine-grained distinction of the intermediate space between mere bodily movement and full-blown intentional action. This gradualness partially is asked for because several features that are linked to the distinction between mere bodily movement and intentional action are (a) spelled out as orthogonal and independent of one another, and/or (b) gradual distinctions.

Section 3.2 concerns the relation between control and self-control. The notion of self-control is often discussed in the context of temptation and weakness of will and is more directly connected to normativity and control over our desires and intentions, rather than over our bodily movements. People are said to be tempted if they are more strongly motivated to act by their impulses or spontaneous desires than by their judgments about what is desirable, rational, or best (O'Brien, 2015; Horstkötter, 2015). Intuitively, self-control appears to be a matter of mental strength, whereas lack of it is attributed to a weakness of will. This basic idea dates back to an ancient philosophical legacy. In Aristotle's *Nicomachean Ethics*, for example, people are argued to be self-controlled if they act with restraint in the face of temptation, whereas those who lack continence suffer from weakness of will (Aristotle, 2011).[23] Current discussions in social

---

[23] Mele has established a corresponding contemporary account of self-control according to which self-control and weakness of will (*akrasia*) appear "as two sides of the same coin" (Mele, 1995, p. 5).

psychology, which focus on the automaticity of many of our actions, have raised doubts about our capacity of self-control (see Horstkötter, 2015, for a discussion). So, again, our understanding of automaticity plays a role in the conceptualization of control.

3.1 Control and Mere Activity

The distinction between mere bodily movement and action has been commonly motivated by the intuitive distinction between the things that merely happen to people – the events they undergo – and the various things they genuinely do. The doings are the acts or actions of the agent, and the problem about the nature of can be stated as follows: what it is that distinguishes an action from a mere happening or occurrence. A majority of accounts works within a causal framework and argues that an intention makes the difference (Chan, 1995). How to characterize these intentions has been discussed for many years and is still debated (O'Brien, 2015).

Intentional action can be divided into bodily and mental action. Intentional bodily actions involve bodily movements. "If I move my body, then my body moves" (Haddock, 2010, p. 26). Philosophers of action have reflected on this apparent truth and been concerned with the relation between events of this sort and actions. Usually philosophers of action take a non-disjunctivist conception of bodily movements, assuming that the bodily movements are all the same (Haddock, 2010) writes:

> Even if I move my body with the intention of doing something, the movement of my body does not intrinsically involve my intention of doing this thing; it is just like the movement of my body in a case in which my body moves but I do not move my body with the intention of doing something. (Haddock, 2010, p. 26)

Intentional bodily actions are then taking to be identical to, or to involve, beliefs and desires (Smith, 1998), intentions (Bratman, 1984; Velleman, 2000), or tryings[24] (Hornsby, 1980).

In relation to this question philosophers of action have often defined their topic by quoting Wittgenstein:

> What is left over if I subtract the fact that my arm goes up from the fact that I raise my arm? (Wittgenstein, 1953, §621)

---

[24] On this account the most basic description, in the causal sense of "basic", of an action is as a trying. Not all tryings are actions, only the successful ones are.

If you move your leg, your leg has to move. But your leg can move without your moving your leg. So it seems that something else is required for you to move your leg (Davis, 2010). The way the question is set up allows us to draw an intuitive and "simple" dichotomy between mere bodily movement and action, according to which the action has an additional component: an intention. Bratman's theory of planning agency, which provides the ground work for his theory of shared agency, is part of this tradition.[25] The basic principle common to all causal theories is that the agent performs an action only if an appropriate internal state of the agent causes a particular result in a certain way. Not only the presence of certain mental states, but also their relation to the movement is of great importance (Davis, 2010). Within this tradition, intentional action is usually understood as acting for a reason or reasons (O'Brien, 2015).

Understanding the distinction between mere bodily movement and intentional actions through these causal theories is not without its problems. One of the acknowledged problems that arise when we understand the distinction between mere bodily movement and intentional action in terms of beliefs, desires, and intentions is what Bratman coined the *two faces of intentions*. Intention has to capture both (a) normativity and rationality constraints and (b) motoric capacities as intentional capacities (intention in action, present-directed intention, motor intention). We want intention to relate to our bodily movement and our ability to regulate conflicts between different desires and other motivating mental states. As soon as we make space for (b) it becomes difficult to capture (a) and vice versa. Although the distinction between these two faces of intention helps us to some extent, there are also cases that still do not fit into the traditional dichotomy between mere bodily movement and action. For instance, a person may blink or exhibit highly reflexive reactions. These are all things the person has, in some minimal sense, "done", although in the usual cases, the person *qua agent* will have been altogether passive throughout these "doings".[26] Another phenomenon that seems central to understanding action but is problematic to integrate into the standard dualistic picture of doings and happenings are habits and

---

[25] It is this tradition and debate that I will focus on. There are many more accounts of action, some people have devoted their life's work on this topic and I do recon that some of these approaches would be very interesting for the current project. However, due to limited space and time I will focus on the tradition in which Bratman puts himself, including philosophers like Harry Frankfurt and David Velleman. I will not discuss notions such as *a*rational agency (Hursthouse, 1991) and *aliefs* (Gendler, 2008).

[26] This passivity is not to say that intentionality and action always need to go together. Take for example omissions and refraining, which are clearly intentional yet also passive (see Bach, 2010).

skills. I will turn to these in some detail to sketch the problem of dichotomous thinking now and return to them in chapters four and seven as a solution.

3.1.1 Habitual and Skillful Actions

Few scholars would dispute that much of what we human beings do is habitual. Our daily lives are dominated by practiced routines of varying importance, which we achieve quite without thought, conscious decision, or awareness (Pollard, 2010). Habits transform performances which may once have required attention and concentration into actions which come so naturally and easily that we just find ourselves doing them, whilst we think about other things.

These days, discussions of action often focus on the distinctively human kind of purposive action, our capacity to act for a reason. Under the influence of Anscombe (1957) and Davidson (1980), the debate has focused on the nature of intentional actions, e.g. on issues such as the role of the reasons "for which" we act and on the nature of psychological antecedents of actions such as beliefs, desires, and intentions. Habitual and skillful actions do not fit well with contemporary philosophical conceptions of action in analytic philosophy.[27] Habitual actions are not obviously intentional, since, on the face of it, we do them without any intention (though they are not by that token unintentional) (Pollard, 2006, 2008). Neither do habitual actions seem to be done "for reasons", if reasons are to be understood as considerations which lie before the agent at the time of action. Habits, after all, spare us the need for any such consideration. Likewise, they elide the necessity of antecedent beliefs and desires. As Pollard notices about the standard framework:

> In this conceptual framework, if habitual actions are mentioned at all, they tend to be pushed to the margins of human action, where they can safely be relegated to being 'mere behaviors' rather than exercises of agency proper. We are thereby invited to think of them as little more than reflexes or nervous tics. (Pollard, 2010, p. 75)

Equating habitual actions with reflexes and nervous tics is problematic. Even though some reflexes and nervous tics might be described as having some form of purpose, this purpose is more agentive in the case of habits and skills. A tic

---

[27] The words "skill" and "habit" have both been used to describe the domain of practiced and automatized behaviors. Sometimes interchangeably, sometimes to refer to distinct phenomena. I will say more about the distinction in the following chapters, but for now they can be regarded as a cluster of action types that do not fit the traditional dichotomous action theory framework.

or reflex, when it has a purpose, does not have a purpose that has been assigned to it by the agent. We are less able to intervene on reflexes, to control them, nor do we seem to form intentions to perform them (not even at an earlier time).

This skepticism about habitual actions as actions, as well as the idea that they are just "run-of-the-mill" consciously deliberated actions that now run unconsciously is symptomatic of a philosophy of action which he takes to be "intellectualist" (Pollard, 2010; Fridland, 2017; Christensen, Sutton, & Bicknell, 2019).[28] By understanding purposive agency and intentions-in-action through propositional attitudes such as belief-desire pairs and intentions that are also connected to acting for reasons, other forms of purposive agency cannot easily be characterized. Different starting points, different questions to start with, can help to generate more space for these actions that lie somewhere between mere bodily movement and full-blown intentional action. In the next chapter I will focus on levels of control in skillful action as an alternative route to an understanding of action. If skillful actions and habits are actions, it is worth asking whether and what makes such actions intentional actions. And if they are not intentional actions we can ask in which way they are still an expression of the agent (O'Brien, 2015). The three-tier models of intentions (Pacherie, 2008) and control (Fridland, 2017; Christensen, Sutton, & Bicknell, 2019) move away from the dichotomous understanding. Before turning to these positions, however, I will first highlight ways in which those within the currently discussed framework have proposed to work around this problem that habitual and skillful actions give us that seem unfit to be classified as either mere bodily movement or intentional action.

3.1.2 Mere Activity

One solution that enables us to conceptualize intermediate phenomena while staying true to the distinction between mere bodily movements and actions is the idea of distinguishing mere activity from intentional action. Harry Frankfurt (1978) has pointed out that purposeful behavior of animals constitutes a low-

---

28 Merleau-Ponty uses the notion of habit as the central concept of understanding traditional dualisms such as those between active and passive, mind and body, subject and world. He emphasizes the sense in which habits both represent a form of intelligence and are essentially embodied; a knowledge "in the hands" (Merleau-Ponty, 2002, p. 144). Such an account of action has, however, not yet been translated to the case of collective intentionality. For reasons of time and space I cannot do justice to such an account in this book.

level type of "active" doing, thereby introducing an in-between category. He illustrates this category with a spider's movements. When a spider walks across the table, the spider *directly controls* the movements of its legs, and they are directed at taking him from one location to another. Those very movements have an aim or purpose for the spider, and hence they are subject to a kind of teleological explanation. Similarly, the idle, unnoticed movements of my fingers may have the goal of releasing a candy wrapper from my grasp.

Frankfurt's argument for doings in spiders allows for two answers to Wittgenstein's question about raising one's arm. Raising an arm may be something less than an action (but more than a mere bodily movement):

> Actions are instances of activity, though not the only ones even in human life. To drum one's fingers on the table, altogether idly and inattentively, is surely not a case of passivity: the movements in question do not occur without one's making them. Neither is it an instance of action, however, but only of being active. One result of overlooking events of this kind is an exaggeration of the peculiarity of what humans do. Another result, related to the first, is the mistaken belief that a twofold division of human events into action and mere happenings provides a classification that suits the interests of the theory of action.
> (Frankfurt, 1988, p. 58)

According to Frankfurt, all this behavioral *activity* is "action" only in some fairly weak sense. The traditional distinction between mere bodily movement and action is related to certain key terms, such as purposefulness, intentionality, control, awareness and the ability to intervene. Some of these characteristics that are used to describe intentional actions also apply to mere activity. One of criteria that these weaker forms of actions do not necessarily meet are the normativity and rationality constraints that seem to play a role in our understanding of intention. This, however, is only a negative characterization of mere activity; it is lacking something that intentional action has (see Douskos 2019 for a similar point).

The movements of the spider and the agent that shows mere activities, for example, are controlled movements. These mere activities are portrayed with some level of purpose. Yet the reason *why* they acted might be answered in a different way, if answered in terms of reasons at all.[29] This means that both the movements that are categorized as mere activity and those that are categorized as intentional action are controlled and it also means that saying that a movement is controlled is independent of saying that the activity is intentional (that

---

[29] The way we understand the relation between these different concepts has consequences for the way that we think about joint actions. Especially when it comes to the idea of sharing an intention and having control over what one is doing.

there is an intention involved). The threefold distinction between mere bodily movement, mere activity and intentional action that has been introduced because of the observation that certain phenomena cannot be conceptualized well when we stick to a distinction between mere bodily movement and intentional action can be understood in two ways.
A. Activity falls apart into intentional action and mere activity.
B. There is something in between mere bodily movement and intentional action, a third class of movements, a third class of events.

Option A stays true to the idea of a dichotomy between action and mere bodily movement, although not all activity will be object to the same (normative and rational) constraints. Option B breaks more radically with the idea of a dichotomy. Although both options give us a way to better categorize certain phenomena, they also do both not really give a clear conceptualization of the differences and relations between the new category – mere activity – and mere bodily movement and intentional action. If not by means of intentions, how are mere activities to be understood as actions?

We are now faced with a problem. One of the key concepts needed to understand agentic control makes use of desires, beliefs, and intentions. Yet mere activity is action, but not intentional action understood through such mental states. So how can we understand mere activity, when characterizing them positively?

Philosophers have drawn several distinctions regarding the notion of intention to better understand such intermediate activity. Some introduce two types, or faces, of intentions (Searle, Bratman). This mainly serves in an attempt to better understand the differences and similarities between the intention to do something in the (near) future, and the intention that guides action in the here and now. In both cases the action is understood as an action through its relation to a mental state, typically a propositional attitude. O'Shaughnessy introduced sub-intentional actions as an in-between category (O'Shaughnessy, 1980, 2008). O'Shaughnessy's work (both in his 1980 and 2008 versions of *The Will*) on sub-intentional acts is based on Davidson's (1971) idea that actions are intentional under some description and his idea that an act individual is intentional depending on the descriptive heading under which it is brought, which means that being intentional is description-relative (Davidson, 1967). In the first edition of *The Will* he argues that there exist actions that are "intentional under no description; that are not intentional under any description; that are such that there does not exist a description under which they emerge as intentional" (O'Shaughnessy, 1980, p. 59). As an example he uses the case of idle unnoticed tongue movements (which he argues to be a sub-intentional act). Of such idle unnoticed tongue movements we can say that the agent (1) is unaware of (not know of) in either the conscious or unconscious sector of the mind ("there does not exist a *concept-using* state of knowledge that these phenomena are occurring" (1980, p. 66)),[30] (2) does it out of a feeling-like, (3) it is not performed for any reason that is our reason, and (4) the faculty of reason plays neither a positive nor negative causal role in its genesis. Sub-intentional activity is not described in propositional terms, and "such knowledge is incapable of *founding an intention*" (1980, p. 65). First of all, it should be noted that in the second edition of the same book he retracts this idea. In the 2008 edition O'Shaughnessy argues that these actions are still describable under some description, which he relates to (levels of) awareness and attention. Secondly, only a negative formulation of such actions is given (it is the absence of awareness). Thirdly, habitual and skillful action seem to belong to the category of intentional action on this account, where this is problematic for reasons mentioned earlier. To conclude, within the standard theory of action the characterizations of mere activity seem unsatisfying. I will take this as a reason to take skillful action as a starting point in the next chapter. But before that some further clarifications regarding the notion of self-control are in order.

3.2 Autonomous Agency and Self-Control

Philosophical talk about human autonomy is multifaceted. It includes ideas about forms of agency that are considerably more demanding than those involved in "merely purposive agency". Autonomy is often understood as a necessary condition for culpability and accountability. This second puzzle evolves around the different desires or goals that can pull in different directions. The most common example to show that the presence of a desire or intention is insufficient to say that an agent is autonomous comes from Frankfurt's (1971) example of the *unwilling addict*. A heroin addict may shoot up intentionally, while regarding the desire to do so as an alien force. In this case the addict's desire for heroin does cause him to take it, but the addict does not want to act on this desire, suggesting that the causal conditions for intentional action are not sufficient in this case. The desire and behavior are connected, but this in spite of the agent rather than because of the agent being in control. The powers within the agent are conflicted. The agent may have to struggle to overcome contrary desires, and sometimes fail to do so. In those cases the agent shows

---

[30] This leaves open the possibility of sub-propositional knowledge of the action.

weakness of will. There are several ways to understand autonomy, or the lack thereof, including the idea of a higher-order desire that is effective (Frankfurt, 1971), the additional requirement that the agent believes that what he/she desires is right and good (Watson, 1975), the idea that the agent's desire to act must be in accordance with justifying reasons (Velleman, 1992), the idea that the agent must identify with the desire or decision by deciding to treat it as reason-giving or justificatory in practical reasoning and planning (Bratman, 1999), or the idea that the agent consciously acts under the influence of the desire (Hornsby, 2004). In all these cases, the causal theory maintains that agents act for reasons only if an interrelated complex of beliefs and desires causes their actions (Davis, 2010).

For many philosophers, reason-responsiveness is what makes it possible to talk about autonomy and normativity and it is also reason-responsiveness that allows agents self-governance.[31] Autonomy involves more than the control relation between bodily movement and mental state: it does not merely involve the execution of desires and intentions, but the formation of intentions, beliefs, and other attitudes that are integral to the agent. This section is organized around Bratman's conceptualization of self-control and autonomy through self-direction and self-governance for two reasons. Firstly, his theory is a very influential one in the field and, secondly, it plays a crucial role in my discussion of shared agency in the chapters to come. Self-control involves control over one's actions, but more importantly, it also involves control over the agent's evaluations or evaluative judgments about what one should do. Bratman sees all this in the light of two related problems that humans face because of their reflective capacities: the problems of self-management and of underdetermination by value judgment. First, because so many courses of action seem valuable, there is the problem of underdetermination. Value judgments of the different options can be, and usually are, insufficient to determine a course of action. It is up to the agent. The second reason to integrate intentions and plans into our belief

---

[31] The link between autonomy and intentions also plays a role in the debate on collective intentionality, where Schmid (2009) has argued that many still adhere to the idea of individual autonomy. The *individual ownership claim* (IOC) holds that only individuals can have intentions and perform actions. All interpretations of the IOC, and therefore most accounts of collective intentionality, adhere to the idea of *individual intentional autonomy*. This idea holds that individuals are responsible for their behavior as agents and that their behavior can be ascribed to them as actions for which they can claim ownership. Schmid argues that we find this thesis, amongst others, in authors such as Bratman, Tuomela, and Gilbert. When we understand the individual agents to be autonomous in such a way while acting together, the possibilities of acting together become limited by a notion of autonomy and control that is not specifically argued for.

and desire structures, especially in relation to diachronicity, is the problem of self-management. Bratman argues that we are "creatures who are affected and moved by complex forms of motivation, and we sometimes find ourselves needing to reflect on, and respond to, these forms of motivation" (Bratman, 2007, p. 165), especially when we encounter contradicting desires. Take the example of a student who has to write a term-paper and is invited to a party. The writing of the term-paper will serve some long-term goals which the party will not. This long-term goal has higher priority, which could be explained through understanding it as a core value that the student ascribes to herself. Such long-term plans usually are the result of reflection (even if they might sometimes have to be re-evaluated). Another way of understanding the importance of the paper-writing goal is that doing so would allow the agent to express and constitute herself as she understands herself.

Autonomous agents have the ability to act in accordance with their evaluative judgments. Bratman writes:

> In autonomous action [. . .] an agent directs and governs her action. Note that there are two different ideas here: *agential direction* and *agential governance*. As I see it, in agential direction, there is sufficient unity and organization of the motives of action for their functioning to constitute direction by the agent. Agential direction that appropriately involves the agent's treatment of certain considerations as justifying reasons for action involves a form of agential direction that also constitutes agential governance.[32]
>
> (Bratman, 2007, p. 177)

An agent directs and governs both her practical thought and action. Governance implies direction and, both in the case of governance and in the case of direction actions are controlled by the agent through the involvement of intentions. The agent must be guided by the relevant kind of attitudes, i.e. those that fit into the hierarchy of conative attitudes and have the authority to speak for the agent (Bratman, 2007, p. 4). This idea is known as the autonomy-hierarchy thesis. In autonomous action the agent herself directs and governs the action.

Bratman's autonomy-hierarchy thesis is set up as a set of sufficient conditions for autonomous action. He explicitly leaves it open whether there are

---

32 Without appealing to a homunculus account, my strategy is to see agential direction and governance as being realized by appropriate forms of psychological functioning. There is agential direction of action when action is under the control of attitudes whose role in the agent's psychology gives them authority to speak for the agent, to establish the agent's point of view – gives them, in other words, agential authority. This agential direction of action is, furthermore, a form of agential governance of action only when these attitudes control action by way of the agent's treatment of relevant considerations as justifying reasons for action, that is, as having subjective normative authority for her.

other forms of functioning that could also realize human autonomy and therewith self-governance. If there are other such forms that can be spelled out, then we will want to understand their relation to the hierarchical model (Bratman, 2007, p. 163). However, Bratman assumes that the form of self-governance he has spelled out is the most general, or most common. He writes:

> I believe that higher-order conative attitudes play a significant role in central cases of autonomous agency, and so we should accept the AH thesis [Autonomy-Hierarchy thesis].
> (Bratman, 2007, p. 164)

At the end of chapter two we also encountered a relation between control, governance, and purpose (Fujita, Trope, Cunningham, & Liberman, 2014). It should be clear that Bratman has a more normatively embedded understanding of these two concepts and couples them to autonomy. They are embedded in his view of human agents as planning agents, according to which governance and purpose have to be organized by certain attitudes that are justifying reasons for action. In Fujita et al. the coherence is not subject to the same normative standards.

Recent work by Horstkötter (2015) is helpful to connect these different, yet related, concepts. She makes a point similar to Bratman's, arguing that a goal or commitment[33] is different from a desire because it does not only explain the action, but also justify the action. Desires alone cannot give us such justifications. She develops her argument on the basis of an example of a person desiring to eat cake. An agent wishes to follow a diet and therefore has formulated a goal not to eat cake. When the agent desires to eat cake and consequently eats it, this desire offers an explanation for the action but not a justification. Therefore, Horstkötter argues:

> ... although both desires and goals constitute reasons for action, there is, in terms of justifiability, a significant difference between mere motivational reasons that consist of desires and normative reasons which are constituted by a person's goals.   (Horstkötter 2015, p. 31)

The distinction that Horstkötter makes here is between different roles reasons can play. Reasons can *motivate*, they have a guiding role in reasoning about whether someone ought to φ (relative merits of the reasons), but we also use reasons to *evaluate/justify* and we use reasons to *explain* the occurrence (or

---

[33] Horstkötter (2015) uses the terms goals and better reasons, following Kennett and Smith (1994). Kennett and Smith added better reasons to the basic two-tiered picture of action-explanation pointed out by Davidson (1980), they argue that not only desires, but also goals or better judgment can give rise to an action, because they also constitute a reason for the person to act accordingly.

non-occurrence) of an event, the obtaining (or non-obtaining) of a state of affairs (Alvarez, 2010). It need not be the case that a reason fulfills all these roles. Hence a desire can explain, without justifying, why an agent did something. A desire in such a case could be described as a pro tanto reason, it is a reason that could be (or should have been) defeated. Where Horstkötter uses a person's goals Bratman would refer to the agglomeration of intentions in plans and policies (see chapter five for an extended discussion). In both cases there is control over the bodily movement, but only in one of the two cases is there also self-control. Whenever there is self-control, there is also control in the way Fujita and colleagues conceptualize control. This strategy, however, has the consequence that lower-level purposes that are not connected to these agglomerations are not considered controlled by the agent, or at least not autonomously so.

Researchers in psychology and cognitive science have experimentally discovered many cognitive/neural processes that typically hardly fit in with Bratman's strict (normative) coherence-framework. Nevertheless, they enable us to understand coherence in different ways and at different levels. A theoretical integration of these levels of coherence may offer a conceptual framework in which control and self-control can be integrated. When we can integrate these levels, this might provide us a story which allows us to integrate control and self-control. In the introduction to this chapter I pointed at several ways in which an agent can suffer from a loss of autonomy and self-control as proposed by cognitive science. Here, instead, I want to look at ways in which the mechanisms of control proposed in social psychology do not only reduce such control, but might offer forms of control by means different from self-governance.

Take, for example, the work of Fujita and colleagues, which point at several mechanisms that allow for structuring. They rely on the idea of cohesion to bring structure to agency. This is in contrast to structure understood as practical reasoning that results in a picture of coherence focused on the agglomeration and coherence of attitudes. Although coherence is not through agglomeration of attitudes, it gives us ways to intervene.

Fujita and colleagues work with examples such as someone trying to lose weight. They never discuss how the agents in their examples got their goals and desires in the first place. Their focus is rather on the way in which an agent that has a goal can automatically seek to fulfill this goal once it is in place. Bratman gives us a more encompassing story, in which we can understand how we come to have specific goals. He gives us *one* way in which the agent arrives at goals. In order to better understand these ideas, we have to turn to his theory of planning agency. This will be discussed in great detail in chapter five, but here I will discuss Bratman's ideas on planning agency as far as they are connected to the notions of autonomy and control.

3.3 Diachronicity and Control

Self-governance is a key aspect in Bratman's understanding of autonomy. It is intimately linked to his ideas about planning agency and coherence. The understanding of the agent as an agent is one that is relatively constant over time. Many of the things she will commit to take time to complete and up to that moment when the goal has been reached the agent should not (or not too often) act against that goal or plan.

As a first step towards understanding self-governance Bratman points out that the agent herself has to direct and govern her practical thought and action. To direct and govern are then defined as follows:

> Begin with agential direction. As a first step we can say that for the agent to direct thinking and acting is for relevant attitudes that guide and control that thinking and action to have authority to speak for the agent – to have agential authority. In this way, the idea of agential authority serves as a bridge between, on the one hand, appeal to attitudes that guide and control and, on the other hand, appeal to the agent as directing. When relevant attitudes with such agential authority appropriately guide and control, the agent directs.
> (Bratman, 2007, p. 4)

One key ingredient to understanding these capacities is the temporal extendedness of human agency. Bratman takes a broadly Lockean approach to personal identity, holding that personal identity is a matter of psychological continuity. He understands identity to unfold over time and as presupposed in our practical thinking. The second key factor is the idea of hierarchical structures that we are already familiar with from his planning theory. Bratman uses Frankfurt's idea of higher-order conative attitudes (see chapter five, most specifically section two and four), where the higher-order desire plays a motivating role. Reasons to accept higher-order conative attitudes as a key element to understand human agency are the problem of underdetermination and the problem of self-management that I briefly touched upon in section 3.2.

On Bratman's account of autonomous action an agent directs *and* governs her action. There are two different ideas here: agential direction and agential governance.

> . . .in agential direction, there is sufficient unity and organization of the motives of action for their functioning to constitute direction by the agent.[35] Agential governance is a

particular form of such agential direction: agential governance is agential direction that appropriately involves the agent's treatment of certain considerations as justifying reasons for action. (Bratman, 2007, p. 177)

When an agent acts autonomously this involves a form of agential direction that also constitutes agential governance.[34] There is agential direction of action when action is under the control of attitudes whose role in the agent's psychology gives them authority to speak for the agent, to establish the agent's point of view – gives them, in other words, agential authority. This occurs only when these attitudes control action by way of the agent's treatment of relevant considerations as justifying reasons for action (see section 5.3 for an extended discussion of justifying reasons for action). This leads Bratman to the view that motivational hierarchy is at the heart of at least one important realization of human autonomy.

3.4 Synchronic and Diachronic Self-Control

What do Bratman's *agential* governance and direction as ways to control have in common with Fujita and colleagues' proposal of governance and direction as elements of control mechanisms? And where do they differ? One theory is motivated by concerns about autonomy and responsibility. Another theory is driven by psychological and cognitive findings regarding the way human agents organize their behavior. Both give us functions that can help us understand coherence. In Bratman's case the coherence is understood in a more normative manner, leading to an account of *self*-governance and autonomy. Fujita and colleagues are more open about the possible functions that lead to coherence and what sort of coherence such processes are after also due to the underspecified ways in which purposes (direction) get defined. Bratman's proposal could be *one* of the many ways coherence is possible in Fujita and colleague's account. The coherence spelled out by Fujita et al. falls short to these requirements. What they have in common, is the idea that hierarchical structures can provide coherence, but the means by which they do, and the standards such coherence is held up to is different.

Spelling out the differences between synchronic and diachronic self-control is another way that shows us the differences and potential relations between Bratman's work on self-control and Fujita and colleagues' proposal on control. Synchronic self-control refers to self-control in the moment and in circumstances

---

[34] Bratman (2007) proposes a functional account, making sure the does not fall prey to the homunculus fallacy.

of vulnerability whereas diachronic self-control pertains to self-control over time. Diachronic control is often created though consistency over time of self, intentions, and plans. Intentions, plans, and commitments are to keep the agent from giving in to current desires that would divert her. In social psychology there has been a focus on solutions that also succeed if the agent is less strong-willed.

For example, someone who is addicted to a certain series and would be tempted to binge-watch a full season of the series may be unable to resist watching another episode, especially with online platforms that automatically play the next episode once the previous one has finished. This person is unable to exercise synchronic self-control. Nevertheless, her binge-watching tendencies need not also prevent her from forming a second and incompatible desire. In such a case, agents might purposively leave their laptop charger at work, allowing themselves only two hours before the battery runs out, and in doing so creating a situation that will allow them to act as they perceive best. By exercising such diachronic self-control, they enable themselves to circumvent situations they cannot handle. Horstkötter (2015) writes:

> Exercising diachronic self-control, if one finds oneself unable to exercise synchronic self-control, is not merely a conceptual and practical possibility, rather, it constitutes a normative requirement. The self-control failure of those who fail to achieve their goal, because they lack a suitable psychological strategy or capacity, does then not consist in not having tried hard enough. Instead, it consists in having failed to enable themselves and to put themselves in a situation in which the capacity they lack would not be required.
> (Horstkötter, 2015, p. 34)

Creating the right circumstances becomes part of the normative obligations that come with self-control. Implementation intentions could be part of such stage setting. Goals are not pre-given, but their formation is part and parcel of the very exercise of self-control, especially when they allow the agent to set up the situation as such that they automatically, or at least with little effort, act in line with their previously determined goals. This is how they might get to play a role in Fujita et al: the other processes do not give us the goals. We can now also see how control that doesn't live up to the normative standards as spelled out by Bratman, can play a role while an agent exercises self-control as defined by Bratman.

This chapter looked at the issue of control, with a focus on philosophy of action, specifically Bratman's approach. Two relations took central stage: (a) the relation between mere bodily movement and intentional action and (b) the relation between agency, control, and self-control. Referring to the discussion on the binary distinction between automatic and non-automatic that was treated in chapter two, I proposed to be more careful when introducing mere activity as an intermediate category between mere bodily movement and intentional action. Instead of a (clear-cut) threefold distinction, I proposed to see the distinction as a more gradual one, which is in line with the discussion in the current chapter. Then I had a closer look at the agential notion of self-control and the more widely interpretable notion of control. Again, the notion of automaticity was important for the discussion. I argued that if we better understand the relation between control and self-control and the diachronic relation between the two, we can see how control and self-control can be conceptualized as different yet highly interdependent functions. While we now have a way to relate the different types of control, it should be clear that mere activity, or anything on a spectrum that would be closer to mere activity than to intentional action, does not come with the same kind of autonomy as intentional action. Autonomy and self-governance, as understood by Bratman, does not apply in these cases. Self-direction might, in some cases, be in place, but even that is not a given. This leaves us solely with a negative definition of mere activity: it is not mere bodily movement, nor is it intentional action. In the next chapter I will look for ways in which we might be able to understand such forms of control from the perspective of motor control and skill. If we want to relate this to autonomy and self-governance, we will have to find ways to connect the mechanisms in skillful action to reason responsiveness.

4 Motor Control and Skillful Action

This chapter's main focus is on skill acquisition and skillful action, which will be key ingredients in my approach to skillful joint action. Orthodox theories of skill acquisition and skillful action put a heavy emphasis on the automation of certain movements. Recent theories by Fridland (2014) and Christensen and colleagues (2016, 2019) focus on the integration of several levels of control. They go against the traditional picture of automation. This is in line with my suggestions in chapter two on our understanding of the automatic/non-automatic distinction. To understand these novel theories of skillful action, we must first be acquainted with the more general background of motor control and motor cognition. The chapter is set up as follows. First, I will introduce relevant details of generally accepted views of motor control. Then skillful action will be discussed. The third part of this chapter focuses on the degrees of freedom problem and its relation to skill acquisition as well as joint action theories that will be discussed in chapter six.

4.1 Motor Control

Standard accounts of action are silent on the role of motor cognition and motor intentions. Yet interest has grown over the last two decades with several authors looking at the functions motor cognition can fulfill (Butterfill & Sinigaglia, 2014; Christensen, Sutton, & McIlwain, 2016; Fridland, 2014; Mylopoulos & Pacherie, 2017; Pacherie, 2008).[35] In my brief review of motor cognition below, I will mainly focus on its role in the *acquisition of skills* and *performance of skillful action*.[36] The recent debate on skillful action creates conceptual room for actions

---

[35] Assuming that propositional attitudes play a role in our behavior on at least some occasions, how do we solve the interface problem? (Mylopoulos & Pacherie, 2017; Butterfill & Sinigaglia, 2014). On these views, cognitive representations are propositional in structure, while sensorimotor representations have an internal structure that maps to the perceptual and kinematic dimensions involved in an action context. This way of thinking has resulted in worries about the interface between cognition and sensorimotor systems – that is, about how representations of these distinct types might interact in performing actions.
[36] I will have a different focus than most people working in that field. Two key issues, for example, are the *sequencing and timing problem* (how are behaviors ordered in time?) and the *perceptual-motor integration problem* (how are perception and motor control combined?) (Rosenbaum, 2009). Although these are highly interesting problems of their own, their details do not bear consequences for my account of action and joint action.

that are neither automatic nor non-automatic, which will be helpful for my discussion of joint action in this intermediate space. Moreover, the three levels of control that Fridland (2014), Christensen et al. (2016, 2019), and Pacherie and Mylopoulos (2019) introduce will allow us to conceptualize three levels of coordination between interacting agents.

My discussion of skill acquisition and skillful action will also touch upon another important problem for motor cognition: the problem of *degrees of freedom*. Degrees of freedom can be metaphorically understood as the number of joints we can move in order to reach a certain goal. The guiding question here is how an agent selects *specific* movements in order to achieve particular tasks when, as is almost always the case, the range of potential movements with which that task can be completed is near infinite. Put differently: how does an agent reduce her degrees of freedom? The problem of degrees of freedom has been used as a paradigm for understanding joint actions. In the joint case the main idea is that, although the total number of degrees of freedom (the amount of joints involved) is larger, the degrees of freedom of individuals interacting are mutually constrained by the degrees of freedom of the partaking other(s).

Before turning to skill acquisition, skillful action, and the degree of freedom problem, I will briefly review the hierarchical division of tasks that most cognitive scientists use in their models of (skillful) motor cognition.

4.1.1 Hierarchical Division of Labor

Successful locomotion, or smooth movements, have been understood through the fluidity and correctness of the sequence and timing of the movement (James, 1890). Cognitive scientists in general and scholars working on motor cognition in particular are concerned with how agents are able to time and sequence their behavior. Most current theories assume that elements of response sequences are organized hierarchically (Schack & Messner, 2006; see Rosenbaum, 2009 for a discussion), which is in line with the proposals of skillful action that I will discuss below. The distinguishing feature of a hierarchical organization is that it has distinct levels of control. A considerable amount of evidence suggests that hierarchical models provide a useful explanatory framework for understanding motor control. For example, in the context of the sequencing and timing problem, a hierarchical model does much better than any other model (Rosenbaum, 2009).

Earlier attempts to model how agents sequence and time their behavior had difficulties to accommodate our ability to follow and apply rules.[37] These models relied on sequencing and inhibition (see Rosenbaum, 2009). More recent models, which introduce a hierarchical dimension, allow us to understand a rule as a function applied to any of a large number of possible instances. The function can be assumed to occupy a "higher" level in the hierarchy that allows us to skillfully and fluidly act, and the sequences to which the rule applies can be assumed to occupy, or be represented at, "lower levels" (see Rosenbaum, 2009). Hierarchical models give us a way to understand the appearance of schema-like patterns in our behavior.

In a hierarchical structure schema-like patterns are understood through ascending level that each contain more abstract information, and in that sense fewer and fewer (more basic) elements. Different levels will have different representations. Low-level units could promote the formation of higher-level units, which in turn could promote the formation of still higher-level units, which would allow us to understand skillful action (Rosenbaum, 2009). Skillful action accounts that work with hierarchies assume that more abstract information is processed by the higher levels processes that allow for more flexibility in the processing. The timing of the different elements that are involved in a certain action can also be explained by such hierarchical structures. When we engage in behaviors that have several distinct elements, such as speaking, typing, or walking, the elements of the behaviors must be ordered correctly in time. The best conceptualization of the fluidity and correctness of the sequence seems one that includes a hierarchy of different levels with (micro-)plans (Rosenbaum, 2009).[38]

Different types of grouping are used on different levels of the hierarchy and different "chunks" are generated. A chunk is a combination of moves or letters that is easier to remember. When people are asked to recall certain sets of letters, for example, they are better at this task when they can easily chunk the letters together. FB IC IA might be harder to remember than FBI CIA, even though the amount of letter, as well as the order of the letters are exactly the same. This is

---

[37] The oldest solution to the sequencing and timing problems was offered by William James (1980) who suggested that one movement provided the stimulus for the next movement. Inhibition was later added, solving some of the problems that were left open by James' solution, such as the problem that one starting point can be followed by different outputs (Rosenbaum, 1985).

[38] The existence of schemas and rules underlying our behavior is hard to prove. Hierarchical models give us a way to understand the appearance of schema-like patterns in our behavior. A schema can be conceptualized as a knowledge structure that can be instantiated in different ways depending on the values of its underlying variables or parameters.

only the case because FBI is a chunk, on some level. If no such chunk is available we have to recall the individual items, on a lower level of the hierarchy. Research suggests that different sorts of "chunks" and different types of grouping occur in hierarchically organized information related to memories subserving motor control as well as memories subserving more symbolic activities like chess playing (Miller, 1956).

Speech provides a clear and well-studied example of the existence of a hierarchical structure in the way we produce speech. When we make a mistake in the pronunciation of a certain word, consonants only get replaced with other consonants, and vowels only get replaced with other vowels. Similarly, nouns tend only to exchange with other nouns, and verbs tend only to exchange with other verbs. The structured way in which we make errors suggest that there are distinct levels of representation in the planning and production of speech (Fromkin, 1980) and errors occur within such levels. The kinds of speech errors that people make indicate that speech is not simply produced by planning and then executing one utterance at a time. Rather, a general plan is set up for an extended sequence of forthcoming utterances (Lashley, 1951).

This logic also applies to actions. Consider, for example, the typical kind of errors that occur when we are distracted: pouring the sauce into one's glass rather than next to the fries, or swapping letters while writing down a word. Such errors are indicative of the fact that our bodily actions, like our speech, are based on plans with distinct functional levels. The error arises because an abstract description of the task to be achieved exists in the mind of the actor and the specifics of the task situation are misidentified (Norman, 1981).

Scholars have shown that the different kinds of mistakes that are made in different languages are highly dependent on rules of grammar and pronunciation, which indicates that a theory of sequencing in general must account for *psychological* as well as *physiological* constraints (Jordan, 1986). These results fit well with the idea that there are different levels that provide structure to our behavior, giving us the capacity to organize and time our behavior appropriately. This idea is also assumed in skillful action, where, as in the examples given above, the different levels of the hierarchy are closely integrated.

4.1.2 Skill Acquisition

At least since the time of Plato the question what defines skillful performance in terms of specific capabilities, knowledge, competence, and expertise has concerned us. The debate on skill acquisition and skillful action as it is carried out in psychology and cognitive science, on the other hand, was shaped around two fundamental assumptions. Firstly, it was assumed that innate talent accounts for skilled performance (Galton, 1979). This assumption is still widely accepted by many athletic coaches and music teachers today, but mostly refuted by cognitive scientists (see Rosenbaum, 2009). Secondly, theories on skillful action and skill acquisition adopted a strict distinction between those actions which we are capable of performing skillfully and those where reflection on what the agent is doing is needed while performing the action (Anderson, 1982; Fitts & Posner, 1967; Shiffrin & Schneider, 1977). It was assumed that skill acquisition was mainly, if not only, a process of automation. The agent would start learning a movement in a reflective manner and the process automatize incrementally. In short, the main question was *how* we automatize, i.e. how we can perform the same action without need for reflection or attention. Recent findings put pressure on this idea that there is full automatization, and they further suggest that automation is not the only key to understanding skillful acquisition (see Fridland, 2017, for a discussion).

Potentially due to, or next to, automaticity, there are other skill-related improvements including better timing, tuning, and coordination (Rosenbaum, 2009).[39] An alternative understanding of skill acquisition and skillful action that is receiving more and more support is that deliberate practice is of substantial importance. In addition to, or instead of, sheer talent, the amount of deliberate practice one devotes to a skill accounts, to a large extent, for how well the skill develops (Ericsson, Krampe, & Tesch-Römer, 1993). Learning is aided by practicing *deliberately*. Skill development is aided by practicing often and with concentration on those aspects of performance that need improvement. In order to account for the relation between deliberation and automation, a more sophisticated conceptual framework must be developed in which not all of the change that accounts for skill acquisition is explained by automatization. Before I turn to the role of automaticity in skillful action (section 4.2) I will first briefly discuss a popular view on skill acquisition.

Paul Fitts (1964), a pioneer in the field of skilled performance, suggested three principal stages of skill acquisition. During the initial *cognitive phase*, one learns the basic procedures to be followed, often using verbal cues. Talking to oneself is common at this early stage of skill acquisition, and a considerable

---

[39] Research in skill acquisition and skillful action is linked to memory research. Overall a link is assumed between automated action sequences and non-declarative (procedural) memory, and between reflectively performed actions and skill acquisition and declarative memory (Anderson, 1982; Dreyfus & Dreyfus, 1986; Squire, 2009). The details may differ, i.e., Dreyfus and Dreyfus argue that intuitive responses are based on holistic pattern-recognition, Anderson argues that we build associative links between successive actions.

amount of attention is also usually required in this early stage. The second stage, the *associative phase*, represents a transition from reliance on verbal, conscious control to more automatic control (Fitts, 1964). Fitts believed that during this stage the learner tries out various task components and associates them with the success or failure that follows. Through this associative process, task components that contribute to success are preserved, whereas task components that contribute to failure are eliminated (Johnson, 1984). In the third stage, the *autonomous* or *automatic phase*, behavior is performed quickly and consistently with little conscious involvement. Performance at this stage is possible even while one is engaged in other tasks simultaneously. Besides varying the timing of muscle events, skill learners alter patterns of inter-limb coordination.

The automation of action is thought to open up capacities for different (simultaneous) tasks. Skilled typists can repeat what is said to them while they type (Shaffer, 1975), and with enough training, adults who have had extensive practice reading and writing can read intelligently while simultaneously writing down and even categorizing words presented to them at the same time (Spelke, Hirst, & Neisser, 1976). This might be related to the fact that skilled agents shift from continual to intermittent reliance on feedback (Pew, 1966).[40]

In terms of understanding the factors that contribute to skill learning, the findings of Ericsson, Krampe, and Tesch-Römer (1993) indicate that there is a clear intellectual component to skill acquisition throughout the process. Rote practice does little good compared to focused exploration of alternative ways of performing. Deakin and Cobley (2003) asked figure skaters to complete diaries about their skating practice habits. The diaries revealed that elite skaters spent 68% of their practice sessions rehearsing risky moves. Lower-ranked skaters spent only 48% of their time rehearsing risky moves. Attention plays a role both while acquiring a skill and, as we will see in the next section, while acting skillfully.

---

40 There is an entire field in philosophy and cognitive science that is devoted to these differences. There are interesting links between the literature on skill acquisition and different types of knowledge (knowing how and knowing that, procedural and declarative knowledge), which bear important consequences for the representational format that they are thought to be in (Ryle, 1949; Squire, 1987). And there are important discussions regarding the different types of memory that are involved. Although these definitely bear consequences for the discussion here, it is beyond the scope of this book.

4.2 Skillful Action

4.2.1 Reasons for Less Automation – Stepping away from the Dichotomy

One of the standard reasons to assume that skill acquisition is related to automation is that control was conceptualized as a slow process. Since skillful action often involves very rapid responses, it would therefore be near impossible to exert control over them. In what Papineau (2013) calls the speed argument, it is argued that cognitive control doesn't govern action execution because the latter occurs too quickly. He uses cricket batting as an example. At the elite level the time from the release of the ball by the bowler to its striking the bat is between 0.4 and 0.8 seconds. The argument relies on the assumption that this is too fast for controlled processes: these processes need to be automatic. As Christensen et al. (2019) point out, however, there exist controlled processes that occur within even shorter time spans, so the speed argument in itself is insufficient to assume that (agentive) control does not play a role in skillful action. Furthermore, Christensen and colleagues also point at the fact that there are plenty of skillful actions that are not taking place at such high speed.

Another argument against the idea of full automation comes from the *action execution complexity argument* that has been put forward by Christensen et al. (2019). They argue that many skills are too complex and context dependent to be fully automated. Agents need flexibility because their skills are exercised in constantly changing and new situations where new combinations of possible action responses are required. They use braking on a mountain bike tour to illustrate this flexibility. Many factors influence braking, such as the topography, type of surface, equipment, and braking technique. It seems unlikely that for each specific situation we have an automatized response in the sense of "automatic" described above. Schack and Mechsner (2006) found that individuals with a great deal of tennis-playing experience had more structurally elaborate mental representations of the observed serves than did low-level players or non-players. These findings support the hypothesis that skill acquisition is associated with the formation of ever more elaborate hierarchical structures. This goes against the idea that skillful action is skillful and efficient because there is only one step of memory-retrieval (Fitts, 1964). We cannot conclude that no attention is required to carry out a task once it has been practiced, just because its carrying out now requires *less* attention (Strayer & Drews, 2007). It seems rather that attention shifts to different aspects of the activities the agent is performing (Christensen, Sutton, & McIlwain, 2016). Instead of a strict distinction between experts and novices, there are more gradual distinctions, just as with the distinction between automatic and non-automatic processes. During skill acquisition, and later during skillful performance, the attention will shift between different aspects of the action the agent is performing. This is in line with a subset of alternative approaches to skill that propose there is substantial involvement of (higher-level) cognitive components (e.g., Christensen, Sutton, & McIlwain, 2016; Ericsson, 2006; Fridland, 2014; Papineau, 2013; Pacherie & Mylopoulos, 2019).

4.2.2 Three Levels of Control

It is a relatively common idea that the automation that occurs during skill acquisition frees up attention. Once we have learned how to cycle or how to drive a car, we can easily have a conversation whilst driving. While we are still learning to shift gears, we might not be able to hold such a conversation, the conversation or the driving would go awry. In cognitive tests such automation is often tested through the simultaneous performance of the target task and an unrelated (cognitively demanding) task. Several authors have recently stepped away from this picture of complete automation and suggested that attention becomes available for higher-level aspects of control of the skillful action at hand (Christensen, Sutton, & Bicknell, 2019; Schmidt & Wrisberg, 2008; Vallacher & Wegner, 1987; William & Harter, 1899). In other words, rather than attention disappearing from the scene, attention shifts.

To better understand how attention might shift and in what way the agent can focus on higher-level aspects of the task several authors have distinguished multiple levels of control (Pacherie, 2008; Fridland, 2014; Christensen, Sutton, & McIlwain, 2016). Each of these different theories distinguishes *three levels of control*.[41] Although there are differences in the details, their theories show large overlap in comparison to the previously described theories on skillful action. The trichotomy below follows the presentation by Christensen and colleagues. Then I will discuss some of the main differences between these various theories.

- *Strategic control*: Governance of an extended course of action so that it achieves one or more goals.
- *Situation control*: Determining what actions need to be performed in the immediate situation in order to achieve the overarching goal.
- *Implementation control*: Governance of the execution of the actions specified by situation control.

---

[41] It should be noted that Christensen et al. (2016) are not committed to the division of three strict levels. It should, rather, be understood as an idealization, where the number of levels of control can vary with the activity and it may not always be possible to clearly differentiate levels.

Apart from these three levels of control, Christensen and colleagues propose that the (situational) awareness of the expert changes. I come back to this idea below. Fridland (2014) roughly follows the same distinction, but relies on top-down, automatic attention to integrate situation control and situational awareness.

Fridland nicely characterizes the highest level, strategic control, as "the goals, plans, and strategies that the agent uses in order to guide various instantiations of motor skill" (2014, p. 18). These are the kind of states that are, at least in principle, accessible to the agent and can be integrated uncontroversially with conceptual, propositional, personal-level states.[42]

Christensen et al. (2016, 2019), have argued for the integration (meshing) of these different levels of control. The three levels of control taken together give us a conceptualization of what they call *online control* (Christensen, Sutton, & McIlwain, 2016; Christensen, Sutton, & Bicknell, 2019). The main idea is that agents control their actions through several control processes that function in unison. The model assumes a broadly hierarchical division of labor, in line with Rosenbaum's proposal and Schack and Mechsner's findings, thereby stepping away from the idea of full automation. Online control is more closely linked to Bratman's idea of self-governance than older theories of skillful action because it leaves room for decisions made by the agent while acting skillfully. Yet it is less reason-based, partly because there is no time to deliberate at the moment of acting, and the entire situation could not be planned in advance. Cognitive control is not eliminated, but rather shifted to a more abstract level, such as long-term goals, or the combination of a goal with the specific requirements of the current situation. At the same time these new views are committed to the idea that many cognitively controlled actions (and skills) can have a great deal of automaticity.

A good example of situation control, and how it interacts with strategic control, comes from descriptions of mountain biking by Bicknell (2010). I will discuss this example of situational control and online control in mountain biking and directly follow up with my example of dancing together. It will demonstrate the relevance of the interaction of different levels of control in the case of dancing together, showing the applicability of the theory of online control to

---

[42] There is another issue in the debate on skillful action and the relation between different levels of control and their different formats, which has been called the interface problem by Butterfill and Sinigaglia (2015). They argue that the two processes have to function mainly independently of one-another because they have different formats and therefore cannot communicate well. Christensen et al. (2019) argue that propositional representation may not be the only format employed by cognitive control. Mental imagery (Kosslyn, Ganis, & Thompson, 2001) and mental models (Johnston-Laird, 1983) are *prima facie* examples of non-propositional representational formats.

joint action performances. During a race a mountain bike rider might exert strategic control both with respect to the race itself but also with respect to goals for the season and more general personal goals (Bicknell, 2010). Now take a moment where another mountain bike rider falls and the rider that is right behind this person must change path. The person still riding must quickly adapt to and navigate the altered path in front of them or they will likely crash as well. Given the unlikelihood that the competitor still riding has the possibility to safely jump over the fallen rider, it's more probable they'll find another way around so as not to injure that rider, or themselves. Depending on specific situational features, they may be able to cycle around the fallen rider on the side of the track (an area not previously practiced) or have to stop and get off their own bike to pass by. These options rely on different skillsets and a rapid assessment of the situation in relation to goals for the race.

This example can easily be translated to the case of ballroom dancing that I presented in the introduction. Any dancing couple will have long-term plans, including the choreography, but potentially also an important upcoming show or competition. As with the case of the mountain biker that is right behind someone that fell, ballroom dancers will often have to adjust their plans because of the other couples on the floor. What the couple will do will depend on their skill and a rapid assessment of the situation.

As I indicated earlier, next to a trichotomy of levels of control, Christensen and colleagues introduce a second important factor: *situational awareness*. They propose that attention goes to information that is of importance for a skillful performance in this specific situation (which is only possible if the agent has experience, is skilled). Relying on studies on Naturalistic Decision Making (NDM), they show how the awareness of one's surroundings change with the skills one has.[43] In Fridland we find a similar idea regarding changes in the agent's attention due to skill acquisition. In Fridland's theory this is included as the second level of control, which she calls situational attention.

NDM is of particular interest for my project because it is helpful in understanding skillful action in other situations than elite sport performance. Both skillful action as approached by Fridland and by Christensen and colleagues, as well as NDM give ways to understand how else joint action can be organized. This helps us to step away from the traditional distinction between emergent coordination and planned coordination, which I will turn to in the next two chapters. Situational awareness, as presented in Christensen and colleagues, is

---

43 In section 7.3.3, I will say more about NDM and how it fits in my proposal.

the least developed concept in their framework of online control.[44] The key idea is that situational awareness highlights parts of the environment based on someone's expertise and current tasks. This occurs without explicit inferential reasoning processes (Christensen, Sutton, & McIlwain, 2016). This makes it possible to talk about cognitive control without the need of referring to explicit decision making, explicit reasoning processes, and traditional rationality theories.

Fridland (2014) combines the notions of situational control and situational awareness (as spelled out by Christensen and colleagues, 2019) in her conception of *selective, top-down, automatic attention*. She draws inspiration from Wu (2011, 2014) and Pylyshyns's (2003) work on attention and the role attention plays in action.

Wu (2011) argues that attention is an overlooked aspect of our agency that helps with action selection. He maps the many inputs that we get and the many outputs that would be suitable to these inputs on what he coins *the behavioral space*. A behavior is the actually chosen path in the behavioral space. Which path to take in this map is a problem that agents must solve. Perceptual attention is a necessary part of Wu's solution. Not all choices that are made need not to be intentional, they can also be habitual, automatic, involuntary, or unintentional actions. The *role* of habits, skills, attention, and intentions is to aid appropriate path selection in an agent's behavior space. On the level of neural structures, this could be understood as biasing the mental processes, altering and strengthening specific routes.[45] What skillful agents are capable of, on the basis of their input-output coupling profile, are *more* types of controlled behavioral outputs than available to less capable players (they have a bigger map), and better selection of this larger variety of controlled outputs (they have a selection of good routes available).

The role that attention plays in skillful action is then twofold: (1) it structures and coordinates multiple lower-order, automatic processes toward the completion of a represented goal, and (2) continuously sustains the goal's representation (Fridland, 2014; Christensen, Sutton, & McIlwain, 2016; Bermúdez, 2017). Loss of attention can cause the agent to wander from the current goal or intention. While

---

[44] This is partly due to the kind of literature Christensen et al. (2016) use (NDM) to conceptualize situational awareness. NDM is studied in field experiments, making it much harder to support claims that differentiate cognitive processes that are involved in the process of making a decision. Rather, it shows us how it *does not* work, but that, as a theory in itself might not be very satisfying.

[45] Wu introduces *intentions as standing states* that persist over time (rather than events that occur at a time). It is not the case that for these to influence, they must be events. Intentions can then be states that structure how the many-many problem is solved.

the action evolves over time several other possible actions have to be inhibited or blocked, even if they are very strongly present (Bermúdez, 2017; Fridland, 2014; Wu, 2011, 2014). Top-down cognitive control allows the agent to keep her goal in mind and not get distracted by other possible actions.

Fridland integrates this idea into an account of skillful action. She writes:

> The second variety of control that is relevant for any theory of skill to take into account is what I call, following both Wu (2014) and Pylyshyn (2003), selective, top-down, automatic attention. This kind of attention is responsible for selecting the relevant features in an environmental array that a skilled agent should gather information about and respond to, given her goals, plans, and strategies. This requires learning how to control one's attention, which means learning to attend to the right things at the right times.
>
> (Fridland, 2014, p. 22)

Selective attention is deployed automatically once the trained agent initiates intentional action. Although it is automatic, it is also semantically integrated with the personal-level, intentional states of the agent. It cannot be construed as a cognitively impenetrable process and must be sensitive to the content of the goal states and strategies that the agent possesses at the level of strategic control.

Before I will draw more general conclusions based on this threefold distinction of levels of control, including a more close-up discussion of the expert decision-making outside sports, using studies in naturalistic decision-making paradigms, I will first turn to another major discussion in the field of motor cognition that has yielded interest by theorists working on joint action: the problem of degrees of freedom. For now, I will mainly discuss the problem that degrees of freedom pose in relation to motor control. In section 6.1, I will discuss the joint action approach by Tollefsen and Dale (2012) that uses degrees of freedom in their conceptualization of joint action.

4.3 Degrees of Freedom

When an agent picks up a cup there are many different ways in which she can do this. The degrees of freedom problem occurs whenever there is a many-to-one mapping (Bernstein, 1967). There are many, sometimes even infinite, ways of getting things done. The degrees of freedom in a system are the number of ways the system can independently vary. The degrees of freedom are dependent on the number of joints involved in a movement. The phrase "degrees of freedom problem" is used by motor-control researchers because generating a physical action generally involves going from many possible degrees of freedom to just the few that characterize the task that is selected.

Although explaining which degrees of freedom are used in solving a certain task raises the question how we select specific movements over others, having many behavioral options in itself is not a curse but a blessing. If you come home with your arms filled with groceries and need to turn the light on in your apartment, you may do so with a nudge of your shoulder. You wouldn't flip the switch with your shoulder if your hands were free, however. Having many possible ways of performing a task gives the option of performing the task in a way that makes sense at the moment, in a situationally suiting manner. Rather than a problem, it is an opportunity for adapting to changing environmental conditions (Rosenbaum, 2009). Researchers in motor cognition have tried to define how agents solve the problem, how they reduce their degrees of freedom. There are three options that seem to occur in everyday life and when we acquire new skills: 1) soft constraints through synergy; 2) interdependency; and 3) efficiency. I will discuss these in more detail.

(1) *Synergies* are interactions between different joints or movements of joints. Synergies can reduce the degrees of freedom that must otherwise be independently controlled. Consider the following commonplace phenomenon. If you are like most people, no matter how hard you try, you probably cannot keep your eyes open when you sneeze. This interaction seems "hard-wired" in the sense that there is nothing you can do about it. It is, however, not hard-wired in the sense that mouth and eye movements always are interacting in such a way. Only in the case of sneezing does a particular combination of mouth- and eye movement occur. This example illustrates how one kind of motor activity can automatically dictate what other activities may occur (Bernstein, 1967).

(2) Our joints also have functional yet flexible *interdependencies* that help us coordinate our actions such as the coupling between our arms and legs while walking. The activity of one extremity affects the activity of the other extremity (Amazeen, Amazeen, & Turvey, 1998; Swinnen, Massion, Heuer, & Casaer, 2013). There are many such functional linkages between different parts of the body. These linkages influence what movements can and cannot be done at the same time. Such interactions have ancient evolutionary origins (Rosenbaum, 2009). Physical properties of the body can eliminate the need to control each feature of neuro-motor control (Bernstein, 1967; Bizzi & Mussa-Ivaldi, 1989).

Both synergies and interdependencies do not actually eliminate degrees of freedom because they are not necessary connections. Rather, they bias the neuro-motor system to perform in certain ways (Rosenbaum, 2009). They are a so-called soft constraint. They help reduce the degrees of freedom

through their interdependence, but there is the option to act differently (even if this would require a lot of concentration).
(3) The final approach to the degrees of freedom problem relies on *efficiency*. The efficiency of a movement is determined through the reaching of a) an end position, and b) the smoothness of the movement. The idea here is that the movements we make are usually more efficient than the movements we don't make but would allow us to reach the same goal (Rosenbaum, 2009). Efficiency also includes taking into account future movements that become more/less available when we make the first movement in a certain fashion, or the general openness to new movements even if they are undefined yet. People are sensitive to this fact. They deliberately adopt awkward initial postures when taking hold of objects if those initially awkward postures let them end the maneuvers in comfortable or easy-to-control final postures.

Degrees of freedom can be spelled out in relation to certain goals. Which goals are selected, however, cannot be explained by degrees of freedom. Degrees of freedom in our current posture can constrain what follows, for example when I am leaning on my arm and I simultaneously want to grab something, it will be easiest to use my other arm: my position shapes my future movements. but the very fact that there are degrees of freedom problems left despite these three constraints shows that they in themselves cannot be fully determining what will happen: there is still something (the goals) to be accounted for.

4.3.1 Degrees of Freedom and Skill Acquisition

Bernstein (1967), who introduced the problem of degrees of freedom, suggested that novice performers try to reduce the complexity of the problem by locking joints, and then, with experience, involve more joints and letting the joints move more freely. This has been called the uncontrolled manifold hypothesis. This transition has been observed in an experiment that analyzed the motion and stability of people learning to shoot handheld pistols (Arutyunyan, Gurfinkel, & Mirskii, 1968). Novice shooters first held their wrists and elbows rigid but unlocked their wrists and elbows as they practiced more, allowing their firing accuracy to improve. Several studies have found such unlocking of joints. However, other studies have not found this same progression of unlocking mechanical degrees of freedom, indicating that this is not a general pattern. Given that unlocking joints as the agent becomes more skilled is not the only explanation in our understanding of improvement of skillful action, the degrees of freedom approach seems compatible with the suggestions of Fridland (2014) and

Christensen and colleagues (2016, 2019) that focus on the role of attention, automation, and control.

The learning of novel skills, viewed through the lens of degrees of freedom, has not only focused on this pattern of freezing and freeing degrees of freedom while we learn a new skill. We can also learn new synergies through practice, which is something that is found in dancers:

> Sometimes synergies develop naturally, such as the pattern of arms and legs in walking and running. In other circumstances, synergies develop through practice and training, such as the tendu and dégagé in ballet and modern dance, or the hand and foot coordination in classical Indian dance. (Krasnow & Wilmerding-Pett, 2015, p. 156)

Such synergies can serve several functions. For example, they can facilitate movements and improve the esthetic quality of the movement.

4.3.2 Degrees of Freedom in Joint Action

Joint action can be understood as inter-limb coordination between agents rather than within agents (Tollefsen & Dale, 2012). In a study where participants were free to decide to lift particular planks alone or together and were required to make their decision on the fly as the plank passed by on the conveyor belt the degrees of freedom of the couple were taken into account (Richardson, Marsh, & Baron, 2007). Individual action systematically depended on the ratio between plank length and the groups' joint arm span. Participants with a longer arm span took into account the shorter arm span of their partner and the transition from individual action to joint action followed the same dynamic principles as the transition from uni-manual to bi-manual action in individual plank lifting. Mottet, Ferrand, Bootsma, and Reinoud's (2001) study provides evidence that actors can jointly optimize performance to particular object sizes and particular distances between objects. Just as is the case in individual actions, it seems that some of these constraints can be better understood as soft constraints, rather than hard constraints.

Degrees of freedom in individuals are only hardwired to some extent. Many of the inter-limb relations that help us reduce the degrees of freedom are soft constraints. In the joint case all constraints are soft constraints. This, however, can be perfectly well combined with high levels of automaticity or difficulty of doing it differently.

Although the total amount of degrees of freedom becomes larger if we are acting with several agents together, there has been a focus on the reduction of degrees of freedom because there are other agents involved that limit the available (viable) options. This reduction of degrees of freedom can easily be translated to the case of ballroom dancing. Apart from the reduction of degrees of freedom for esthetic reasons that I already pointed at in other forms of dancing, ballroom dancing often involves two agents bending their knees to the same degree, having the same amount of sway to one side (a sway is a stretching movement of the body side. Sway describes a dancer's body position in which the entire body deflects from the vertical). This reduction of the degrees of freedom, however, does not solve the puzzle *how much* the couple will sway their bodies.

4.4 Conclusion

The last part of this chapter will sketch some of the implications that theories on skillful action have on other domains that are less associated with fast-paced bodily movement. As I pointed out before, not all forms of expertise are so strongly related to bodily control and to speed. The hierarchical division of different tasks that has been proposed in motor cognition theories in general, and applied to theories of skill acquisition and skillful action more specifically, allows for a translation to less speed and motor-control related skills and expert decisions.

Naturalistic Decision Making (NDM) is a field of literature on decision making that focuses on experts in the field. NDM research has defined itself in contrast with formal decision-theoretic approaches to decision-making, and NDM researchers have the view that experts don't typically make decisions by generating and analyzing an extended list of options (Klein, 1993). In that sense they divert from the traditional picture of practical deliberation where "all options" are considered in order to determine what should be done best. The general gist of this field of research is that experts often do not seem to evaluate *all possible action options* in order to determine which is best.[46] Rather, they look for an *action option that is good enough*. This fits with Simon's (1983) idea of bounded rationality.

The ability to recognize good-enough options depends on (trained) situational attention, as described in Christensen and colleagues' and Fridland's paper. NDM research has arrived at a picture of expert performance where experts often engage in quite extensive cognitive processes (Christensen, Sutton, & McIlwain, 2016). In part, it is argued that full automaticity would be problematic because the situational requirements will be different at each occasion that

---

[46] The research is interesting but also hard to compare because they often involve field studies. It gives us ecologically validity, but because the situational factors are less controlled, it is also less clear what cognitive components can be distinguished in the process (Klein, 1993).

decisions must be made. In chapter seven, where I will propose an understanding of skillful joint action, I will discuss the resources we can get from NDM.

The previous chapter focused on a brief discussion of control and self-control in philosophy of action and how the standard theory of action divides behavior into two categories. Based on the discussion in chapter two on automaticity and the problems of a strict dichotomy between automatic and non-automatic processes, I suggested to focus on direction and governance and how this relates to control in agency. I did this partially to avoid the problems that are created by introducing the "mere activity" category. I ended with a proposal for implicit intentional action, which might give us one way of understanding the "in-between". We saw how theories of skill acquisition and skillful action used to follow the same dualistic division but have moved away from this view. This gives us a first idea about how to think about the intermediate case and the complex case of ballroom dancing.

In this chapter we saw that the phenomena that we want to describe, skillful actions, are best captured with a concept of action control that is hierarchically organized, with (roughly) three levels of control. These three levels are highly interdependent. I will return to this threefold distinction as building blocks for chapter seven, where I will introduce my own account of skillful joint actions. Before getting there, I will focus on four proposals regarding joint action that focus on more "low-level" cognitive functions.

5 Planning Agency and Shared Agency

5.1 Introduction

In the upcoming chapters there is a stronger focus on collective intentionality and joint action. This, rather long chapter, will discuss Bratman's normative account of shared agency. In the following chapter (6) I will discuss theories of joint action that are inspired by cognitive and psychological research, taking a descriptive approach. These theories are also set apart by their respective focus: planning coordination and emergent coordination. The work in the previous chapters will give us a lens to look at several problems that already have been pointed out on each "side" of the debate. After discussing these two different branches of collective intentionality and joint action I will make a first proposal towards skillful joint action, integrating planning agency, coordination that emerges on the spot, and something that lies in between: situational coordination.

Before looking at Bratman's account of *planning* agency and *shared* agency two things must be said that explain my approach to his work. First of all, it has often been said that Bratman's planning theory of shared agency is over-intellectualized (Butterfill, 2012, 2015; Tollefsen, 2005).[47] I agree, to some extent, with this critique and will argue that it also extends to Bratman's underlying picture of individual agency. To better understand what is at issue, I will also discuss Bratman's methodology and some of the key elements in his account of individual agency. The second thing that must be accounted for, is my choice for Bratman's theory as the only theory I treat in detail. I already pointed out my reasons in section 1.2, but will briefly recap them here. First of all, Bratman has one of the most developed and most discussed positions in the field. Secondly, the fact that Bratman has a fully developed account of individual agency as well as a fully developed account of shared agency is important for the kind of work I want to do here regarding the over-intellectualization. Last but not least, Bratman's work has been a starting point for many working in closely related fields, such as the work by Michael Tomasello and his lab on joint action and social understanding.

In this chapter, Bratman's action theory and theory of collective intentionality will take center stage. Bratman's action theory is best described as a planning

---

47 This does not only apply to Bratman's theory, but to the general debate on collective intentionality where the approaches start with the assumption that a propositional attitude is shared in some way.

theory of action. The core idea is that human agency is directed at and structured by future plans, a cohesive self-image, and social embeddedness:

> We are purposive agents; but we – adult humans in a broadly modern world – are more than that. We are reflective about our motivation. We form prior plans and policies that organize our activity over time. And we see ourselves as agents who persist over time and who begin, develop, and then complete temporally extended activities and projects. Any reasonably complete theory of human action will need, in some way, to advert to this trio of features – to our reflectiveness, our planfulness, and our conception of our agency as temporally extended. (Bratman, 2007, p. 21)

A planning agent is distinguished from a purposive agent through several extra constraints to the choices she makes. Both agents show goal-directed behavior. The simplest version of a purposive agent that Bratman describes would be an agent that acts on her strongest current desire, assuming she believes this is feasible. A planning agent takes her future plans and future self (including, for example, ideas about future regret) into account:

> . . . structures of planning agency of the sort I am trying to describe are basic and, perhaps, distinctive aspects of our agency. Many animals, human and nonhuman, are purposive agents – agents who pursue goals in light of their representations of the world. But we – normal adult human agents in a modern world – are not merely purposive agents in this generic sense. Our agency is typically embedded in planning structures.
>
> Second, appeal to such planning structures allows us to articulate basic features of intention and decision, features that distinguish such phenomena both from belief and from ordinary desire. We characterize important and distinctive roles of intention and decision in shaping ongoing reasoning and action without appealing, as Davidson says, to "mysterious acts of the will".
> (Bratman, 1999, p. 5; Davidson, 1980, p. 83, as quoted in Bratman, 1999)

Diachronic and synchronic coherence, or the possibility to agglomerate beliefs, intentions, and plans, is a key element for understanding planning agency. Being a planning agent allows humans to exercise self-control as discussed in chapter three.

Bratman mentions a trio of features (reflection, plans, and temporal extendedness) that together are closely related to the idea of consistency. Temporal extendedness of our agency helps us better understand why the other two features, planning and deliberation, are both desirable features. They can help us engage with the environment in a successful way through anticipation of future regrets and consequences of our actions and actions that seem tempting in the here and now but might be downgraded through this future perspective. Furthermore, certain goals and desires are only obtainable if we can arrange our behavior such that we do not undermine our own plans. We plan because we foresee the future, and because we foresee the future we plan. This idea of temporal extendedness, together with planning agency is not only relevant for the individual, but also the starting point for his account on shared intentions. The temporal extendedness of our agency as individual and as part of a group is an important factor in understanding why we engage in deliberation and planning in the individual and the joint case.

I will follow Bratman in his suggestion that the function of planning intentions[48] should be understood in their forward-looking orientation. This future-directed orientation differentiates his theory from other accounts of human agency, such as Anscombe (1957), Goldman (2006), and Davidson (1971, 1980) who give methodological priority to "intentions in action".

There are further reasons why Bratman's theories of planning agency and shared agency are central to this book. I endorse his assumption that it is reasonable to assume that the human capacity for planning agency allows us to interact and act jointly in ways that other animals are incapable of. I also agree with him that it is exciting and necessary to explore what the implications of our specific capacities are for understanding shared agency. Further, Bratman offers one out of a few complete and comprehensive theories on collective intentionality. He has been named "one of the big four" thinkers of collective intentionality (Chant, Hindriks, & Preyer, 2014) and has been influential outside philosophy, including debates on the development of joint action skills in children (Butterfill, 2012; Tollefsen & Dale, 2012; Tomasello, Carpenter, Call, Behne, & Moll, 2005).

The chapter follows the ensuing order: the last part of the introduction will reflect on how Bratman's theory fits into the current trend of naturalizing philosophy. Section 5.2 discusses Bratman's methodology and his account of (individual) planning agency. This will set the stage for section 5.3 that deals with his account of shared agency. Sections 5.4 to 5.7 zoom in on specific parts of his account of planning agency and shared agency that are relevant to my project: the importance of diachronic coherence (5.4), the introduction of policies (general applicable intentions, 5.5), cognitive limitations and purposive agency (5.6), and control, autonomy and agentic purpose in both the individual and the shared case (5.7).

---

48 Intention is a very widely used and discussed notion. Bratman has introduced an argument to distinguish intentions from desires and beliefs by alluding to the specific functionality of intentions. His notion stands in relation to planning and justifying reasons for action. To preclude ambiguity, I will use the term "planning intention" when I talk about the notion of intentions as defined by Bratman. Other accounts that will be discussed usually focus on less demanding notions of intention, such as being able to answer what it is that one is doing.

A Route to Naturalizing Intentions

Before looking in greater detail at the relation between planning agency, shared agency, and heuristic thinking there is another point that needs clarification. There are several ways in which one can understand Bratman's theory. The most minimal, or modest, interpretation is that he offers a how-possibly model. How-possibly models describe how a set of parts and activities might be organized such that they exhibit the explanandum phenomenon (Craver, 2006, p. 361). Intentions have often been described as mysterious. One way to make them more plausible to play a role in human action is to show that they can be conceptualized in a metaphysical plausible way. This is the approach taken by Bratman. He formulates metaphysically plausible building blocks that allow for such complex functions to be demystified. The most maximalist way to read Bratman's theory is to read it as a proposal of how our psychology works all of the time. This latter interpretation is highly unlikely to give us a model of human agency in everyday activity. The first reading yields underwhelming results. I take Bratman to position himself somewhere in between (Figure 2).

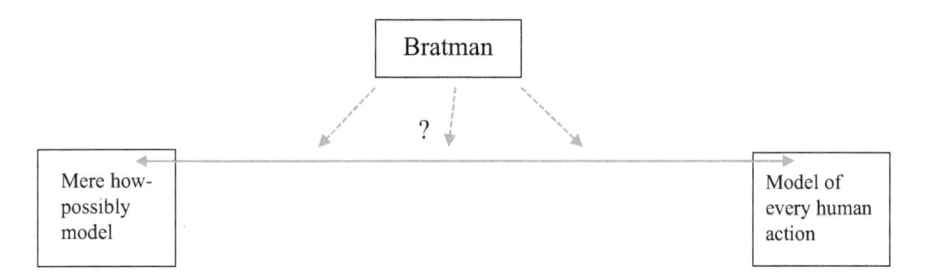

Figure 2: Positioning the model: From mere how-possibly to a description of all human agency.

We need to clarify to what extent Bratman is taking his own account to be an adequate conceptualization of human action. At this point I am not talking about what happens in our brains. The most minimal understanding of what I am interested in, is to what extent many of our every-day activities can be captured by Bratman's conceptualization of human agency. A second question is whether such a conceptualization does right to human agency. For this second question I will depend on certain findings in social psychology and cognitive science. I will argue that he does take his account to have descriptive value, at least as a "minimal model" (Metzinger, 2004). This is important because I question the psychological adequacy of Bratman's theory. Such a critique would only stand if we are not supposed to understand his model as a mere how-possibly model.

In order to position myself in relation to Bratman's shared agency three elements of his theory will be central in my rendition of his theory: (a) his methodology, which involves modeling through creature constructions, (b) his account of planning agency, and (c) his account of shared intentions.

These three elements are strongly connected. Bratman takes his account of shared intentions to be an extension of his theory of planning agency, and he achieves both positions through creature construction. Creature construction is a methodological approach introduced by Grice (1975) that allows us to build how-possibly models. The basic idea of a creature construction is that we start with a simple agent that is assumed to be metaphysically plausible. Both Grice and Bratman start with a creature that can respond to desires. New features are introduced as metaphysically plausible building blocks. By adding new functions – that are again thought to be metaphysically plausible – we can show that a combination of simple building blocks can get to complex forms of agency, such as we find in human agency and shared agency.

The status of Bratman's creature construction, and where it puts him on the scale I displayed above, will be discussed in section 5.3. At some points he seems intent on merely demystifying complex forms of agency. At other points his models appear to be models of our (human) actual psychological functioning. In demystifying complex agency, one is not necessarily concerned with the particularities of *human* agency. In that case it suffices to show how complex forms of intentionality and valuing could be realized without taking into account how this is done in human agents. But if Bratman is committed to the idea that he gives an adequate conceptualization of (a part of) human agency, as I will argue he is, his theory should be able to answer the set of questions I set out below. Before I set out these questions, let me start by saying that Bratman's creature construction is highly useful because his redescription allows for naturalization of intentions as planning states. Demystification opens the possibility to naturalize, and this is partly what my project is about.

An aspect that has not gotten enough attention in his theory is what human agents are doing in those cases where they are not acting as described by his planning theory of action. When we accept that we sometimes – but not always – act as outlined by his creature construction of planning agency we need to know how behavior based on planning agency relates to other forms of agency that we also find in human agents. Do human agents act following earlier, simpler, versions of his creature construction? Or do they act based on a completely different principle or set of building blocks? The second question concerns the fact that Bratman's approach functions through coherence in action and thought. If, however, agents sometimes (or often) act following another principle, the question rises what the consequences are to this notion of coherence. The overarching idea of coherence seems to push towards a picture of humans trying to be coherent over all our actions. And although I think that this might be a normatively adequate picture of what we want ourselves – and others – to do, it is not a descriptively adequate picture of the actual motivation of all of our behavior. We should reengage with his theory to better understand the relationship between the (normative pressure from) planning agency and other forms of agency.

Bratman's account of shared intentions is centered around three guiding ideas, which partly repeat what we saw in his approach to planning agency. The first idea is that we have to "try to understand aspects of mind in terms of characteristic roles and associated norms" (Bratman, 2014, p. 26). This means that we must wonder what fundamental roles shared intentions play in our lives, and what norms are associated with them. These roles are primarily "roles in temporally downstream social functioning, including later shared reasoning and bargaining shaped by these shared intentions" (Bratman, 2014, p. 27). The norms that are associated with these social roles of shared intentions are norms of social agglomeration and consistency, social coherence, and social stability. Secondly, he uses his theory of "intentions of individuals as elements in partial, coordinating plans" (Bratman, 2014, p. 26). The third guiding idea is, again, Grice's methodology of creature construction. Bratman argues "we should be struck by the analogues, in the shared case, of the coordinating, structuring, organizing, guiding, and settling roles of intention in the individual case!" (Bratman, 2014, p. 27)

Sections 5.4–5.7 discuss specific aspects of his theory that stand in relation to the ongoing exploration regarding the relation between planned coordination and emergent coordination. Bratman has ideas on how to include bounded rationality and heuristic thinking into his theory of planning agency. I will argue that the integration of skillful action, heuristics and bounded rationality, as proposed by Bratman, fails to recognize the unawareness of the agent to the functioning of the processes involved. This has implications for the way we can integrate, or relate, heuristic thinking to Bratman's theory of planning agency, and it has implications for the way we think about the relation between emergent coordination and planned coordination.

Since Bratman's account of shared agency is built on his account of individual agency, these points concerning bounded rationality and policies have important implications for his theory of shared agency too. Some problems are even more pressing in the shared agency case, exactly because the intention is shared and several people are contributing to a shared goal, which has consequences for the understanding of (individual agentic) control.

5.2 Planning Agency

5.2.1 The Methodology of Creature Construction

Humans are one – known – type of agents that show complex forms of agency which seem best described by functions such as intentions that stand in complex relations to one another. Some have argued that the assumptions that are made in action theory, such as the existence of intentions, are metaphysically implausible. Gilbert Ryle (2009), for example, argued that volition and intention were at best unnecessary reifications of some of our ways of talking about action. Elizabeth Anscombe (1957) felt that intentions were very mysterious. Bratman's demystification project should be understood as an argument for plausible metaphysics that give us agency that is as complex as human agency. Such a demystification, however, does not have to be evolutionary adequate or descriptively adequate.

No matter how important such a claim of plausibility is, in the end we want a theory to do more than demystify. We want to be able to say more than planning behavior is possible on such an account, we want to say that this is also the way human adult agents – at least partially – structure their behavior. I realize that a descriptive adequacy is compatible with pluriform conceptualizations. However, as will become clear below, Bratman is committed to the idea that his conceptualization adequately captures many of our actions. Bratman's demystification, so I will argue, indeed seems to aim at a theory that is conceptually adequate when describing human agency in a range of cases.

I will discuss the relation between Bratman's action theory and conceptual adequacy in further detail by looking closer at his discussion of this demystification, and what he says about his creature construction in relation to conceptual adequacy. I will do so mainly based on a specific paper by Bratman that focuses on the different steps and building blocks, but will also discuss further work, especially "Shared Agency: A Planning Theory of Acting Together" (2014), where shared intentions take central stage.

Demystification is accomplished through what Bratman calls a creature construction (Bratman, 1999, 2000, 2014). He takes the concept from Grice. A creature construction is a construction:

> ... according to certain principles of constructing, a type of creature, or rather a sequence of types of creature, to serve as a model (or models) for actual creatures.
> (Grice, 1975, p. 37)

In Grice's approach we see that the models are supposed to describe actual creatures. In this sense they differ from how-possibly models that only show the metaphysical plausibility without necessarily saying anything about the similarity in functionality and functions in the model and what is modeled. Demystification does not concern the actual psychological functioning or the usual functioning of human agency. Its primary focus is on showing mere possibility:

> The general idea is to develop sequentially the psychological theory for different brands of pirot [prototypes or creatures], and to compare what one thus generates with the psychological concepts we apply to related actual creatures. (Grice, 1975, p. 37)

An important part of creature construction is starting with simpler agents. One then adds metaphysically plausible additional building blocks that help generate more complex forms of agency. Note how Grice, whom Bratman takes the methodology from, includes a link to the psychological concepts that apply to the agent we try to model. For Grice the method clearly has a wider scope than creating mere how-possibly model. Although Grice envisions these models to have this wider scope, these models are not supposed to show the evolution of planning agency or shared agency. Nor are they supposed to describe brain structures. The models are describing psychological functions that we refer to in our folk psychology. They do so with specific attention for different conative states, states with a world-to-mind direction of fit:[49]

> The idea is not that this is how our planning agency actually emerged within an evolutionary, historical process. The idea is only that such a hypothetical series of constructed creatures can help us understand complex elements of our actual planning agency, elements that are compatible with our limitations and build on but go beyond less complex elements in ways that respond to basic concerns with cross-temporal coordination.
> (Bratman, 2014, pp. 25–26)

Demystification serves to show that something complex can be understood based on more simple notions, making it plausible that we are, for example, planning agents that act on policies, plans, and intentions. For example, creature two will have all the features of creature one, and something additional that allows us to understand more complex forms of agency. Each additional feature, or building block, is supposed to be metaphysically plausible, and in this way the total construction (the result, not the process) is also supposed to be metaphysically plausible. Other complex notions that are made metaphysically

---

49 The technical term "direction of fit" is used to describe the distinctions that are offered by two related sets of opposing terms: mind-to-world and world-to-mind (Searle, 2001, pp. 37–38). A belief has a mind-to-world direction of fit. A belief depicts the world as being in a state of affairs such that the belief is true. Beliefs aim to fit the world. A desire, on the other hand, normally expresses a yet to be realized state of affairs and so has a world-to-mind direction of fit. A desire, unlike a belief, doesn't depict the world as being in that state; rather it expresses a desire that the world be such that the state is true. Desire is a state that is satisfied when the world fits it.

plausible include free will and our capacity of valuing desires and beliefs and their relation to justifying reasons for acting.

When creating a creature construction empirical adequacy is not the main objection. This is especially the case for the way in which one model is built by adding onto another earlier model in a non-evolutionary order. So, on the one hand, Bratman uses creature construction as a method to show the metaphysical plausibility of complex forms of agency. On the other hand, he often seems to imply that his account can give a description of how we actually act, intend, and plan (Bratman, 2000) and the target phenomenon, the inspiration for creature construction, is human agency. This implication is further supported in the way the elements of his creatures include limitations that Bratman introduces as limitations to human agency. Think of the limited time that we have available to reflect, or the limits of our cognitive capacities.

The impression that Bratman offers more than mere demystification is further confirmed in conclusions following creature constructions that include wordings like "I think this picture depicts human agency", "In these respects our model of Creature 8 seems to me to capture important core features of our agency" (Bratman, 2000, p. 259), and "this model of Creature 8 seems in relevant respects to be a (partial) model of us" (Bratman, 2000, p. 260). In all these cases one could argue that Bratman is still merely committed to a mere how-possibly model: he does never say something like "this is describing core human functions", but rather talks about "depicting", "capturing", and "modeling". Nonetheless, the implications suggest that he aims at more than a mere how-possibly model. Secondly, the limitations on cognition and time that Bratman takes into consideration reflect human limitations in our capacities as planning and intending agents. They have no use in a strictly metaphysical argument on the possibility of planning agency.[50]

Bratman uses creature construction at several points in his work (Bratman, 1999, 2000, 2014). He uses such constructions when he tries to demystify intentions and plans, and to show that we can understand complex human tendencies such as valuing and the will through building a specific kind of creature with basic building blocks (Bratman, 2000). In Bratman's book on shared agency (2014) he pursues three interrelated aims: (1) a conceptual aim, (2) a metaphysical aim, and (3) a normative aim (Bratman, 2014, p. 4). He does not, unfortunately, explicitly define as a fourth aim the psychological adequacy of his theory. By the

---

[50] Not only Rational Choice Theory faced a problem from naturalism, but any theory on rationality does: infinite processing is needed to get to rationality in the traditional definition. So, even if we are not modeling human agents, we might want to make room for bounded rationality, including limitations such as time constraints when constructing "merely" a demystification.

aim of psychological adequacy, I mean that the theoretical implications that we can draw from investigations from cognitive science and social psychology are taken into account. Although Bratman does not seem to be opposed to the idea of integrating such an aim, it is not a central aim of his project. A closer inspection of his metaphysical claim, which uses creature construction, suggests that he is indeed not opposed to this idea. He writes about the metaphysical aim:

> What is the metaphysics of human agency and what is its place in the natural world? This aim includes questions about the basic elements of the world that constitute our shared agency, and the relation to those that constitute our individual agency.
> (Bratman, 2014, p. 4)

Bratman specifically inquires after the metaphysics of *human* agency, not *any* agency. To do so Bratman also includes the time-constraints and cognitive limitations that human agents face. Overall, I think it is safe to say that for Bratman demystification does more than merely demystify. It is also supposed to give a conceptually descriptively adequate theory of human agency – or at least an important and influential part of human agency. Now we are faced with a second question: What is it a description of? Is it a description of most of our agency? Or should we think of it as a model of a possibility for agency we rarely use? Assuming that it is desirable to act based on our capacities as planning agents, but also taking the point that we do not always manage to do so, how can we understand the relation? In sections 5.4–5.7 I argue that this has consequences for his theory. Looking at theoretical work in skillful action, for example, can show us different routes to intelligent and flexible behavior that could (and should) be integrated with Bratman's account.

5.2.2 Eight Steps to Planning Agency – A Creature Construction

In the paper "Valuing and the Will" we find a more extended version of human (planning) agency understood as a creature construction (Bratman, 2000). The idea that we are planning agents is taken as the explanandum; the steps and different creatures are the explanans. The construction aims to show why we need planning agency, and also why planning is primary. Bratman starts the construction with an agent that is only a minimal agent (Creature 1), that has

> . . . beliefs about its world and various desires concerning different possible states in that world, including different possible acts it might perform. (Bratman, 2000, p. 251)

From there he adds capacities and limitations so that the model recognizably applies to us: to represent core human features. Through adding new psychological functions, Bratman arrives at more complex (and closer to humans, or so he argues) models of agency. Thus, when I discuss the capacities of the creatures that follow after a simpler creature, they all have the capacities of the earlier creatures too. It is an accumulation of capacities, not a replacement. The modifications and additions come from observations about what such a (simple) model would lack. For example, a relatively simple creature with desires and beliefs, such as Creature 1, lacks future regret. This lack, Bratman argues, makes its behavior incomparable to the behavior seen in human agents. The first four creatures Bratman constructs are relatively simple creatures, they are based on beliefs and desires. Let's have a look at the models from creature one to creature eight. Creature one only acts on the strongest desire, that is the desire that is strongest at particular time t. This creature can have several contradicting desires and the desires and beliefs are not organized in any "systemic" way. This agent, Bratman argues, is only an agent in a limited sense. The first characteristic that Bratman builds into the follow-up creatures is robustness, or stability. This is achieved through adding reflectivity. Creature 2 takes direct consequences of desired behaviors into account, Creature 3 treats desired ends as justifying. "[M]any of Creature 3's considered desires will concern matters that cannot be achieved simply by action at a single time" (Bratman, 2000, p. 252). But in order to be able to keep to such desires that extend over time, it needs other capacities.

To take all this into account is a relatively big requirement. And in order to make this less cognitively demanding and time consuming, Bratman includes the capacities to settle in advance on complex but partial plans of action. Creature 4 settles on partial plans of action in advance, extending the agency over time. This makes Creature 4 a planning agent. Once a plan is in place Creature 4 can simply continue with what it had earlier planned to do rather than step back and reconsider what present action is best supported by its current beliefs and considered desires (Bratman, 2000, p. 253). Nevertheless, at time t Creature 4 will often rather not do what was planned. Bratman's example is a person who has a policy to work out every day, yet never gets to it, because on that specific day she does not feel like it. This temporal discounting, he argues with Ainslie (1992), is quite common. Therefore, we need an extra step in the creature construction. He introduces Creature 5, which takes its future self into account. Bratman suggests this is done through anticipated future regret. Knowing that one will later regret abandoning a plan works as an additional motivational force to stick to the plan. Creature 6 takes the consideration of one's future self a step further through reflective endorsement and rejection of desires, which is made possible by introducing the capacity and disposition for hierarchies of higher-order desires, in line with Harry Frankfurt's ideas on higher-order desires. Having a higher-order desire does, however, not explain why this bares more power than the first-order desire. The basic point is that Creature 6 is not merely a time-slice agent. It is and understands itself to be a temporally persisting planning agent, one who begins, continues, and completes temporally extended projects. On a broadly Lockean view, its persistence over time consists in relevant psychological continuities (for example, the persistence of attitudes of belief and intention) and connections (for example, memory of a past event, or the later intentional execution of an intention formed earlier) (Bratman, 2000, pp. 256–257).

Particularly policies that reject certain desires are relevant to explain the interaction between "first-order" and "higher-order" desires as we find them in Frankfurt (1988). To give authority to these higher-order desires Creature 7 not only has plans and policies concerning action, but also concerning desires. This creature "exhibits a merger of hierarchical and planning structures" (Bratman, 2000, p. 257). Creature 7 is, however, limited in deciding which desires and policies should motivate our behavior, it is limited in the capacity to take a "stand concerning how he will treat his desires as reason-providing in deliberation" (Bratman, 2000, p. 258). An agent needs to be able to commit herself to certain policies, plans, and desires. The last and final step that Bratman thinks to be important to get close to the core capacities for human agency, is the:

> . . . capacity to arrive at policies that express its commitment to being motivated by a desire by way of its treatment of that desire as providing, in deliberation, a justifying end for action. (Bratman, 2000, p. 258)

Desires have become reason-providing, and for the creature to be in control, is for such policies to be in control:

> [Creature 8] is an agent with considered desires and beliefs, stable plans and policies, and higher-order self-governing policies some of which may be reflexive in the way just highlighted. In these respects, our model of Creature 8 seems to me to capture important core features of our agency. (Bratman, 2000, p. 259)

Such stability is arrived at partially because the agent tries to form a coherent set of desires, intentions, plans, and policies. These policies are crystallization of complex pressures and concerns, some of which are grounded in other policies or desires. The table gives a brief overview of the steps from Creature 1 to 8 and includes the step to social agency (Figure 3).

To Bratman Creature 8 seems "to capture important core features of our agency" (Bratman, 2000, p. 259). On the other hand, a bit later he states, that Creature 8 "seems in relevant respects to be a (partial) model of us" (Bratman, 2000, p. 260). So how should we understand this claim that Creature 8 captures *core* features of our agency? Bratman gives some clarifications on how we should

Bratman's Creature Construction of Planning & Shared Agency

Model/ Creature #	Key new capacities and limitations on each level
1	Moved by strongest desire or cluster of desires
2	Moved by strongest desire(s) and their direct consequences
3	Treating desired ends as justifying
4	Settle on partial plans of action in advance
5	Taking one's future self into account (anticipated future regret)
6	Reflective endorsement and rejection of desires (through higher-order desires)
7	Plans and policies apply to intentions, plans, and desires
8 = Human agency	Policies express commitment by desires by way of treating the desire as providing, in deliberation, a justifying end for action (Bratman 2000)
Social	Sharing desires, intentions and plans as justifying ends for action, having common knowledge of these shared intentions (Bratman 2014)

Figure 3: Bratman's creature construction of planning agency and shared agency.

not understand this claim. He writes that he does *not* claim that all the complexity of human agency is explained by appeal to planning structures. "My claim is only that planning structures are one salient and theoretically important aspect of the psychology that underlies our agency" (Bratman, 2014, p. 4). On this understanding planning agency is the feature that determines a large part of the agent's behavior. In that case it is a core feature in the amount of behavior and thought is organized and/or caused by these capacities.

Planning agency also tells us something about the uniqueness of human agency in comparison to other types of agency that we find in the natural world. In the same book he also writes the following:

> The claim is not that the intention-like roles I have been high-lighting are realized in all forms of agency, or that the associated norms on intention apply to all agents. Not all agents are planning agents. There can be purposive agents – dogs and cats, perhaps – who do not have the organizational resources of planning agency. But it seems plausible that we – adult humans – are, normally, planning agents, and that this is central to characteristic forms of cross-temporal organization in our lives. The planning theory is a theory about the nature of intentions understood as central elements in this fundamental form of human, temporally extended agency. (Bratman, 2014, p. 23)

On this understanding of planning structures as the core feature, it is understood as the distinguishing feature of human agency. It is what makes human agency special. Of course, these two ways of understanding planning agency to be at the core of human agency can be adhered to simultaneously. And it appears to me that Bratman is indeed committed to both understandings of planning agency being a *core* feature.

Both interpretations, however, leave us with the question of the relation between those moments where we act in line with Bratman's account of planning agency, and those cases when we don't. What about those occasions where human agents act as purposive agents, rather than planning agents? In those cases where Creature 8 does not capture human agency, what would be the best way of conceptualizing what the agent is doing? Would it be best conceptualized as through one of the earlier creatures that Bratman provides us with? Or should we start from completely different principles or building blocks? Planning states are at the core of Bratman's theory, yet they only come into the picture through a complex combination of building blocks. Planning agency relies heavily on coherence, consistency, and agglomeration, in time and over time. Such constraints make most sense when coherence and consistency concern the overall picture and not when we consider them for individual actions. A more basic model cannot integrate this – core – aspect of his theory. It seems that when we act based on a different functionality than planning, we are left with the question how this combines with planning agency. I will reflect on these issues in sections 5.4 to 5.7.

5.2.3 Creature Construction of Social and Shared Agency

Creature construction is also used as a method to show that collective intentionality is a concept that is not mysterious (Bratman, 2014, pp. 25–35). Planning agency is used as the conceptual foundation on which Bratman builds his theory of collective intentionality:

> When we see planning agency as such a step in creature construction, it will be natural then to see the step from individual planning agency to shared agency as yet a further

> step in creature construction. And that is what I will do. Further, I will argue that this step to shared agency can be conceptually, metaphysically, and normatively more conservative than the step from individual, temporally local purposive agency to individual temporally extended planning agency.
> (Bratman, 2014, p. 26)

This quote describes how the metaphysical assumptions that are made when we move from individual planning agency to shared agency are supposed to be minimal. Once we introduce planning agency at the individual level, it is easy to see how such planning agents can share intentions. The transition from purposive agency to planning agency is a larger step than the one from planning agency to shared agency.

Together with the assumption that planning agency gives us a better and richer understanding of shared agency, this metaphysical assumption is a reason for Bratman to focus only on shared agency through planning agency. My claim, however, is that we have good reasons to also focus on purposive agency and its role in shared agency. Considering that animals and young children also act jointly, it would be interesting to know how "large" the step is from purposive agency to shared (purposive) agency.

> Constructivism does not suppose that all that is important in shared agency is fully grounded in such broadly individualistic planning structures. Constructivism grants that our shared agency frequently draws on subtly and frequently unarticulated commonalities of sensibility. Think of our sense of conversational distance. Constructivism grants that much of our shared activity takes place within larger moral, cultural, political, and legal structures. Constructivism grants that there can be distinctive social values at stake in shared agency – for example, the value of certain forms of social unity and social governance. Constructivism grants that shared agency raises distinctive issues of trust and trustworthiness, as well as issues about ordinary civility. After all, the stability of a shared intention may well depend on the extent to which the participants can reasonably trust each other. And constructivism grants that there can be complex relations between shared intention and related moral obligations of each to another [. . .].
> (Bratman, 2014, pp. 34–35)

One possible problem for Bratman's creature construction of shared agency is the critique that it is cognitively too demanding to be an adequate description. Young children that engage in joint actions have not yet mastered some of Bratman's building blocks for planning agency, let alone shared agency (Butterfill, 2007, 2012; Pacherie, 2013). Is Bratman's account too demanding for our cognitive capacities and given time constraints? Bratman gives an indirect answer to this potential criticism. He writes:

> The first thing to say is that it is unclear that this concern with psychological demandingness applies more forcefully to the basic thesis than it does to proposals that appeal instead to we-intentions or to joint commitments. [. . .] we might in the end see the capacity of

young humans for modest sociality (if such there be) as itself evidence of the sort of psychological complexity at issue in the basic thesis. (Bratman, 2014, p. 104)

This quote needs some unpacking. Searle (1990) introduces we-intentions as a primitive, distinctive, kind of intentions. Gilbert (1989) introduces joint commitments as a new entity needed to explain shared agency. Bratman's proposal of shared intentionality is based on individual capacities that are already in place for other functions and, in that sense, it does not require us to introduce a new entity. Considering theoretical parsimony, he argues, his theory does better than those that introduce new kinds. Bratman's theory only needs more of the same kind. That is, it needs more individual intentions.

Roles and norms bring us from (a) individual desire belief purposive agency to (b) individual planning agency. Bratman suggests that to go from (b) to (c) shared intention and modest sociality through appropriately interrelated intentions of the individual participants is a more conservative step than to go from purposive agency to shared purposive agency (Bratman, 2014, p. 13). This is because we can build on the capacity of planning agents to understand social agency. As Bratman writes:

> My aim is to provide a construction of interconnected intentions of individuals whose individual-norm-assessable, individual-norm-guided, and individual-norm-conforming functioning (according to the planning theory of individual agency) would constitute and help explain the social-norm assessable and normally social-norm-conforming social function of shared intention. (Bratman, 2014, p. 33)

In this section Bratman deals with this potential problem by arguing that other accounts of joint action face different problems of capacity and complexity. The fact, however, that this might be the case (a) does not tell us anything about the problem his account faces. Furthermore, in describing these other accounts that face similar problems (b) Bratman does not discuss the simplified version of his account that are supposed to be a solution to this problem. Lastly, a lot hinges on the idea that "we might in the end see the capacity of young humans for modest sociality as itself evidence of the sort of psychological complexity at issue in the basic thesis". This is problematic because Bratman does not provide us with an argument that this is the case. And, looking at the discussion on social cognition in young children, the assumption seems problematic. Bratman's account needs the ability to know each other's state of mind, and this seems to be one of the things that young children lack. Bratman gives the following possible route to make his approach viable for young children:

> So we can ask whether certain forms of shared agency involve versions of some but not all of these elements: say, mutual responsiveness and interdependence in the absence of

> interlocking. Some such less-demanding structures might, perhaps, turn out to be common in the sociality of younger human children. (Bratman, 2014, p. 105)

Bratman fails to answer the question why he assumes that the capacities that young children use are later completely replaced instead of complemented with planning agency and shared agency based on planning agency. Once we assume that children act jointly, based on different and likely less cognitively demanding forms of agency, one has to give an explanation why the functions that allow such behavior would extinguish completely (Figure 4).

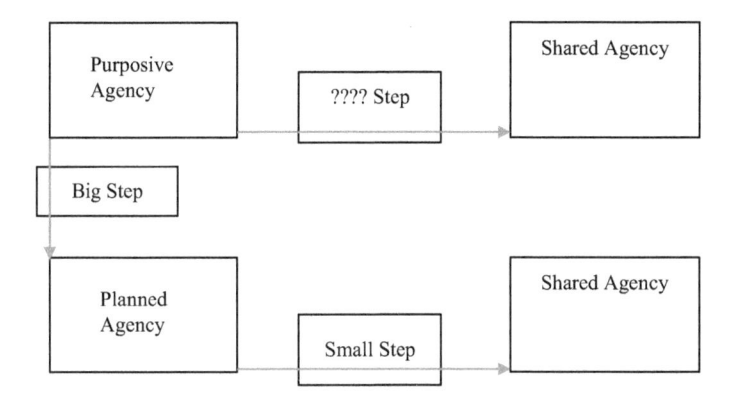

Figure 4: Metaphysical steps and assumptions.

To conclude, the creature construction of shared agency has similar problems with adequacy as a descriptive account as the creature construction of individual planning agency has. Now that Bratman's account of individual agency, intentions, and plans has been discussed to some extent, I will turn to his account of shared agency and collective intentionality in this section. After this section I will discuss several specific concepts that are used in both Bratman's account of agency and shared agency that are of relevance to my account of skillful joint action.

5.3 Shared Agency

I will start this section with describing the target phenomenon that Bratman has in mind, shared cooperative activity, and the functional roles needed for such activity. Examples of the phenomena Bratman wants to capture include painting a house together, cooking a meal together, or dancing together. Paragraph 5.3.1 will present the sufficient conditions Bratman spells out for his account of shared agency. It needs to be stressed that Bratman has an account of sufficiency conditions for one (specific) form of shared agency. Recall also that, in principle, he is open to the idea of other ways of spelling out the relation between the individual's mental states and behaviors and sharedness. In practice, however, as noted in section 5.2, where I discussed individual planning agency, through the way Bratman sets up his account it becomes less clear how different models can be combined. This will be further discussed in Paragraph 5.3.2, which focuses on a technical argument considering the difference between intend *to* and intend *that*. Bratman argues that a shared intention can only have the form "I intend that we". This has several implications for the conception of intention that is involved and the relation between intention, autonomy, and control. But first we need to know more about the functions that Bratman tries to capture with his sufficiency conditions.

Functional Role
Bratman has two considerations in elaborating shared intentions (see also Knoblich, Butterfill, & Sebanz, 2011, p. 25, for a discussion). A theory of shared agency (a) has to specify the functional role shared intentions play and (b) it should give us a substantial account of what shared intentions could be. Regarding the first part Bratman stipulates that the functional role (or job) of shared intentions is to:
(i) coordinate activities;
(ii) coordinate planning; and
(iii) provide a framework to structure bargaining (Bratman, 1993, p. 99).

Bratman (1993, 2014) uses the phrase "shared intention" rather than "collective intention". This is motivated by his individualistic aims when it comes to the nature of intentions. To understand shared intention we "should not appeal to an attitude in the mind of some superagent" (Bratman, 1993, p. 99). The choice to talk about shared intentions is also motivated by the role they play in shaping and informing the behaviors and intentions of the individuals that are involved. Shared intentions help to coordinate our intentional actions. They coordinate our actions by making sure that our own personal plans fit together (mesh) with the plans we make with others.

Shared intentions are a starting point for joint actions. They can, for example, be the background against which bargaining and negotiation about the specificities of a plan with other agents occur. This is partially possible because intentions function as commitments, mainly to the agent herself. This function relates to Bratman's ideas about diachronicity of our agency, plans, and the general wish for coherence. It is also a familiar role for planning intentions; they form constraints on future possible options. Once committed to X, this has implications for further possible actions and plans. An intention or plan constrains future decisions. Bratman illustrates this with the example of two people who plan to paint a house together. Painting requires (at least) two tasks: applying masking tape and the painting itself. Thus, the two painters can now coordinate who will carry out which task. They do not need identical individual intentions or plans in order to coordinate their actions. Suppose that Wendy wants to start painting and Matt wants to start taping, and their individual intentions and ensuing plans to do so mesh, this is sufficient (the individual goals are coordinated through the shared intention of painting together). But now suppose that Wendy wants to paint the house in a different color than Matt. In this case their plans do not mesh and the shared intention cannot be satisfied. Note that meshing and especially knowledge about meshing is important for these examples. Regarding non-meshing subplans, Bratman argues that the fact that Wendy and Matt intend to paint the house together provides a background for bargaining. This might be compared to the individual case where an agent might have two incompatible desires and needs to adjust something in order to have a coherent, or meshing, set of desires and intentions once more. Considering that they still plan on painting the house together, Wendy and Matt will have to find a way that suits both: they will attempt to mesh their intentions. In this case they need to settle on a color for the paint.

5.3.1 Sufficiency Conditions of Shared Cooperative Activity

Philosophy on collective intentionality centers on the debate about what is necessary and/or sufficient for joint action. Bratman studies *one* kind of shared agency; *shared cooperative activity*. Shared cooperative activity is shared intentional activities of (a) small, adult groups, which (b) composition remains stable over time and in which (c) no asymmetric authority relations exist (2014, p. 7). According to Bratman, a shared intentional activity is a coordinated activity that is the outcome of a certain pattern of intentions and beliefs that are distributed among the participants. It is this pattern that Bratman identifies as the shared intention. He does not give an account of several other common group setups and their potential for action, such as groups in institutional settings (corporate agents), nor an account of infants and animals that act in groups.[51]

---

[51] His account has been criticized for not being able to handle actions that occur without prior planning (i.e. "emergent coordination" and joint actions that are initiated without previous planning or commitments).

> We seek [. . .] a construction of interconnected intentions and other related attitudes [. . .] that would [. . .] play the roles characteristic of shared intention. (Bratman, 2014, p. 32)

Shared intentions, which allow for shared cooperative activity, have the three aforementioned functions. Shared intentions serve to (a) coordinate activities, (b) coordinate planning, and (c) structure bargaining. These functions can be understood as *necessary* conditions to be able to speak of shared agency. Note how these three functions are the social equivalent of intentions and plans in the case of individual agency: intentions give us norm-assessable and norm-guided behavior. Intentions and plans coordinate the activities a group plans, in the same way that they do for the individual. They coordinate planning, especially when there are several intentions and actions at play. Although an individual might not have to bargain (function c), she might have to consider one desire or intention in the light of another, in the same way a collective might.

5 Conditions of Shared Cooperative Activity

Bratman (2014, p. 103) then spells out five conditions that must be in place, that together generate these three functions. He is not committed to these conditions being necessary conditions. Instead he spells them out as sufficient conditions: when these five conditions are in place we have shared agency. There might be other conditions that also, when fulfilled together, provide us with the guarantee of shared agency. These are the five Bratman offers:

A. Intention condition: We each have intentions that we J; and we each intend that we J by way of each of our intentions that we J (so there is interlocking and reflexivity) and by way of relevant mutual responsiveness in sub-plan and action and so by way of sub-plans that mesh.
B. Belief condition: We each believe that if the intentions of each in favor of our J-ing persists, we will J by way of those intentions and relevant mutual responsiveness in sub-plan and action; and we each believe that there is interdependence in persistence of those intentions of each in favor of our J-ing.
C. Interdependence condition: There is interdependence in persistence of the intentions of each in favor of our J-ing.
D. Common knowledge condition: It is common knowledge that A–C.
E. Mutual responsiveness condition: our shared intention to J leads to our Jing by way of public mutual responsiveness in sub-intention and action that tracks the end intended by each of the joint activity by way of the intentions of each in favor of that joint activity.

Only in combination these conditions are functionally sufficient for shared agency. For example, without common knowledge we might be very close to Searle's ideas of we-intentions and the possibility to be radically mistaken. It should be noted that Bratman studies a very specific type of shared agency: shared intentional activity or sharing an intention in shared cooperative activity. So, firstly, there might be other sufficient conditions to conceptualize shared cooperative activity. Secondly, very similar, yet different forms of shared agency might not be captured by these sufficiency conditions.

The Effects of Shared Intentions
Once shared intentions are in place they give us: (1) commitment to the joint activity, (2) mutual responsiveness, and (3) commitment to mutual support (Bratman, 1999, pp. 94–95).
(1) If two or more agents successfully share an intention, the required/ensuing web of interrelated intentions they form guarantees commitment to the joint activity. Just as individuals that are acting alone are committed to their individual goals and intentions, cooperating individuals are committed to shared goals and intentions. Note how this implies some history between the agents, for example a conversation. Because of this commitment (which each participant can have for different reasons) both individuals feel mutual responsiveness.
(2) Mutual responsiveness means that each participating agent attempts to be responsive to the intentions and actions of the other. "Each seeks to guide his behavior with an eye to the behavior of the other, knowing that the other seeks to do likewise".
(3) The last characteristic of shared activity is mutual support. "Each agent is committed to supporting the efforts of the other to play her role in the joint activity". Both are prepared to provide help if they believe help is needed, which will heighten the chance of a successful joint activity. This too can be traced back to the idea of individual commitment to one's plans and intentions.

5.3.2 I Intend That We J

The five sufficiency conditions are connected to a specific formulation of the intention that we J (the intentions that individuals have when engaged in shared cooperative activity) and the common knowledge that is present between the agents that intend that they J. The formulation is as follows:

1(a)(i)   I intend that we J
1(a)(ii) I intend that we J in accordance with and because of meshing subplans of 1(a)(i) and (1)(b)(i)

1(b)(i)   You intend that we J
1(b)(ii) You intend that we J in accordance with and because of meshing subplans of 1(a)(i) and (1)(b)(i)

1(c)   The intentions in 1(a) and in 1(b) are not coerced by the other participant

1(d)   The intentions in (1)(a) and (1)(b) are minimally cooperatively stable

2   It is common knowledge between us that (1) (Bratman, 1999, p. 105).

Note that 1(a)(i) and 1(b)(i) do not require that our subplans are in fact consistent. All that is required is that each of us intends them to be consistent. This makes us committed to act in such a way that we can find a solution that we can agree on, possibly only after a process of bargaining or negotiation. The common knowledge condition is necessary for the agents to commit to the shared intention.

5.3.3 Two Problems Concerning "I Intend That We J"

I take it that these conditions indeed allow agents to act together, but only as one of the ways in which we can. One of the criticisms of Bratman's approach to collective intentionality comes from philosophers working on accounts of emergent coordination. Emergent coordination provides opportunities to act (and possibly also intend) together based on lower-level cognitive capacities. Deborah Tollefsen argues that:

> [i]t may be that there is a core notion of shared intention which helps to explain joint action of various types (planned or unplanned) and by various subjects (adults, children, animals) and upon which one could then build a theory to understand the more complex forms of joint action and shared intention we find in adult human interactions.
> (Tollefsen, 2015, p. 44)

Bratman's account would then describe one way of acting together amongst other forms of collective intentionality. These critiques are relevant because it seems that the ways in which young children act jointly and the cases of adults interacting based on lower-level cognitive capacities reveal that adults partially continue to use more basic psychological mechanisms that do not fulfill Bratman's sufficient conditions, yet apparently allow us to act together (Butterfill, 2012; Pacherie, 2013; Tollefsen, 2015). This idea, that there are other ways in which (adult human) agents act jointly, fits to the general approach I am taking. My focus, on understanding the other types of joint action that adult human agents are capable of, however, is different. These criticisms mainly focus on development and highly automatic processes that allow for coordination amongst agents (for short, emergent coordination). My focus is on processes that are less highly automated and more flexible (for short, bounded rationality and skilled agency). Both emergent coordination and bounded rationality, however, pose the same problem to Bratman's approach of creature construction of shared agency through planning agency.

The second problem that critics have pointed at in Bratman's work is the necessity of an intention that is specifically shaped as "I intend that we J". Several scholars have argued that an individual cannot have an intention of that form. Baier (1997), Stoutland (1997), and Velleman (1997) all argue in this vein, although with slightly different objectives. Bratman needs this construction because when I intend to do something, the action I intend to do must be under my control. The intention settles, to some degree of detail, what I will do. Intentions and planning structure our behavior as we strive for consistency in our desires and intentions and strive to act on the basis of the plans that form a consistent whole. Intentions are strongly connected to actions. When an agent forms the intention (a plan to do X) she is committed to act according to this intention. Thus, commitment seems to be implied in, or is a virtue of, the concept of intention. This means that intention is more than merely a predominant desire.

Yet, when I intend that we J, there is something in the action that I intend that is out of my control. My intention cannot settle what *we* do. Since you have your own intentions, *you* settle what *you* do (Bratman, 2007, chapter 8). In order to see whether this is problematic we need a better understanding of the type of control the agent does or does not have. As was discussed in chapter three on the notion of control and self-control, there is an important distinction between control on an agentic level and control on a causal level. There are plenty of cases where we would want to say that the agent is in control, although causally a lot is under no-one's control. Take the specific details with which we perform many actions. For Bratman there seems to be a distinction between such cases of "motor implementation" which the agent does not control and the intentions of agent A that, in some way, includes the intentions and/or actions of agent B. Considering a third layer of control, situational control, is helpful when conceptualizing cases that are not fully under intentional control as spelled out by Bratman (on either the individual or shared level), yet are (i) joint actions and (ii) more than motor implementation or fully automatic emergent coordination.

Now that we have looked at planning agency and shared agency in some detail, I want to highlight some parts of Bratman's theory that are highly relevant for both the singular and the shared action case. I will discuss the relation between diachronicity and coherence (5.4), policies and shared policies (5.5), cognitive limitations and bounded rationality (5.6), and Bratman's notion of control (5.7).

5.4 Diachronic and Synchronic Coherence

Bratman stresses the necessity of synchronic *and* diachronic coherence for understanding human agency and argues that beliefs and desires are insufficient to fulfill the necessary demands of human agency. Synchronic coherence refers to the idea that the desires, intentions, and plans that the agent has are coherent *at this moment in time*. Diachronic coherence is about coherence *over time*. Given that many plans cannot be executed immediately, or unfold over time, diachronic coherence is important for human agency. Plans are not only the outcome of reasoning; they are also a starting point for further reasoning. They are the basis and result of diachronic and synchronic coherence.

Given how many things are worth pursuing, the value (which could be expressed as the desire to perform a certain action) of certain action possibilities might be insufficient to direct and govern our actions for at least two reasons (Bratman, 2007). First, there is the problem of underdetermination. Because so many courses of action seem valuable, value judgments of the different options can be insufficient to determine a course of action. The second reason to integrate intentions and plans into our belief and desire structures, especially in relation to diachronicity, is the problem of self-management. Bratman argues that we are "creatures who are affected and moved by complex forms of motivation, and we sometimes find ourselves needing to reflect on, and respond to, these forms of motivation" (Bratman, 2007, p. 165), especially when we encounter contradicting desires. Contradicting desires are more likely to occur when an agent is committed to certain desires over time (Bratman, 2000). When one is, for example, committed to dinner later in the evening one might forego on a five o'clock snack. Our coordinated responses to problems of underdetermination and self-management are part of the deep structure of our ordinary practical thinking. To handle these two problems, Bratman proposes that human agents tend to incorporate policies and plans into their practical thinking. Policies are intentions that are general in relevant ways (Bratman, 2007). These policies (in action and attitude) constitute the agent's response to the problem of fashioning a life with a coherent shape in the face of underdetermination by value judgments. In other words, policies are a kind of valuing that constitutes a unified response to problems of self-management and underdetermination. I will say more about policies in section 5.5.

The fecundity of planning structures, "the idea that planning structures ground a wide range of fundamental practical capacities that are central to our human lives" (Bratman, 2014, p. 4), is at the basis of a deep continuity between individual and social agency in Bratman's work. These planning aspects include our capacity for complex, temporally extended activity, our capacity for self-governance (autonomy), and our capacity for sociality. About the organizing role of intentions, both synchronically and diachronically, Bratman writes:

> Associated with this web of plan-like roles are characteristic norms of intention rationality. Primary among these norms are norms of consistency, agglomeration, means-end coherence, and stability: intentions are to be internally consistent, and consistent with one's beliefs; and it should be possible to agglomerate one's various intentions into a larger intention that is consistent in these ways. (Bratman, 2014, p. 15)

Of course, this is an ideal description of what human agency is: fully coherent and consistent behavior, over time and all the time, is tremendously complicated to achieve. Given Bratman's focus on the limits of time and cognitive capacities that a human agent faces Bratman clearly thinks these norms are not always met. The most minimal claim Bratman seems committed to, is the idea that norms, at least in part, are involved in our perception-action coupling, as distinct from mere causal regularities. How strong his claims regarding consistency, agglomeration, and means-end coherence have to be understood is probably something that is open for discussion. It is, however, something that an agent aspires to. The ideal of Bratman's future-directed intentions, or planning intentions, plans, and policies, is based on these norms of intention rationality. As human agents face limitations in the time and cognitive capacities they have available for reflection Bratman introduces policies as a solution for agents that face such constraints (section 5.5). Next to policies Bratman also integrates heuristic thinking into his account, to lower the cognitive load of planning agency (section 5.6). As a normative description, however, planning agency still stands.

The motivation for consistency over time, which seems to have both a normative component and a psychological descriptive component, gives us reason to accept planning agency as an adequate description of (some of) our thoughts and actions. Bratman sketches a picture in which an agent's reasons for acting (the outcome of practical reasoning) and the pursuit and maintenance of a balance of practical reasons are just as important. This has to do with his understanding of the concept of valuing and the importance of valuing for human agency. Bratman argues that valuing in the way human agents do has a strong relation to consistency of beliefs and plans, both synchronically and diachronically.

5.4.1 Synchronic Coherence and Guiding Desires

Bratman (1987) argues that there is at least one other way in which our behavior can be guided by conative attitudes. However, this alternative is structured differently from planning agency, namely through guidance by guiding desires. Guiding desires are another element that share some characteristics with planning intentions, but are, according to Bratman, less cognitively demanding. Actions based on guiding desires are an example of action that are not strictly speaking part of Bratman's planning agency, yet Bratman considers relatively typical human agency. I will follow Bratman's example, which includes someone who wants to marry two different people (Bratman, 1987, chapter 9). At the moment of planning this is still lawfully possible, but midway through the rules change and the agent can now only marry one person. One option would be for the agent to reach a decision in favor of one of the two partners. But, Bratman argues, the agent can also proceed by continuing to plan on ways of persuading each of them to marry her and *let the world resolve the conflict.* In this case the world would refer to the two partners of choice. The option where the world resolves the conflict is different from the situation where the agent makes a decision because the two guiding desires (marrying X and marrying Y) are incompatible given the agent's beliefs. The two particular subplans that the agent forms, based on each guiding desire, still need to be compatible within themselves. Rather than giving us an understanding of how guiding desires can be less cognitively demanding, these subplans give us a way to understand how we can follow up on two different – incompatible – desires without being inconsistent. Guiding desires can be used to describe a situation where "several different strategies for the resolution of practical conflicts" (Bratman, 1987, p. 138).

For an agent to perform an intentional action many potential conflicts must be resolved. Bratman argues that these conflicts can be resolved at different levels, such as the level of habit (his example is which foot we use when we step out of the car), or more (situation) specific intentions (for example whether to stop the car at this restaurant or to keep on driving). In some cases, there will be conflicts that need not be settled by the agent for her to proceed. At other times, she can wait a while and let her decisions depend on how other things work out.

In the case where she lets the world decide how the conflict will be resolved she continues to be guided by both (conflicting) guiding desires and does not settle for an intention for one of the two desires. The way things work out will then decide which desire will be fulfilled (Bratman, 1987, pp. 135–136). An example might be to have the guiding desire to have breakfast at home alone, or with a friend in a bar if this friend calls before nine in the morning. The two desires are inconsistent – assuming that the agent will not have breakfast twice – and the agent can leave it up to the world, which would be her friend in this scenario, to see which guiding desire will be acted on. As soon as the world decides in favor of one guiding desire the other guiding desire is dropped. Bratman seems to apply this idea not only to guiding desires, but also to habits that might guide our behavior. We could of course easily imagine how different habits could guide our behavior but also potentially stand in conflict with each other.

5.4.2 Coherence through Planning. Too Demanding?

Scholars endorsing the usefulness of intentions as planning states have raised questions regarding some consequences of accepting the concept (Knoblich, Butterfill, & Sebanz, 2011; O'Brien, 2015; Preston, 2012; Vargas & Yaffe, 2014; Velleman, 2000). These questions run in two directions. Velleman argues that Bratman's planning intentions are insufficient to give us stability. We need a further motivation to settle in advance (Velleman, 2000). This does not necessarily make Velleman's theory more demanding, but it gives it an additional backdrop of motivation. An agent, Velleman argues, feels uncomfortable when she does not make up her mind regarding issues that she deems important. This unease with oneself is the reason agents are willing to settle in advance. The other question that has been raised concerns the observation that we do not always act on planning intentions (Knoblich, Butterfill, & Sebanz, 2011; O'Brien, 2014; Preston, 2012). Children that have not fully developed planning capacities and adults that act spontaneous or improvise both seem to be badly captured by a theory of planning agency. Especially in children planning agency is understood as being too demanding. When accepting the importance of planning agency, but also accepting this pushback on the general applicability of the theory, one is forced to think about the relation of action captured by planning intentions and actions that are not described by planning intentions (Knoblich, Butterfill, & Sebanz, 2011; O'Brien, 2015; Velleman, 2000). Bratman himself also recognized that his theoretical focus on planning and intentions may seem to

> ... point at a caricature of human agents as constantly planning, eschewing spontaneity, and rigidly following through with prior plans. [. . .] But of course these planning capacities are embedded in a complex psychic economy that also involves abilities to characterize one's plans in schematic and conceptually open ways, and to be spontaneous and flexible as time goes by. A basic challenge for a theory of human agency will be to do justice both to the centrality of planning in the constitution and support of fundamental forms of organization, and to our important capacities for conceptual openness, spontaneity, and flexibility. (Bratman, 2014, p. 24)

For Bratman the solution lies in the open-endedness of the agent's plans and intentions. So Bratman agrees that he has to specify how we should think about openness and spontaneity. He encapsulates his solution into his theory on planning agency. Starting from the planning agency perspective, he tries to understand how we can still leave room for spontaneous and flexible behavior.

Through this encapsulation Bratman evades the question what the relation between other forms of intentional or purposive agency, and planning agency might be like (see also section 5.5 and 5.6). Nor does he have to react to Preston's (2012) theory on flexible spontaneous actions. Preston argues that creative and flexible behavior might arise through spontaneous build-up of plans, or through purposive decisions. Such build-ups have different "styles" of deciding and she assumes that human agents use both styles. This is also the case for group agents. Bratman specifically wants to build shared agency on top of individual planning agency, not on purposive agency or creative agency. Bratman refers to swarms and flocks that show purposeful group behavior. He says that collective agency based on purposeful behavior is indeed to be understood as collective and as agency. However, Bratman aims at understanding human agency. Human agency, Bratman argues, presents a twofold challenge in the context of shared agency:

> First, we are interested in our shared agency, and this is shared agency whose participants are, it is plausible to suppose, planning agents. Why is this so plausible? The basic answer is that this is a way of understanding and explaining the striking richness of our temporally extended and organized individual agency. And once these planning capacities are on board we should expect them to play important roles in our sociality.
> Second, the ability of the theory to refer to and exploit these planning structures allows it to provide a rich model of robust forms of shared agency without introducing fundamentally new and discontinuous elements. This is an aspect of the fecundity of planning structures, and supports the thesis of continuity. (Bratman, 2014, p. 26)

To summarize, planning structures are central to the kind of temporally extended individual agents that Bratman argues people are. Bratman combines this thesis (that humans act jointly on plans and intentions) with the earlier discussed continuity thesis: the idea that once we have those planning structures on board they play a central role in our sociality. Planning is not only that which seems to make us unique compared to other animals, but it is the most fundamental way to understand human beings in their social context.

The implicit assumption at work in Bratman's theory of planning agency is that planning agency is thus key to an understanding of human shared agency that an account of such forms of shared agency is sufficient to capture those shared phenomena that are interesting in the case of human cooperation. This approach brings with it a disregard for the relation between other types of purposive agency and planned agency. This goes for both the collective and the individual account. When arguing that other animals act together as purposeful agents, this can either be understood to mean that there is a strong discontinuity between human animals and any other animals, or it poses a problem for his argument of theoretical parsimony. I follow Bratman in his assumption that planning intentions are essential in understanding human agency and human shared agency. Nevertheless, and this is where I depart from Bratman, I do not share his implicit assumption that purposive action should not require more attention in our understanding of human agency. This means that I take it that we often act purposefully, either as individuals or as groups. Therefore, I argue that we need a clearer picture of (a) how we do this, and of (b) how such actions relate to our planned actions and planning agency. These ideas will be further discussed in chapter seven of this book.

The next two sections of this chapter will discuss two ways in which Bratman deals with the impossibility to reflect on one's actions. Section 5.5 discusses policies and shared policies. Policies are general plans that will be useful multiple times. They regulate our behavior in advance, as intentions do, but in a more general way. In this way they can provide relief from the "caricatural picture" of planning agency. Section 5.6 looks at Bratman's discussion of cognitive limitations and relates this to his ideas on purposive agency, again zooming in on ways in which Bratman's model allows us to think about human agency outside of, and in relation to, planning agency.

5.5 Policies and Shared Policies

5.5.1 Policies in Planning Agency

Next to planning intentions as intentional structures that help with diachronic coherence there is another structure that plays an important role in Bratman's theory of planning agency; policies. Policies are intentions that are general in relevant ways. They contrast with the particularity of plans, which are specifically made for one situation. We can have policies about actions and policy-like attitudes (Bratman, 2007, p. 168). Policies play a role both in Bratman's account of planning agency and in his account of shared agency. They fulfill the same role as plans in the following sense: they help us to be consistent and have means-ends coherence. They help us deal with the rational pressure that we face (Bratman, 2014, p. 18). I will first discuss the more basic idea of policies and its relation to planning agency and then continue with a discussion of policies and their role in shared agency. I will end with some critical notes on the distinctions that Bratman draws between shared policies and social values.

Policies are general rules or directions the agent lives by. Bratman gives several examples of policies, such as buckling up before driving, having only one beer at dinner, avoiding deception, and not giving in to anger (Bratman, 2014, p. 20). They apply to more than one instance in time, whereas plans are more specifically connected to a specific moment in time. Plans typically concern relatively specific courses of action extended over time. It is important, though, that sometimes one's commitment is to a certain kind of action on certain kinds of potentially recurrent occasions. They allow an agent to act consistently in similar situations. Policies will often have implicit unless-clauses, so they are general but not necessarily performed (Bratman, 2007, p. 27). An example of such an unless-clause would be an agent that drinks only one beer at diner, except for festive occasions. Bratman distinguishes two forms of policies (1) those about actions, and (2) those that tell us "what to treat as having more or less weight in the context of certain relevant deliberation" (Bratman, 2014, p. 20).

Bratman distinguishes two ways in which we can relate to our desires. Firstly, we can hold higher-order desires concerning first-order desires, which tell us something about how to act in response to desires that might arise. Secondly, we can take a stand with respect to the functioning of a given desire (Bratman, 2007, p. 23). Policies share characteristics with plans in the way they relate to our desires. There are also further similarities between plans and policies. For example, they are subject to distinctive rational norms of consistency, coherence, and stability (Bratman, 2007, p. 27). This distinguishes them from desires, or most forms of purposive agency. Policies, unlike intentions and plans, are "explicitly concerned with the functioning of relevant desires generally in one's temporally extended life" (Bratman, 2007, p. 34).

When we couple this to his creature construction, only Creature 8 is "in control" in the way Bratman understand control in human agency. Such control can then be through both plans and policies. As pointed out before: desires become reason-providing because Creature 8 treats desires as providing, in deliberation, a justifying end for action (see section 5.2.1). A well-functioning policy has to be specific to some degree. At the same time, we want policies to be general to some extent, to make sure that they can guide behavior in various circumstances. It should be clear which situations are similar enough to allow the agent to apply the same policy. Potentially also in new situations. As with plans they allow the agent to determine what to do at an earlier point in time. This helps the agent to overcome limitations it would otherwise face because of the lack of available time and cognitive capacity. Such strategies are also available to groups.

5.5.2 Shared Policies

Shared policies play a similar and similarly important role in Bratman's account of shared agency as they do in his account of individual agency. They provide groups of agents general ways to respond to situations. More technically Bratman defines a shared policy as a shared weight given to a certain aspect, consideration, or motivation that plays a role in further deliberation. Shared policies should not be confused by general (social) rules that many or all people follow: they are particular ways of responding to a certain situation that is specific that group of agents. This means that they have to come about through some form of a deliberative process. I will say a bit more about this deliberate process in the case of group policies, and then continue by arguing that these policies might indeed be useful conceptual tools, but they leave us wanting for other tools to explain more spontaneous cases of agents acting together.

When discussing shared deliberation (Bratman, 2014, chapter 7), Bratman highlights three features: (1) deliberation is embedded in an ongoing shared intention activity of the group, (2) the shared deliberation is itself a shared intentional activity on the part of the group, and (3) shared deliberation should be distinguished from "ordinary bargaining", where there is "no common ground of shared commitments to treating certain considerations as mattering in our shared deliberation" (Bratman, 2014, p. 132). This means that when something matters to us we give it a certain weight in our considerations in our shared reasoning. In the example of painting a house together, this shared intention would have a greater weight (compared to other possible (joint) actions). Policies can be about the way the participants of a group interact (for example that there should always be consensus, or, in a group bigger than two, that the majority will get its way), or they can be about giving more weight to certain considerations. In Bratman's example, a couple might decide that the environmental impact of the choices they make while building a house together is involved in all further decisions. They give weight to this general policy in their future deliberations. Regarding the relation between policies and other structures of practical reasoning he adds that there are

> . . . significant questions here about the exact interrelations between these and perhaps other structures of practical reasoning. I put these issues aside here.
> (Bratman, 2014, p. 133)

He does not give an example of the action-related policies in the case of joint action (policies that are directly related to actions, rather than weights of certain considerations). Presumably they also involve reaching an agreement to act in a certain way when situation X and closely related situations occur.

Policies are distinguished from (general) social rules that we expect everyone that we encounter to follow. Policies are formed by the group, by means of a deliberative process. This implies that shared policies can only exist when a group of agents has been interacting or acting jointly before. Given the more general nature of policies it seems reasonable to assume that they play a major role in creating stability and to reduce the cognitive load that our aim for coherency puts on us. This goes for both the individual and the shared case.

Shared policies are a specific background of common knowledge that help agents mesh their plans and shorten deliberation and bargaining. Policies are not shared through social structures. Public known weights share the same value indeterminacy as values for the individual do. On the other hand, policies are specific for a specific group. Given this feature, they will not play a role in spontaneous actions.

The example of shared commitments to weights (which can be understood as policies) Bratman discusses mainly concerns policies of highly structured organizations. The examples about smaller groups typically include two individuals already having plans together. The examples he uses: building a house and deliberate about earthquake safety, a scientific research team giving weight to the short-term public benefits of science, a start-up enterprise might have a shared commitment to giving more weight to market share than to short-term profits. After going into detail regarding some of these examples Bratman writes:

> As these examples suggest, such shared commitments about weights in shared deliberation will normally be part of a larger package of shared intentions. (Bratman, 2014, p. 135)

The shared policies and shared weights are assumed to be part of (the knowledge of) the group, they are group dependent. They could emerge through a consistency of actions over time that implies a policy, but are mostly understood to follow from deliberation. In either case, a group is already defined. These groups already have a plan to paint a house, there already is a research team that is embedded in the university structures, etc. Amongst relative strangers these policies would be impossible to exist. In those cases the individuals that might act jointly have to rely on shared values. Shared policies are different from public known weights because (1) a shared weight informs us that we also want each other to give weight to R, and (2) there is an interdependent intention to do so.

> We might try saying that such shared commitments are a matter of converging judgments of value in a context of common knowledge: our shared commitment to our giving weight to X consists in our each judging that X is valuable, in a context of common knowledge of these judgments. The problem, however, is that sameness of value judgment, in a context of common knowledge, seems neither sufficient nor necessary for a corresponding shared commitment to weights in shared deliberation. (Bratman, 2014, p. 36)

The problem is that knowing that we both share a value judgment is no guarantee that we both also think this value deserves a certain weight. Even when there is public consensus with respect to certain value judgments, this might still not mean that we appeal to those judgments in our shared deliberation. Take two people that both care about the environment but still decide to take a plane for a city trip instead of a train. The shared judgment, or policy, is not translated to a motive for acting in a certain way. As Bratman writes: "Sharing a commitment to certain weights seems closer to a kind of shared intention than to a common value judgment" (Bratman, 2014, p. 137).

Agreement in beliefs and judgments is insufficient. This, according to Bratman, shows the primacy of shared intention and shared policies for our sociality. Shared intentions and shared policies provide the agent with a level of certainty that cannot be gained from mere overlap of value judgments. Given the general applicability of policies, they can provide a different form of stability to groups than shared intentions can. Bratman writes about this difference:

> So there is a web of social pressures in favor of explanatorily intelligible, predictable, and reliable similarity of application of the shared intention about weights. And a basic way to respond to those social pressures will involve generality in the content of the shared intention: it will be a shared intention not just about a specific weight right now in this temporally local particular situation, but rather a shared intention to give weight to a certain kind of consideration – collegiality, say – on various occasions that may arise in our ongoing shared deliberation. This is to respond to these social pressures by appeal to shared, general policies about weights. (Bratman, 2014, p. 138)

This mirrors the importance of policies compared to plans in Bratman's model of individual agency. Generality brings stability and reduces our need for reconsideration. This seems particularly relevant in the joint case:

> Our model of shared commitments to weights as shared policies about weights aims to provide in a clear way for these phenomena [manage to reason together in the pursuit of shared projects despite significant background differences]. And it does this in a way that highlights the central role of intention in our sociality. (Bratman, 2014, p. 140)

Policies, on Bratman's account, may also play a constitutive role:

> Many times it will be by virtue of our shared policies about weights that there will be something that counts as where we stand on certain relevant issues [. . .]. Our shared policies about weights are, in such cases, not merely useful coordination devices; they are, as well, partly constitutive of what we can plausibly call the standpoint of the group on relevant matters. (Bratman, 2014, p. 142)

There are two questions regarding the function of shared policies that have to be answered. Firstly, we have to answer how shared policies function in relation to other theoretical postulates such as intentions, policies held by the individual, shared intentions, and the like. According to Bratman shared values do not allow us to say whether the agent that shares a value with another agent will also use this value as a motivation to act on. Although the length and explicitness of deliberation amongst agents that belong to the group that share a policy is not explicitly discussed in Bratman's texts, it seems evident that these policies are created or confirmed explicitly. Any "implicit shared policy" remains undistinguishable from shared values.

Given the distinction that Bratman draws between general social conventions and weights and shared policies, they are not a solution for on the spot and spontaneous joint actions. I am doubtful whether we can make such a strict distinction between social values and shared policies. I assume that we do not always need to spell out such shared policies for them to play the role Bratman wants them to play. Presumably social values are often assumed as policies in longer existing groups, and in that sense only implicitly reinforced. Furthermore, in cases where agents act together spontaneously Bratman's framework excludes the possibility that they act jointly based on shared policies and on his account social values are underdetermining what the group will do. It seems to me, however, that shared values (in combination with assumptions about how these shared values feature in the (joint) "deliberation" about what to do on the spot, seem to fulfill a rather similar role as shared policies do in longer existing groups. Or that shared values are commonly known and picked up as soon as one agents uses this to guide their behavior in the social setting, leading to a set of agents to act jointly.

In such a case, social values can function as a proxy in spontaneous group action and this would allow for a more natural and fluid transition between parallel action and joint action. Assuming that some of these social values that play a very similar role as Bratman's shared policies are presented in a more heuristical way, it seems that deliberation and explicit sharedness fall away, yet the functionality remains largely intact.

5.6 Cognitive Limitations and Purposive Agency

In the second half of the twentieth century, rational choice theory came under pressure from two directions. Bratman's work on planning agency is an adaptation of rational choice theory which tries to overcome this critique. First, empirical work in psychology and behavioral economics (Kahneman, Slovic, & Tversky, 1982) established a variety of different ways in which human beings do not make choices in the way predicted by the rational choice theorist's model (e.g., Kahneman, Slovic, & Tversky, 1982; Kahneman & Tversky, 1979; Tversky & Kahneman, 1981). To give some examples: people quite often do not choose that to which they assign the greatest expected utility; they quite often have intransitive preferences; and they frequently discount future goods on a schedule that results in making abrupt reversals of policies merely as a result of the passage of time. Together this showed that rational choice theory was not descriptively adequate. Rational choice theory is a normative frame, and from this perspective such deviations are perceived as limitations. It could be maintained that such results show, simply, that human beings are not always rational. Yet the normative pressure and aim remain in place. Empirical results speak to how things are, not how they should be, and so if the rational choice theorist's model is a model of how things should be, it could not possibly be falsified by any empirical results.[52]

The availability of this line of response depends on the adequacy of rational choice theory as a prescriptive account. On this point, however, a second attack on the model emerged – most notably in the work of Herbert Simon (1982). Simon formulated a critique of rational choice theory's adequacy as a prescriptive theory. He recognized that rational agents diverge in their choices from what was predicted by traditional rational choice theory under a variety of conditions. Simon's main idea is that agents often rationally diverge from what traditional rational choice theory would predict because they are limited in their cognitive and psychological capacities. This has had a major influence on Bratman's approach to understanding agency, as is also evident in his creature constructions. The planning theory of intention can be thought of, and was thought of by Bratman, as a description of the psychological mechanisms through which rational agents acting in pursuit of goals overcome, or at least mitigate, the impact of cognitive and agential limitations that Simon pointed out (see Vargas & Yaffe, 2014, for a discussion).

---

52 Note that although it is a normative theory that cannot be falsified, it is still used in fields such as economy that at least partially are committed to being empirical founded.

5.6.1 Bounded Rationality and Planning Agency

Bratman explains how the mental state of intention makes it possible for rational agents to overcome the cognitive limitations identified by Simon. Bratman's account, however, was not limited to that project. He also identified further cognitive and agential limitations. Each limitation can be overcome with the help of planning intentions. For instance, Bratman argues that one of the great virtues of the stability of intentions – their resistance to reconsideration even in the face of some new information – is not just that agents thereby avoid wasting resources on re-deliberating but also that they are thereby able to coordinate their activities with other agents by making it possible for other agents to predict their behavior without having to predict how they would deliberate. Vargas and Yaffe write about Bratman's theory:

> The theory is compatible with the empirical results uncovered by psychologists like Kahneman and Tversky, and it harmonizes with the efforts by Simon and economists to build formal models of decision making consistent with the recognition that human beings are limited in their cognitive and agential capacities. (Vargas & Yaffe, 2014, p. 4)

While the planning theory might be recognized as an innovation in rational choice theory – it includes a distinctive account of the norms of rationality governing intending agents that is incompatible with the account offered by traditional rational choice theory – it was also, and perhaps more so, an innovation in the philosophy of action. To get to an adequate theory of human agency, one that is more adequate than rational choice theory, Bratman takes both the capacities that we find in human agents *and* their limitations and puts both central stage.

Bratman points at four limitations human agents face. These partially interrelated limitations are that (1) we are time-constrained and (2) we have cognitive, (3) conative, and (4) affective limitations (Bratman, 2014, p. 24; 2007, pp. 53–54, 263, 289; 1999, pp. 4, 52–54; 2000). Bratman wants a systematic account that gives us "reasonable stability" (Bratman, 1999, p. 4). The stability that we gain by plans and policies has always been thought to be important for coordination, constant reconsideration of our actions is highly disrupting in social situations. It gives us tools that help us decide when to reconsider and when not to. Otherwise said, it gives us non-reflective (non-)reconsideration. As Bratman puts it:

> I presented a two-tier, pragmatic theory – a theory I saw as part of what Herbert Simon had called the theory of bounded rationality. We need general habits, strategies, and policies concerning such nonreflective (non)reconsideration. We can assess such general

mechanisms in terms of their expected impact on our achieving what we (rationally) desire, given our needs for coordination and our cognitive limitations. We can then see the rationality of a particular case of nonreflective (non)reconsideration of a prior intention as dependent on the acceptability of the underlying general mechanism.

(Bratman, 1999, p. 4)

Why do we need stable intentions and plans to support coordination? Why don't we simply figure out, at each moment of action, what would then be best given our predictions about what we and others will do in the future if we act in certain ways in the present? One answer echoes the work of Herbert Simon (1983): We are agents with significant limits on the resources of time and attention we can reasonably devote to reasoning and calculation. Given these resource limits, a strategy of constantly starting from scratch – of never treating prior decisions as settling a practical question – would run into obvious difficulties. A second, related answer is that coordination requires predictability, and the actions of planning agents are more easily predicted. (Bratman, 1999, p. 36)

Treating prior decisions as settling our issues spares time and cognitive capacity, or allows us to use the time and cognitive capacity when we need them most. This also generates stability which is helpful in coordination. The list of four limitations is almost all the explanation he gives of the kind of the limitations that human agents face while engaging with the world as planning agents. He continues by saying that we act:

in a way that is responsive to our need many times to choose among conflicting options in the face of underdetermination of our choice by relevant considerations. And we do this in a way that is responsive to our needs for self-control and selfmanagement in the pursuit of organization and coordination and in the face of conflicting sources of motivation.

(Bratman, 2014, p. 25)

The explication of limitations in our planning agency is important because this explication tells us something about the kind of limitations that Bratman deems important to be considered when describing human cognition and action.

I see three challenges for Bratman's approach. These are not the type of challenges that render Bratman's proposal problematic, but rather the kind of challenges that require additions and changes to his theory, which I will explore in the last two chapters of this book. These challenges mainly relate to the skillful, sometimes fast-paced, joint actions, and purposive joint actions.

Before discussing these challenges, I would like to point at several ways in which we can talk of limitations and their potential relation to normativity. There seem to be two senses of limitations. The first is limitations on the extent to which we are ideally rational (heuristics are constitutive of these limitations). The second is the use of limitations on our resources (problems that the heuristics are solutions to). In the first case heuristics are non-optimal, in the second case they are optimal because the agent needs to solve a problem and heuristics might allow us to decide what to do. I have three suggestions for an alteration of Bratman's understanding of cognitive limitations and how we should understand bounded rationality within a framework of planning agency. They rely on an integration of both understandings of such limitations.

a) I propose to change the emphasis from cognitive limitations to cognitive capacities that have rational limitations. This means that the – rationally speaking sub-optimal – cognitive functions such as heuristics are, most of the time, well-functioning mechanisms that structure our behavior. These are other forms of cognition that can also help agents exert control. From a rational choice theory perspective, they might be sub-optimal and non-ideal, but they can also be characterized in a more positive way. Usually heuristics work, and that is precisely the reason we rely on them and are not scrutinizing them all of the time.

b) By putting the emphasis on (limited) cognitive capacities – rather than limitations – a second aspect also changes. We no longer need to ask how to *overcome* such limitations all of the time, but we rather ask how different functions that are related to our behavior interact. This opens up the space to discuss both positive and negative contributions of all cognitive capacities, and the interaction between different cognitive capacities.

c) Incorporating these cognitive limitations into a theory of planning agency as is done by Bratman appears to be problematic. Bratman understands policies and habits to be like bounded rationality: they help us cope in those moments where we lack the time and cognitive capacity to form a judgment on the spot. Since we will have found ourselves in (very) similar situations before, we know that having such policies is useful. Although it seems plausible to me that heuristics and policies can be understood in such a way, there are also cases where this bundling together does not work. An aspect of bounded rationality that Bratman seems to overlook is our inability to control the way these heuristics and the like work. Policies, and also habits, as spelled out by Bratman fit into the larger idea of planning agency: just like plans they can be agglomerated. Many heuristics, however, are thought to be automatically activated and automatically run through (Cialdini, 1984). It is also not a given that the habits an agent has and the heuristics that she uses are there *because* of earlier decisions or installments of policies and the like. Whether they are compatible with the agent's beliefs, desires, intentions, and plans, will often be something that is hard to judge by the agent. Although the agent might reflectively discover certain heuristics and reflectively recreate some of them, many are there without explicit formulation and potentially without explicitly ever knowing about them. In many cases there may be no way for the agent to know whether such forms of bounded rationality fit in with her deliberation. This seems to block Bratman's idea that we can integrate them into the agent's planning agency.

Understanding the role of bounded rationality as proposed by Bratman seems to deviate too strongly from the way in which bounded rationality is today assumed to play a role in our decision-making and behavior. At least to be the sole interpretation of bounded rationality. What Bratman sets out to explain is larger than the capacities of his model. Once we are seeing this difference between bounded rationality and Bratman's way of integration of bounded rationality, it becomes clear why we need to accommodate the integration and interaction of purposive agency and planning agency.

To conclude: Bratman wants to take Simon and Kahneman and Tversky seriously. He does so by pointing at certain limitations in our rational agency that have implications for our capacities as planning agents. Our agency is bounded in time and by our capacities, and this can be taken into account beforehand by making plans. The primacy, automaticity, and self-completion of lower-level processes is missing in the rendition of bounded rationality that Bratman gives us. Rather than a model with open-ended plans, we need a model where things are filled in by bounded rationality (processes that are usually thought to be non-inferential). Apart from the question which conceptual framework we want to adopt (see the critical discussion on dual-process theories in chapter two), I take it that the least we can learn from this debate is that not everything is working as proposed by Bratman. And once we accept that there is something that is agentic (the agent knows what she is doing) but not inferential, we need to understand the combination. We need a smart use of "deliberative control" in the context of many other (often also highly intelligent and flexible) processes. I will develop a first proposal for such smart use of deliberative control in chapter seven, where I propose skillful joint action along the line of skillful action as proposed in chapter four.

5.6.2 Purposive Shared Action

Planning intentions play an important role in many aspects of Bratman's theory. At several points intentional actions are compared to purposive actions. Planning agents are compared to purposive agents. Shared agency based on planning intentions is compared to shared agency based on purposive agency. These comparisons are used to show what is special, unique, or needed for an explanation of the richness of human agency. Understanding purposive action as an important part of human agency, while taking into account the points made in the previous section regarding the integration of bounded rationality, needs an account of human agency as purposive agency. Bratman spells out several versions of purposive agency in his creature construction but does not specify which, if any, creature construction he understands as applicable to human agents. This is also explained by Bratman's focus on integration of bounded rationality into planning agency. In the discussion of social agency and shared agency an account of purposive agency is absent for reasons discussed in section 5.2.3. Instead of this contrast, Bratman formulates a social analogue of Wittgenstein's question about the difference between my arm's rising and my raising it. The social version would be "What is the difference between a contrast case (painting alongside each other) and corresponding shared intentional activity (painting together)?"

Bratman swiftly acknowledges that there are also phenomena of group or collective agency within which the distinctive social organization is grounded in causal mechanisms of a very different sort than that of shared intention. Examples are swarms of bees and flocks of birds. Such social organization, he argues, is grounded in causal mechanisms "of a very different sort than that of shared intention" (Bratman, 2014, p. 10). His conjecture is that:

> in central cases of small scale human shared activity – cases naturally described as ones of shared intentional activity – the concept of shared intention does point to important, internal explanatory structures, and that it is these internal explanatory structures that are central to our answer to our social analogue of Wittgenstein's question.
> (Bratman, 2014, p. 10)

Bratman gives us three reasons to assume shared intentional acting as the central case of human joint action.
1)   Creature construction and metaphysical leanness.
2)   It is typically human to plan, and this element is key to our understanding of shared agency.
3)   The continuity thesis.

Re 1) Bratman writes: "I will argue that this step to shared agency can be conceptually, metaphysically, and normatively more conservative than the step from individual, temporally local purposive agency to individual temporally extended planning agency" (Bratman, 2014, p. 26). Two earlier discussed concerns come up: it remains unclear whether planning agency, as the only type of agency discussed, is a conceptual adequate description of human agency. Furthermore, does the leanness of the step from planning agency to shared (planning) agency not give us any information about the leanness of the step from purposive agency to shared (purposive) agency.

Re 2) Bratman takes our capacity to plan as a crucial step in understanding the kind of agents we are. Assuming that planning is a critical capacity that human agents possess, however, does not give an answer how this capacity relates to other capacities and their role in joint action.

Re 3) The continuity thesis only works when 2 is assumed. The continuity thesis holds that "the conceptual, metaphysical, and normative structures central to such modest sociality are [. . .] continuous with structures of individual planning agency" (Bratman, 2014, p. 8). The only thing that he presupposes together with the continuity thesis is social cognition, or "relevant knowledge of each other's minds" (Bratman, 2014, p. 8). This continuity thesis contrasts Bratman with other important authors in collective intentionality such as Margaret Gilbert and John Searle. Both see the step from individual to shared agency as involving a new basic practical resource. In Gilbert's work a new relation is introduced, the relation of joint commitment between the participants, in Searle's case it is a new attitude of we-intention that is necessary to understand collective intentionality.

First of all, Bratman's reasoning depends a lot on its leanness, with the implicit assumption that this gives us an inference to the best explanation. However, many have argued that his starting point (planning agency) is too cognitively demanding. In that sense, critics have argued, it is not lean at all (e.g., Butterfill, 2012; Pacherie, 2013). As pointed out in section 5.2, Bratman argues that the step from planning agency to shared agency is small. This, however, does not tell us how small the step would be from purposive agency to shared agency. Bratman agrees that other animals also act jointly, and that they are not planning agents. From an evolutionary perspective it seems implausible that such routes to joint action are not available to human agents too. And if they are available, it will be highly interesting to know how they work in human interaction, and how they can be incorporated into a picture that also allows for planning agency and shared agency that is based on planning agency. Looking at skillful joint action is one way to create room for an interaction between deliberative (planning) agency and other forms of agency.

5.7 Control, Autonomy and Agentic Purpose

This section focuses on the tension between autonomy and shared agency. This tension goes back to the ideas about self-control discussed in chapter three. Autonomy and agential control are highly related concepts. In this section I discuss control and purposive agency and their relation to shared agency.

Autonomy and self-governance are important topics for theories of action. They bear important consequences for the way we conceive moral responsibility, culpability, and accountability. To understand the relation between responsibility and *shared* agency often involves discussing autonomy. But in a different way than in the individual case. The view that the intentional states of individuals are their own is in tension with the view that the intentional states are in some way collective or shared. To act and intend together can easily lead to a situation where it seems that one agent intends for the other. Although individual (intentional) autonomy is often invoked in theories of collective intentionality, individual autonomy is almost never defined or explained. Contemporary discussions of personal autonomy[53] are rooted in the 1970s work of Frankfurt and Dworkin. Both argued that an agent's decisions are autonomous if they are rooted in the agent's values, commitments, and objectives, whereas they are not autonomous if they run counter to those. Thus, such accounts of personal autonomy locate autonomy in the process of reflective endorsement itself. The aim of such an account of personal autonomy is to protect individual agents who pursue actions that accord with their self-consciously held values, commitments, and objectives from external influences.

Frankfurt's and Dworkin's hierarchical accounts of autonomy form the basis and background for the contemporary mainstream discussion, including Bratman's position. In general terms, the account of personal autonomy these hierarchical models put forward is that an agent is autonomous, for example regarding an action, if her first-order desire to act is sanctioned by a second-order volition endorsing the first-order desire (Frankfurt, 1988, pp. 12–25). In what follows I do not attempt to do justice to this rich and complicated debate, but rather try to highlight how autonomy and self-governance play a role in Bratman's theory. I only do so insofar this has implications for our understanding of being able to intend and act together.

Coherentist accounts of autonomy, the category to which Bratman's theory belongs, argue that any account of autonomous agency requires a clear conception of the self and of what counts as the self's "own" reasons to act (Ekstrom, 1993).[54] Coherentist accounts work with hierarchies of attitudes. Ekstrom's coherentist account is understood in terms of the endorsement of preferences, Frankfurt talks about higher-order desires, and Bratman prefers the terminology

---

[53] Which must be distinguished from (Kantian) moral autonomy. Personal autonomy is committed to a neutral metaphysics and adheres to – at least – a procedural individualism. Contemporary accounts of personal autonomy judge actions to be autonomous based on features of the action and the mental process preceding the action internal and particular to the agent.
[54] A clear self-conception can avoid the problem of infinite regress (or *reductio ad absurdum*).

of intentions and planning agency. The accounts overlap in their assumption that an agent has a preference or higher-order propositional attitude if she holds a lower order desire to be good. A self, on this account, is thus a character with specific beliefs and preferences which have become endorsed in a process of self-reflection. A true self, on this account, consists of those beliefs and preferences that form a coherent whole. This coherence provides the authorization for the separate preferences – a preference is endorsed if it coheres with the agent's character. This account requires an ability or capacity to reshape one's beliefs, preferences, etcetera in the light of self-evaluation. A certain level of insight into one's own motivations is needed.

Looking at the literature on autonomy,[55] two dominant characteristics can be noticed. Most accounts are "identity-based" and rely on notions of (taking) ownership (Benson, 2005; Christman & Anderson, 2005). The pervasive idea is that autonomous agents act upon wills that are fully their own. This implies that autonomous agents possess a "self" that is capable of acting and has a coherent and sustained identity over time. To be autonomous, an agent has to be "herself" in acting. Agents are autonomous if and only if they take ownership of their actions, or at least have the capacity to do so and regularly exercise that capacity. Taking ownership is done in relation to an agent's desires or pro-attitudes that bear on how she wants to live (Oshana, 2005, p. viii). Thus, a "capacity for unimpaired critical self-reflection is included in the standard accounts of autonomy" and "a person is autonomous if she is moved by values, desires, beliefs, and attitudes that would withstand unimpaired self-scrutiny" (Oshana, 2005, p. 77). Bratman's "identity & identification-based" account of autonomy, more or less subscribes to these standard features.[56] His theory holds that agents take ownership of what they do when they identify with the motives that lead them to act.

The literature on autonomous agency differentiates between "merely intentional action" and actions that are, in the fullest sense, the agent's own and thus autonomous (Benson in Christman & Anderson, 2005, p. 101). In other words, an

---

[55] The literature distinguishes between "local autonomy" and "global autonomy".
[56] Identification-based theories are the core target of our argument. Benson (2005) identifies four popular accounts of autonomy. They are respectively based on: identification, evaluative self-disclosure, whole-self, and reflective non-alienation. We think that our argument applies to all four, because they all rely to some extent on the agent's capacity for introspective access to her beliefs, desires, i.e. on the assumption that (unimpaired) self-reflection is possible. Benson, whose argument and characterization of autonomy theories is congenial to ours, criticizes identity-based accounts on different grounds than our own, and develops a "social account of autonomy" as an alternative.

autonomous agent controls the operation of her own will and is not reduced to a passive bystander by the forces that move her (Benson, 2005, p. 101; Schmid (2009, part III) argues against this idea).

This picture of individual autonomy, in broad lines, lies at the basis of the main theories of collective intentionality by Tuomela, Gilbert, Pettit, Searle, and Bratman. It is also the main reason that most authors remain wary of strong conceptions of collective intentionality, agency, and action. Such conceptions, it is argued, would impair the autonomy of the participating individuals because it would deprive them of their "intentional ownership", i.e. of them "owning" their reasons for acting. These individuals would no longer be directed by their authentic self, but rather (at least partially) by the collective or plural self and hence be directed by "desires, conditions, and characteristics" that are "imposed externally" and that cannot be considered part of one's authentic self (see Schweikard & Schmid, 2013, for a similar point).

5.7.1 Agential Direction and Agential Control

When Bratman discusses the possibility and importance of agential control, he is led by the questions "What is self-governance?" His initial answer is that "in self-governance the agent herself directs and governs her practical thought and action" (Bratman, 2007, p. 4). To direct thinking and acting it is important that the relevant attitudes guide and control the thinking and acting. That way we can say they have authority to speak for the agent (agential authority). Agential authority serves as a bridge between the appeal to attitudes that guide and control and the appeal to the agent as directing.

It is not sufficient that the agent directs her thinking and acting. The directing has to be shaped by justifying reasons for action. These should be understood as higher-order conative states of the agent that are in accordance with the higher-level models that Bratman worked out in his creature construction. These reasons need to have subjective normative authority. Such authority has an important relation to the diachronicity of our agency:

> . . . one and the same agent persists over time, and there are complex continuities and connections that help constitute the organized interweave of our action and practical thinking over time. (Bratman, 2007, p. 4)

Temporal extended agency needs such authority, also in the form of policies, in order to constitute a cross-temporal identity. This identity is presupposed in much of our practical thinking. Bratman follows a largely Lockean approach in the way he interweaves authority, personal identity, and temporal extendedness.

Furthermore, he is strongly influenced by Harry Frankfurt's work on higher-order volitional states. Another term for higher-order volitional states is higher-order conative attitudes. Frankfurt's original version of this idea is that in acting of one's own free will one desires one's desires to be motivating. In other words, the idea is that one is not acting simply because one desires so to act, but also desires a desire to fill such a motivational role, to be guiding the action.

Bratman argues that these higher-order conative states are sufficient for cases of human autonomous agency,[57] but he leaves room for potential other ways to conceptualize autonomous agency. This sufficient condition, he then continues to argue, is one that plays a major role in cases of autonomous agency in human beings:

> ... one central kind of psychological functioning that can constitute or realize human autonomous agency involves motivational hierarchy. (Bratman, 2007, p. 163)

and:

> Indeed, I believe that higher-order conative attitudes play a significant role in central cases of autonomous agency, and so we should accept the AH [Autonomy-Hierarchy] thesis.
> (Bratman, 2007, p. 164)

So, again in a similar fashion as with planning agency and shared agency, Bratman takes these sufficiency conditions not only to bear a metaphysical point of plausibility of such a structure, but also to provide us with good tools to conceptualize most of these occasions concerning autonomy.

Bratman offers two reasons, or problems that we face, that entice us to adopt the autonomy-hierarchy thesis. It is also here that Bratman argues that humans face different problems from most nonhuman agents because we are "reflective in certain ways" (Bratman, 2007, p. 165) which involves practicing reflective self-management.

Problem one regards the many motivations we may find ourselves to have, and their potentially conflicting nature. An agent might find herself in an angry state but might – upon reflection – realize that she does not want to act on this anger. This is what Bratman calls the problem of reflective self-management. This is a problem that agents face in their everyday activities, although their awareness of the conflict might not always be present.

The second problem is the problem of underdetermination by value judgment. To illustrate this problem Bratman uses Sartre's now famous example of

---

[57] In a similar vein as his sufficient conditions for shared agency are spelled out as sufficiency conditions.

the young man that has to choose between fighting with the Free French or stay with his mother (Sartre, 1975). Both choices would be valuable and reasonable choices, and the options themselves do not dictate what the agent should do. In many less extreme cases we will face two options that are both worthwhile pursuing, yet we cannot do both and we will have to make a choice based on something else than the mere value of both options. This indeterminacy might be either because the values are incomparable or because they are the same. According to Bratman a "wholehearted commitment" can help us to live a coherent, temporally extend life.

About both problems Bratman writes the following:

> They are pervasive, practical problems faced by ordinary human agents. This is not to say that these problems are normally ones with which we are explicitly and consciously concerned in our everyday practical thinking. Rather, much of our ordinary, day-to-day practical thinking takes for granted background structures that help constitute our solutions to these problems. (Bratman, 2007, p. 166)

In both cases Bratman thinks that a motivational hierarchy can constitute or realize human autonomous agency. A more or less unified agent will help solve both these problems.

Bratman's notion of autonomous action is connected to two different ideas: agential direction and agential governance. Agential direction brings us sufficient unity and organization of our motives of action so that they can constitute direction by the agent. Agential governance is a particular form of such agential direction. It is direction that involves an agent that treats her considerations as justifying end for action. We saw this notion earlier when I discussed Bratman's creature construction. To treat a desire, intentions, or plan as a justifying reason for action the agent has to commit herself to being motivated by a desire or intention.[58]

This section has shown that Bratman understands autonomy in terms of a certain relation to our desires and beliefs, which closely correlates with commitments, plans, and policies. All these are defined as sufficiency conditions, not necessary conditions. At the same time Bratman supposes that these

---

58 For such an account to not fall prey to the homunculus fallacy Bratman suggests that such agential direction and governance are realized by appropriate forms of psychological functioning.

"There is agential direction of action when action is under the control of attitudes whose role in the agent's psychology gives them authority to speak for the agent, to establish the agent's point of view – gives them, in other words, agential authority. This agential direction of action is, furthermore, a form of agential governance of action only when these attitudes control action by way of the agent's treatment of relevant considerations as justifying reasons for action, that is, as having subjective normative authority for her" (Bratman, 2007, p. 177–178).

sufficiency conditions are the ones that usually operating. This way of understanding autonomous agency has consequences for the way in which Bratman can spell out shared agency. I will turn to those consequences now.

5.7.2 Intend That and Intend To

The existing literature on collective intentionality recognizes an issue concerning control in the conceptualization of collective intentionality. This issue is described as the problem of the own-action condition (Baier, 1997; Stoutland, 1997; Schmid, 2009). This problem evolves around the fact that an intention needs a causal relation to the behavior that follows from it. In both individual and joint action, the idea is that the agent's intentions lead (to) the action. I cannot intend for another agent. Yet when I say, or think, "we intend . . ." this suggests that I can intend for the two of us, and therefore that I can intend for you. In other words, if Wendy has control over her actions, and Matt cannot control Wendy's actions and vice versa, how can either intend something in the plural?

Bratman has argued against the own-action condition (Bratman, 2014, p. 66) and defends two alternatives; A settle condition and a control condition. When each person intends that we J, there is a control condition than can be specified as follows:

> . . . each will sensibly see her intention that we J as controlling (though not as the sole control of) whether they together J, where this control goes by way of the other agent's intention, one that is itself supported by her own intention given persistence interdependence.
> (Bratman, 2014, p. 66)

Note that there is interdependence of control and of intentions. Bratman uses "I intend that we" as the grammatical structure that allows us to intend together without the possibility of one intending for both. This is in response to the debate on the own-action condition. I will first go through the details of Bratman's argument for "intend that" as a structure that is suitable for shared intentions, before outlining some of the problems with the "intent that" solution that have been discussed in the literature.

Originally, philosophers did not functionally distinguish between intend to and intend that. Bratman introduced a distinction between "intending that" and "intending to", arguing that "I intend to J", where J is a collective action, is grammatically impossible, whereas "I intend that we J" is possible. In the individual case both grammatical structures are allowed. This allows us to make progress in the collective intentionality debate. "Intend to" pertains to individual agency only, whereas "intend that" can pertain to individual and shared agency. A "we" cannot intend to do something because that would either involve a group mind with this mental state or an individual that takes herself to be speaking for the group (which would imply a hierarchical relation).

English grammar allows "I intend that we" do something; the individual subject has an intention that also involves other agents. An "I" cannot "intend to" we do something because that would either lead to a plural subject or a grammatically incorrect structure. Thus, in shared agency and in social contexts we cannot intend to, but I can "intend that we J".[59] In this case the two intentions of the involved agents have *persistence interdependence*. We have persistence interdependence if (a) each of us "will continue so to intend if, but only if the other continues so to intend", and (b) "there is this interdependence because each will know whether or not the other continues so to intend, and each will adjust to this knowledge in a way that involves responsiveness to norms of individual plan-theoretical rationality" (Bratman, 2014, p. 65).

Bratman argues that I cannot only "intend that we", but I can also "intend that you X". In both the "I intend that we J" and "I intend that you X" case there is a less direct connection between the person expressing these intentions and the (joint) agency that will (potentially) follow from the intention. By less direct I mean that agent A, who has the intention, can undertake certain actions (including communicative acts) that might move agent B to perform as A intends her to. In this sense the relation between the intended outcome and the actions that the agent performs always involve an extra step.

We saw in the last section that Bratman's theory of planning agency strongly relies on the idea that intention and action are closely related. Yet the "I intend that we" construction and its implications seems to move away from his original idea of the connection between intention and action. In the collective case the agent is only capable to "intend that we" in combination with intentions about her individual intentions (I intend to) making it seem impossible to act together and putting the focus on intentionality (instead of intentions). The togetherness is in the planning intentions and meshing, not in the acting.[60]

There are plenty of cases where the agent intends to do something, but the success of this action will be dependent on certain situational factors. The agent does not only want to control her own body, or bodily movements, but also tries to make changes in the surroundings, including others, in a

---

59 It is even questionable whether a *we* really exists in Bratman. At least it doesn't exist in the unitary sense, but only a qualitative composition of I's that have a shared intention and meshing subplans.
60 Is this truly better than Searle's we-intentions? Or just a matter of different wording ("I intend that we J" rather than "I we-intend")?

controlled manner. The success of these changes can be beyond the – more narrowly understood – control of the agent. Yet we would not want to say that the agent did not intend to do X. When we are in a well-known and predictable situation, we can say and can feel we have control over both body and context. Through my intentional action I control (with some degree of certainty) my own movements and the changes in the environment. As I am writing this text, it is rather predictable to me how my finger movements will influence what happens on the screen. But it might be that my cat just walked over the keyboard and caps-lock is still on and therefore the outcome is different from what I intended. There are many instances in which it is less predictable what our bodily control will lead to qua effects outside the bodily movement. This, however, does not change the intention of the agent. Forming an intention where the outcome depends on the situation, being that either objects or others, is therefore not something that should make it impossible to intend the outcome. Requiring common knowledge in place seems one way to make it more likely that the outcome will be as desired. There are, however, also other options available, that would not take away the autonomy of other agents involved. Agent A could, for example, start a movement that agent B picks up on and continues, jointly with agent A.

Depending on the situation, a social situation can also come with a high level of predictability and in that sense a high level of control. I know what responses I will get, even without forcing those around me to these responses. In both cases there is intending and control without full certainty. This distinction between the bodily control and controlled influencing of our environment might be helpful when relating to Bratman's discussion of the difference between intend that and intend to. In many cases we might be able to act jointly, foregoing the sufficiency conditions as spelled out by Bratman. What the exact grammatical description of such an intention would be like, is then of less importance. How we can coordinate through different functionalities than those proposed by Bratman will be the focus of the next chapter, where I will introduce four theories that start with more minimal notions of joint action. Before that I will briefly summarize the findings of this chapter on planning agency and shared agency.

5.8 Conclusion

I followed Bratman in his suggestion that the function of planning intentions should be understood in their forward-looking orientation. The core idea is that human agency is directed at and structured by future plans, a cohesive self-image, and social embeddedness. A planning agent is distinguished from a purposive agent through several extra constraints to the choices she makes. Both purposive and planning agents show goal-directed behavior, but they have different constraints. A planning agent takes her future plans and future self (including, for example, ideas about future regret) into account.

Planning agency is important in our interaction with other agents, but it is also the foundation of Bratman's thoughts on shared agency. In both cases the diachronicity of our agency (including our intentions, plans, and policies, and the coherence and agglomeration of all these) is of tremendous importance. Many issues regarding self-control do not arise when an agent does not consider coherence *over* time. This goes for both the individual and the shared domain. The proposal developed in chapter seven is in line with these theoretical foundations, both in the individual and the joint case.

Bratman wants a theory of *shared* agency (a) to specify the functional role shared intentions play and (b) to give us a substantial account of what shared intentions could be. Regarding the first part Bratman stipulates that the functional role (or job) of shared intentions is to:

i. Coordinate activities;
ii. Coordinate planning; and
iii. Provide a framework to structure bargaining.

Together these functional roles allow us to plan for the shared future, act jointly in the here and now, and talk if we disagree. This cannot think of another functional role that we would need for agents to act together. Bratman (2014) then suggests five sufficient conditions, that together generate these three functions.

1. The intention condition;
2. Belief condition;
3. Interdependence condition;
4. Common knowledge condition; and
5. Mutual responsiveness condition.

There is one element that needs further elaboration, and one worry. Regarding the first functional role (the coordination of activities) theoretical proposals on emergent coordination can provide us with useful concepts that help us describe how we coordinate activity without referring to Bratman's sufficient conditions 1–5. Assuming that we can and often do use both emergent coordination and planned coordination we need to spell out in more detail how these different ways of coordinating work together. It can also be conceived how there is a continuity between emergent coordination and planned coordination. The worry that arises is that the distinction between those cases where we coordinate together and those cases where "the we" emerges as we already are coordinating becomes a matter of degree, rather than a dichotomy. This is a consequence that I would like to embrace. My proposal, based on what I discussed in chapters two to four, is to allow for a more multidimensional understanding, encapsulating several aspects that can make it the case that we consider something to be a joint action. I will say more about this in section 6.4 and chapter seven.

The worries that have been expressed regarding the over-intellectualized picture that Bratman introduces, so I argued, has its roots in his understanding of individual agency and how this translates into his account of shared agency. By allowing for a more skillful understanding of our everyday activity, both as individuals and in groups, we can avoid such over-intellectualization.

This entails that an agent sometimes acts against her own plans, intentions, and policies. Bratman wants to incorporate bounded rationality into his theory of planning agency. I argued that, at least in some cases, this is not possible because the agent herself does not realize what the influence of such bounded rationality is. Reflection upon one's own behavior can be of help in those cases, but only after the fact, that is, only after the agent has acted in disagreement with her own intentions.

6 Joint Action and Interaction

There have been several formulations of joint action theories starting from the insights in cognitive science. Cognitive scientists and behavioral scientists are typically not studying the intentions involved. Rather, they focus on "lower-level cognitive capacities" that allow agents to coordinate. For a large part they spell out ways in which human agents *coordinate* their activities. This is different from philosophical accounts, including Bratman's account, which starts with the question of shared *agency*. For most philosophers coordination is not a sufficient condition for shared agency or collective intentionality. The focus of this chapter will be on four theories on joint action. I chose to focus on these four because they offer us not only empirical data, but also a conceptualization of joint action, coordination, and/or collective intentionality based on these data.

Another key aspect that these theories take into account is the development of joint action capacities in children. Tollefsen and Dale (2012), for example, argue:

> Animals, young children, adults, and artificial agents can engage in joint action. Because philosophical theories are modeled on joint actions among human adults they are often unable to account for joint action among different sorts of agents. If, for instance, joint action requires prior planning or joint commitments involving normative demands, it is unclear how animals could be able to engage in joint action, but surely they do. Philosophical theories of joint action tend to over-intellectualize joint agency.
>
> (Tollefsen & Dale, 2012, p. 390)

And they are not alone. Take the following quote from the article on the minimal architecture model that I will discuss in section 6.2:

> Unlike approaches focusing on language and shared intentionality that are mainly concerned with thinking and communicating about acting together, the framework is geared towards explaining how people actually perform actions together.
>
> (Vesper, Butterfill, Knoblich, & Sebanz, 2010, p. 998)

These different theories often position themselves in opposition to, or as the other dimension of, collective intentionality approaches to joint action, contributing to the dualism-thinking in our conceptualization of joint action. I think this is a mistake. When we look closely at the theories these four people provide, we see that they are very rich and that they do not provide "the other side of the spectrum" in comparison to shared intentions as spelled out by many philosophers. Once we recognize this, and also recognize that their depiction of the "over-intellectualized" philosopher might be too much of a caricature, we find room to see how we can understand the interplay of the different forms of coordination that different (sometimes specifically human) capacities allow us to.

I will discuss *emergent coordination*, which mainly deals with highly automatic processes, in section 6.1. A modular approach, the *minimal architecture model*, that supposedly fills the gap between emergent coordination and planned coordination (which are to be understood as shared intentions, commitments, we-intentions, and the like), will be discussed in section 6.2. Section 6.3 focuses on an *enactivist account of interaction and joint action*, with a special focus on dancing together. While the first three approaches give us insight into the coordination, section 6.4 covers a discussion on the *phenomenology of we-agency based on prediction and control mechanisms*. This approach is based on findings regarding prediction and control in cognitive psychology, bearing important relations to both the experienced togetherness in shared agency and on the notion of control. Where the first three sections of this chapter focus on coordination, the first of three elements I discussed in chapter one, section four focuses on the other two features of joint action, control and a sense of agency.

6.1 Emergent Coordination

Cognitive science inspired theories of joint action and collective intentionality frequently used the following definition of joint action:

> ... a joint action is a social interaction whereby two or more individuals coordinate their actions in space and time to bring about a change in the environment.
> (Sebanz, Bekkering, & Knoblich, 2006, p. 70)

When characterizing coordination, a demarcation between planned coordination and emergent coordination is not uncommon (Knoblich, Butterfill, & Sebanz, 2011; Tollefsen & Dale, 2012). Planned coordination involves (explicit, commonly known) collective intentions (as described by Searle, Bratman, Gilbert, and Tuomela).[61] Research on emergent coordination focuses on the co-ordination between agents who are acting on the fly. It studies joint action that

---

[61] Tollefsen and Dale connect their account to Searle's we-intentions. Butterfill, one of the authors of the other main paper by Vesper and colleagues (2010), argues that theories of emergent coordination are often inspired by a Bratmanian approach. Neither, however, is strongly committed to any of these approaches and the critique coming from emergent coordination applies to all "higher-level" cognitive approaches that philosophy traditionally offers.

occurs via perception-action couplings or via lower-level cognitive mechanisms. An example of such lower-level mechanisms is the tendency that agents have to synchronize with others when they are performing the same action. This is, amongst others, happening when people rock in rocking chairs (Richardson, Marsh, Isenhower, Goodman, & Schmidt, 2007). Even when the subjects are explicitly asked to follow their own rhythm while rocking in their chair, they will be inclined to change their tempo to that of the other. Such co-ordination phenomena, which are typically thought to be involved in joined action, are argued to function without shared intentions in place (Knoblich, Butterfill, & Sebanz, 2011; Tollefsen & Dale, 2012; Vesper, Butterfill, Knoblich, & Sebanz, 2010). Many, if not all, of these types of influence of the presence of the other are described as automatic and, therefore, hard (if not impossible) to control. Because of this lack of control planning agency also does not seem to play a role.

In *planned coordination*, as described by cognitive scientists, an agent's behavior is driven by representations that specify the desired outcomes of joint action and the agent's own part in achieving these outcomes. In *emergent coordination*, on the other hand, coordinated behavior occurs due to perception-action couplings that make multiple individuals act in similar, or complimenting, ways (allowing coordination), independently of joint plans (Knoblich, Butterfill, & Sebanz, 2011). Any approach that focuses on emergent coordination has the advantage that it allows us to conceptualize how other animals and young children act jointly. A potential disadvantage is the lack of stability that such coordination can provide the interacting agents with.

Empirical research has shown that people are influenced by perception-action coupling (by means of imitation, synchronization, and alignment) on several levels, including psycholinguistic (Branigan, Pickering, & Cleland, 2000), attentional (Richardson & Dale, 2005), and low-level behavioral signals (Shockley, Santana, & Fowler, 2003). Knoblich et al. (2011) and Tollefsen and Dale (2012) have written the two most influential articles providing a theoretical framework that starts from the distinction between emergent coordination and planned coordination. Both approaches emphasize *several* sources of and routes to joint action. Both contributions argue that the mechanisms that are involved in emergent coordination can be sufficient for joint action; they are not merely enabling conditions.[62] We can be jointly engaged through emergent

---

[62] As suggested by several philosophers working on collective intentionality, including Bratman (2014) and Zahavi (2014).

coordination. Concurrently they also acknowledge how emergent coordination can play an important part in the development of collective intentionality in a more robust fashion, including collective intentions of some form. Knoblich and colleagues explain how we can understand the surfacing of and reaching of shared *goals* through emergent coordination. Tollefsen and Dale are looking to create a more encompassing framework that connects emergent coordination and shared intentions. They, like Knoblich and colleagues, argue that emergent coordination in itself can be sufficient for joint actions. They argue, however, that over time emergent coordination often will result in the formation of we-intentions. One can start acting jointly through lower-level mechanisms (emergent coordination), which might later become supplemented by the deeper commitments of planned coordination and collective intentionality. The initiation and maintenance of a joint action can – but need not be – based on the same mechanisms (Tollefsen & Dale, 2012).

6.1.1 Mechanisms of Emergent Coordination

Studies in cognitive science have identified several cognitive mechanisms that get emergent coordination of the ground (Knoblich, Butterfill, & Sebanz, 2011; Tollefsen & Dale, 2012). Some mechanisms work by facilitating the production of the same movements and rhythms, others by means of complementary movements. An orthogonal distinction can be drawn between mechanisms that help us align and synchronize while we are already acting, and those mechanisms that might help to explain how we get coordination of the ground.

Ecological psychologists have studied rhythmic joint actions in order to determine whether dynamical principles of intrapersonal coordination scale up to the interpersonal case (Marsh, Richardson, & Schmidt, 2009). This research has shown that in many cases, the movement of limbs belonging to different people follows the same mathematical principles as the movement of an individual's limbs (Schmidt, Carello, & Turvey, 1990). The degrees of freedom of one limb can be reduced through the movement of another limb (see chapter four). This, research shows, also applies to the limbs of interacting agents. The movements of the one can reduce the degrees of freedom for the other by means of synergy, interdependency and/or efficiency. These results suggest that specific perceptual, motor, and cognitive processes support joint action (Knoblich & Sebanz, 2008; Semin & Cacioppo, 2008) and that the needs of joint action shape individual perception, action, and cognition (Sebanz, Bekkering, & Knoblich, 2006).

Knoblich and colleagues (2011) argue that emergent coordination is a key facilitator of joint action. They distinguish four different sources of emergent coordination: entrainment, common affordances,[63] perception-action matching, and action simulation.[64] Tollefsen and Dale (2012) mainly focus on alignment (referring to the same studies Knoblich and colleagues use to delineate entrainment) and on dynamic system theories as an explanation of this alignment. The article by Tollefsen and Dale mainly points at five problems that most philosophical accounts of collective intentionality face, aiming less to distinguish the differences between forms of emergent coordination. For this reason, I will follow the conceptual distinctions as introduced by Knoblich and colleagues (2011). The end of this section looks at the "social glue" effect that results from emergent coordination.

Entrainment
In entrainment studies, participants are usually engaged in the same repetitive behavior and are asked to find their own rhythm. They are asked to stick to this rhythm while then turning their attention to the other person who is performing the same movements (at their preferred rhythm). Studies where people were in rocking chairs (Schmidt & O'Brien, 1997) and making tap movements (Richardson, Marsh, Isenhower, Goodman, & Schmidt, 2007) show that resisting falling in synchrony with the other is really hard and that people quickly divert from their preferred initial rhythm.[65] The adjustment of speed of motion to synchronize is an excellent example of entrainment. In dynamical system research interpersonal entrainment is often considered as a particular instance of the coupling of rhythmic oscillators (Schmidt & Richardson, 2008). The evidence for the effect on coordination is comprehensive. In Richardson et al.'s experiment individuals could not resist interpersonal entrainment even if the "natural rocking frequencies" of the two rocking chairs they were rocking in differed. Oullier et al. (2008) propose that a

---

63 Knoblich and colleagues note that joint affordances have not yet been studied, so these have hardly any evidence. Some researchers have started to explore how the presence of another person creates affordances for acting together (Richardson, Marsh, & Baron, 2007). Constantini & Sinigaglia (2011) have identified the importance of peri-personal space of the other agent in perceiving affordances. In general, given the complex nature of affordances, especially in the joint case, not much can be said about underlying mechanisms that support *joint* affordances.
64 Action simulation: once a match between observed and performed actions is established, it enables the observer to apply predictive models in his or her motor system to accurately predict the timing and outcomes of observed actions. One's own action helps predict the actions of someone else through simulation. It is unclear, however, how such predictions in themselves help us coordinate, unless we already take it to be the case that we share a goal.
65 Such contagion can be a stepping-stone towards a sense of us, which will be discussed in greater detail in section 4 of this chapter.

"social memory" keeps participants synchronized when the visual input supporting the coupling is absent.

We do not only synchronize, but also have a keen awareness of others synchronizing. Observers that perceive two agents entrain attributed the highest level of rapport to those pairs of walkers that displayed in-phase or anti-phase coordination,[66] regardless whether information about the walkers' synchrony was conveyed through visual or auditory information (Miles, Nind, & Macrae, 2009).

Such alignment/entrainment processes are automatic and arise even while the agent tries to focus on individual goals. Sensing the presence of another agent, perceiving her actions, and inferring goals from these actions, influences our own actions. Taking the perspective of another into account, or focusing on the other's task, slows people down and makes them more prone to errors. Yet research shows that we track the other's goals and actions even if these are not necessary for the tracking of our own goal (Atmaca, Sebanz, Prinz, & Knoblich, 2008). Taken together, this suggests that, first, we automatically perceive the other's task and perspective and, second, that this perception influences our own behavior, even in those cases where we explicitly try to ignore the other.

Perception-Action Matching
Human agents tend to copy what they have just seen, leading to mimicry of observed actions and postures (Knoblich, Butterfill, & Sebanz, 2011). Emergent coordination can arise through such a perception-action matching as it induces the same action tendencies in different agents who observe one another's actions (Knoblich & Sebanz, 2008). Studies have demonstrated that observing a particular movement in another person leads to an automatic activation of the same movement in the observer (Bertenthal, Longo, & Kosobud, 2006; Brass, Bekkering, & Prinz, 2001). For instance, seeing someone grasp a small object, such as a grape, activates brain processes involved in the grasping actions directed at small, round objects (Rizzolatti & Sinigaglia, 2010). Also in cases where there is no object manipulation we see mimicry and brain activation in the same motor areas as when performing the action. Such matching can also be based on similarity in intransitive movements. For instance, observing someone dancing will activate corresponding action representations if one knows how to dance (Calvo-Merino, Glaser, Grèzes, Passingham, & Haggard, 2005;

---

[66] In anti-phase coordination the involved agents synchronize, but rather than both being at the same point at the same time, they are both at the *other* extreme at the same time. It is comparable to the arms swinging while walking: one will be extended to the front while the other is swung to the back, reaching the most extended position at the same time.

Cross, Hamilton, & Grafton, 2006). Such neuronal activation can explain our understanding of the actions of others, but also our readiness to act in similar and/or complimentary ways. The recognition of what the other is doing, and how one might respond will depends on the skills of the person seeing the movements.

Perception-action matching is not as automatic as entrainment. We can and often do "repress" the urge to imitate what we just saw. Although we tend to pick up postures and movements of others we need not. If the ability to control this would indeed be as hard as in the case of entrainment and alignment, this would indeed have rather problematic consequences. In that sense perception-action matching is better described as *facilitating* imitation. This facilitation, although not completely automatic, can be nonconscious.

Social Glue Effect
We do not only imitate and align with other's behaviors, to some degree we also like being imitated. One of the effects on those being mimicked is increased liking of the other (the "chameleon effect", Chartrand & Bargh, 1999). Studies on the "social glue effect" show us the importance of emergent coordination for understanding more complex notions such as the sense of us and joint action (Knoblich, Butterfill, & Sebanz, 2011). The above-mentioned study involving the rocking chairs showed that people who synchronize more judge each other as more likable and that periods of synchronizing engender a more pro-social attitude in people's interactions with others (even those they did not synchronize with). Burger has coined this the *liking heuristic* (Burger, 2007; Byrne, 1997; Insko & Wilson, 1977; Lakin, Jefferis, Cheng, & Chartrand, 2003). There seems to exist a rater direct relationship between coordination and liking (Hove & Risen, 2009). Entrainment also led to more cooperative choices, and a reported feeling of more connectedness and trust (Wiltermuth & Heath, 2009).

Something very interesting happens when liking occurs: it increases (emergent) coordination. This can lead to a looping effect where successful emergent coordination increases liking, which in turn increases the coordination between the interacting agents. We also find the effect of liking on emergent coordination before agents acted together: when liking is increased beforehand. Liking can be increased by mentioning simple and unimportant facts. For example, when subjects are told they share their sign or birthday with another participant, participants show more synchrony amongst each other (Burger, Soroka, Gonzago, Murphy, & Somervell, 2001). This suggests a bi-directional influence of synchronization and a pro-social attitude (Chartrand & Bargh, 1999; Valdesolo, Ouyang, & DeSteno, 2010). Especially when there is no specific goal or shared intention in place, a pro-social attitude can create room for such goals and intentions to arise (Knoblich, Butterfill, & Sebanz, 2011). We could understand this as a movement towards a sense of us and a willingness to formulate shared intentions. When we judge the other to be aligned with ourselves and feel somehow related, this will further encourage acting together. I will say more about the sense of us in section 6.4.

6.1.2 Conclusion

There is an overwhelming amount of evidence showing the importance of these different mechanisms in coordination and linking their effects to joint action. We tend to do what others do, in a rhythm similar to theirs. This helps two or more individuals to coordinate and therewith interact successfully. Although the route to this type of coordination is very different from the planning agency we saw in chapter five, it is meant to emphasize that not all processes identified as emergent coordination are equally automatic, and not all are equally uncontrolled. This is problematic if one sticks to a strict dichotomous picture. Within a heterogeneous and multi-dimensional picture this divergence is not a problem. In chapter seven I will say more about the way in which we can fit emergent coordination, in its all-encompassing way, into my proposal.

6.2 Minimal Architecture Model of Joint Action

We now move towards another approach to coordination in joint action. Vesper, Butterfill, Knoblich, and Sebanz (2010), have introduced a minimal architecture model of joint action. The model consists of several building blocks, or modules, which together purport to explain how agents to act jointly. The minimal architecture model is based on an analysis of differences between individual and joint action and models action at the motor-control level. The model was introduced to fill the gap between the dynamical system approaches to emergent coordination and theories of planned coordination that draw on propositional attitude ascription:

> Unlike the dynamical systems framework that considers interpersonal coordination as a special case of more general coordination principles, the proposed framework assumes the existence of dedicated mechanisms for joint action. Unlike approaches focusing on language and shared intentionality that are mainly concerned with thinking and communicating about acting together, the framework is geared towards explaining how people actually perform actions together.   (Vesper, Butterfill, Knoblich, & Sebanz, 2010, p. 998)

The minimal architecture model should be understood as a model of joint motor intentions (or intentions-in-action) positioned between models based on (highly automated) general interpersonal coordination rules on the one hand and, on (shared) prior intentions on the other hand. Vesper et al. argue that three extra functions that have to be present in the case of joint action, which are not needed when acting individually: agents have to *predict* the behavior of the other, they need to *adjust* our behavior to the behavior of the other, and there has to be (precise) spatio-temporal *coordination* among them.

These three functions are realized through the following four building blocks:
1. *Representation*; both agents have to represent the (joint) goal, their own task, and task x (the task of the other agent, not necessarily the other agent).
2. *Monitoring*; both agents monitor whether the goal and task(s) unfold as expected.
3. *Prediction* of the unfolding; needed in order to be able to monitor and adjust.
4. To further facilitate joint action a *coordination smoother* is added to the model. An agent can facilitate the joint action (simplify coordination) by modulation of one's own behavior or by using an object that affords a particular task distribution.

In the next section, I will discuss these four building blocks in detail.

6.2.1 Four Modules for Joint Action

Representation
According to Vesper et al., the *minimal* representation that we need to cooperate well is that of the goal, the own task and task x. Vesper and colleagues specifically argue that we need not necessarily represent the other agent. For coordination, a representation of the other's task is necessary and potentially sufficient. They appeal to an experiment where two chimpanzees have to pull a rope in order to get a treat. As soon as the goal of the first chimp has been achieved, it will stop the interaction, arguably using the other as a social tool. There appears to be no true cooperation, or shared action, but only the representation of the task of the other in attaining one's own goals, yet there is joint action (understood as coordinated activity towards a shared goal). Vesper and colleagues argue that when two human agents interact they might approach/represent the other as a social tool too. It remains an open question, however, whether representing the other as a tool and representing only the task of the

other are one and the same thing. The representation of the other's task might be implied in the representation of the goal and/or task. Besides this minimal requirement for representation it is likely that many cases will involve richer representations including a representation of the other agent.

Vesper and colleagues use partner dancing as another example to show the lack of necessity of representing the other agent, while representing the other's task. They write:

> To illustrate, consider two people dancing a tango together. In that case, the leader and follower have to coordinate their steps with each other. In principle, the follower might represent the leader's task in a very specific way, including for instance the other's need to make a forward movement with her right foot. This would imply that the follower could in principle switch roles with the leader. But it is more likely that the follower does not represent the leader's task in any such detail, and plausible that she does not represent the leader's task at all. All she requires is a representation of her own task and the goal of moving along a certain trajectory without losing contact between herself and her partner. (Vesper, Butterfill, Knoblich, & Sebanz, 2010, p. 1000)

In this quote they argue that the follower is (a) surely not representing the leader's task in the very same way as the leader is and (b) potentially not representing the leader or his task(s) at all. It is indeed quite likely that the leader's tasks are not represented as such by the follower. The details will not be the same in the representations of the leader and the follower. But from this it doesn't follow that there is not a lot of detail in the representations which includes and goes beyond the task of the other agent. One of the ways in which couples align their goals in dancing is to facilitate certain movements for the other. To do so it is insufficient to represent the goal of the other because how the goal can be reached will depend on their current bodily position and the kind of tasks each has. In order to take that into account one has to represent the other person and how things are from their position.

The distinction between different representations that might play a role in the case of joint action is indeed helpful. In many cases, however, these representations only make sense in relation to one another, and in relation to the shared goal. They have to be embedded in a more holistic understanding.

Monitoring

The second building block Vesper and colleagues introduce is that of monitoring whether the joint goal is unfolding as planned (on the level of motor intentions). This is analogue to the way monitoring works in the case of individual action.

Studies show that observation of others making errors results in a similar slowing down of one's own movements compared to when making an error oneself. It also leads to similar negative brain potentials and activation of similar brain areas (De Bruijn, de Lange, von Cramon, & Ullsperger, 2009; Malfait et al., 2010; Newman-Norlund, Ganesh, Van Schie, De Bruijn, & Bekkering, 2009; Schuch & Tipper, 2007; Van Schie, Mars, Coles, & Bekkering, 2004). Monitoring, an important part of motor-control theories, can be usefully extended to the monitoring of the tasks (and movements) of the other agent. The impact of errors of the other agent are similar to the impact of errors made by the agent herself, pointing at the same motor-control being involved.

Monitoring indeed is very important to coordination in joint action. It is unclear, however, how joint action specific this module is.[67] Monitoring the goal, tasks of oneself and the task of the other are: 1) functions that will often be needed when acting individually in a social environment, and 2) functions that are needed for many more capacities, such as acting more generally and social understanding.

Prediction

The third key building block proposed by Vesper et al. is prediction (of joint action). This has ties to the perception-action links discussed in the previous section. As in the case of individual action, in a joint action an agent makes predictions of movements and end-states. The prediction module that Vesper and colleagues propose for joint action relies on motor simulation and generates expectations about the outcome of actions online (regarding the immediate future). Prediction allows the agent to anticipate the future course of other's actions (Graf et al., 2007). These predictions rely on the agent's own motor experience. Such predictions are thought to bias perception and to help with anticipating the consequences and timing of others' actions (Wilson & Knoblich, 2005). The more similar two agents are in their movements, the better they will be able to predict the immediate future of their coordinated effort. Beside similarity, practice is another route to better prediction because we get familiar with the specificity of the movement and rhythm of the other agent. Repeating a joint action with another agent will help each agent to get a more accurate predictive model of the joint action. This will allow for better coordination.[68] Agents can

---

[67] See also section 6.4, where I use monitoring and prediction as a means to understand the sense of joint agency.
[68] I will say more about prediction and monitoring in section 6.4, when I discuss Pacherie's (2014) ideas on we-agency and the relation between motor cognition and a sense of agency.

also actively make their actions more predictable. This predictability of action is captured in the function introduced in the fourth building block.

Coordination Smoother

The fourth and final module that is part of the minimal architecture model is the coordination smoother. According to Vesper and colleagues it:

> ... is either a modulation of one's own behaviour which reliably has the effect of simplifying coordination, or the use of an object that affords a particular task distribution which reliably has such an effect. (Vesper, Butterfill, Knoblich, & Sebanz, 2010, p. 1001)

Examples they provide include making movements less variable, delimiting and structuring one's own task so that the need for coordination is reduced, imposing structure on a task (turn taking), conventional and nonconventional coordination signals, making certain movements salient, synchronization, and object use. I have trouble understanding the way such diverse functions are to be understood as a single module or cognitive function. I am unsure how this coordination smoother fits with the idea of specifying mechanisms devoted to joint action (as Vesper and colleagues state in their introduction). To make the introduction of a coordination smoother acceptable, (a) it should be spelled out how the functions of this specific mechanism differ from other, similar functions. (b) It should also be made clear what unifies the coordination smoother, if it should be understood as *one* building block. The types of behavior that are currently included in this building block are too diverse and therefore hard to integrate into one kind of mechanism.

6.2.2 Conclusion

The minimal architecture model tries to show minimal aspects, or building blocks, of joint actions with a focus on how people actually perform actions together. It emphasizes how these building blocks can independently be put into play. The model does not provide us with necessary or sufficient conditions for joint action (on the motor cognition/motor intention level). Instead it highlights several joint action specific modules that (1) typically are involved and (2) can be distinguished functionally and content-wise from what is involved in the case of individual action. The functions and the underlying mechanisms that Vesper and colleagues point at are indeed all important for our capacities to act jointly. The first three processes are the cooperative version of motor cognition (intentions-in-action). But most, if not all, of the building blocks that they suggest are also involved in other functions, such as social cognition, self-understanding, acting individually in a crowd, etc. This seems to clash with their claim that their proposed framework "assumes the existence of dedicated mechanisms for joint action" (Vesper et al., 2010, p. 998). The last module they propose, the coordination smoother, faces another issue. It does not seem to present us with one function, nor with one mechanism or process, but rather with several processes and routes that can help us modify our own behavior to help the coordination. The minimal architecture model sets out to specify mechanisms *specifically* devoted to joint action. But what it offers are several, rather general, mechanisms that might sometimes help with coordination in joint action. Both the strict modularity and the specificity claim seem to become less strong upon closer inspection. This makes it harder to strictly distinguish the minimal architecture model and what its building blocks do from the functions discussed in section 6.1. Some of the mechanisms underlying emergent coordination might be functioning only because of the prediction and monitoring mechanisms that have been proposed here. This, however, would require us to see the mechanisms proposed by the minimal architecture model in a more integrated manner than its authors have provided.

The authors of the minimal architecture model argue that their model fills the gap between (1) models that explain long-term planning (based on language, attribution of intention, belief, and other propositional attitudes) and (2) models that explain precise temporal coordination (perception-action links), but, simultaneously, want their proposal to stand on its own as explaining the actual performance of the joint action. Many of their examples of coordination are only comprehensible by combining their model with a goal that is not specified by means of the model. It would be great to see more work on the interrelations between these different capacities that allow agents to act jointly. Such an approach, however, would be less modular and the different functions will be more integrated. Together this means we are moving towards the skillful approach that I will propose in chapter seven.

6.3 Enactivism, Joint Action, and Control

The third approach to joint action that starts with mechanisms or functions that could be described as lower-level comes from enactivism. Varela, Thompson, and Rosch (1991) argued that the standard division between pre-given, external features of the world and internal symbolic representations should be dropped, as it is unable to accommodate the feedback from embodied actions to cognition via the actions of a situated cognitive agent. A key principle of the enactive approach is that the organism is a center of activity in the world. The relation of emergence between novel forms of identity (e.g., integrated sensorimotor engagements as emerging from neural, bodily and environmental dynamics) is one whereby the coupling between the emergent process and its context leads to constraints and modulation of the operation of the underlying levels (Di Paolo, Rohde, & De Jaegher, 2010; Thompson, 2007; Thompson & Varela, 2001). Within this framework De Jaegher and Di Paolo argue that there is a certain form of autonomy to the interaction of two or more agents. This raises interesting questions regarding the autonomy of the individuals involved, and also the type of control that we are talking about. I will briefly discuss the idea of autopoiesis, which lies at the basis of De Jaegher and Di Paolo's (2007) account, with a special focus on the autonomy of the "coupled agents". Enactivism has several central ideas. For the purpose of this section I will focus on two specifically: the idea of autonomy of different levels, and the notion of interaction as spelled out on an enactivist account. I will follow the suggestion by De Jaegher and Di Paolo that the diachronic development of an interaction is crucial for our understanding of the phenomena. This makes it different from the other minimal approaches to joint action and interaction I have discussed this far. It should be noted that this idea of iterativity does not necessarily have to be connected to some of the main claims in enactivism, such as the autonomy claim.

6.3.1 Autopoiesis

According to enactive approaches, cognition is (quite generally) a bodily activity and must be explained in terms of the complex dynamics between mind, body, and environment. In the course of the complex back and forth between action and perception, cognitive processes transform the neutral environment into a meaningful "Umwelt" in relation to the specific needs and purposes of the cognitive agent (Clark, 1997; Thompson, 2007). In this context, the organism's range of sensorimotor skills and the layout of the environment determine the complex set of affordances that emerges specifically for this agent in this situation. To a first approximation, affordances are possibilities for action and perception emerging from situating the agent in an environmental context (Gibson, 1979; Noë, 2004). An important aspect here is the notion of the right kind of *coupling* between agent and world which forces us to treat them as one complex cognitive system where a relevant portion of cognitive processing is *outsourced* by the agent onto the world.

According to one particular brand of enactivism, namely autopoietic enactivism, cognition emerges from the self-organizing and self-producing activities of living organisms. Cognitive structures display the same organizational features as living structures such that mind is life-like and life is mind-like (Thompson, 2007, p. 128ff.). De Jaegher and Di Paolo (2007) have translated the central tenets of autopoietic enactivism into an enactive account of social cognition, i.e. a theory "concerned with defining the social in terms (a) of the embodiment of interaction, (b) of shifting and emerging levels of autonomous identity, and (c) of joint sense-making and its experience" (De Jaegher & Di Paolo, 2007, p. 489).

The original definition of autopoiesis was given by Maturana and Varela:

> An autopoietic machine is a machine organized (defined as a unity) as a network of processes of production (transformation and destruction) of components which: (i) through their interactions and transformations continuously regenerate and realize the network of processes (relations) that produced them; and (ii) constitute it (the machine) as a concrete unity in space in which they (the components) exist by specifying the topological domain of its realization as such a network. (Maturana & Varela, 1980, p. 78)

Thus, the boundary of an autopoietic system is determined circularly by the production of its constituent elements; in this way the organization of, say, a cell is both "circular" and autopoietic because the components that specify the cell are the same components that the organization of the cell secures and maintains. It is this circularity that maintains the cell as a living entity. It is in this sense that an autopoietic system can be considered as a special type of homeostatic system, where the variable to be maintained and controlled is the organization and behavior of the system. For Varela, autopoiesis is both necessary and sufficient to characterize the organization of living, *autonomous* systems, a quite different notion of autonomy than the one we encountered in debates on philosophy of action in chapter three.

To determine whether a system is autopoietic in its organization, Varela, Maturana, and Uribe (1974) developed six criteria that should apply to any system that is considered autopoietic (see also Koskinen (2010) for a discussion of these six criteria).

1) The unity has identifiable boundaries.
2) There are constitutive elements of the unity; components of the unity that can be singled out and described.
3) The unity is a mechanistic system; the component properties are capable of satisfying certain relations that determine the unity, the interactions, and transformations of these components.
4) The components that constitute the boundaries of the unity constitute these boundaries through preferential neighborhood relations and interactions between themselves, as determined by their properties in the space of their interactions.

5) The components of the boundaries of the unity are produced by the interactions of the components of the unity, either by transformation of previously produced components, or by transformations and/or coupling of non-component elements that enter the unity through its boundaries.
6) If all the other components of the unity are also produced by the interactions of its components as in 5, and if those, which are not produced by the interactions of other components, participate as necessary permanent constitutive components in the production of other components, you have an autopoietic unity in the space in which its components exist. If this is not the case and there are components in the unity not produced by components of the unity as in 5, or if there are components of the unity which do not participate in the production of other components, you do not have an autopoietic unity.

6.3.2 Autopoietic Interaction

De Jaegher and Di Paolo argue that these six criteria apply to (individual) human agents and interacting groups. They argue that understanding interaction as an autopoietic organization is helpful for further development of theories of social understanding. It is this understanding of social cognition and interaction that I will focus on, as it allows for a new way of understanding joint action.

Their general take on cognition and social cognition is that the organizational properties of living organisms make them "paradigmatic cases of cognizers" (De Jaegher & Di Paolo, 2007, p. 487). Organizational properties that also protect boundaries have direct relations to agency and autonomy. Such a self-structuring creature seems to fit well to the idea of control that Fujita et al. (2014) have spelled out (see section 2.2). Some form of governance and purpose seems implied in De Jaegher and Di Paolo's notion:

> One such crucial property is the constitutive and interactive autonomy that living systems enjoy by virtue of their self-generated identity as distinct entities in constant material flux. (De Jaegher & Di Paolo, 2007, p. 487)

An autonomous system is defined as a system composed of several processes that actively generate and sustain an identity. This identity is not a given but is in a precarious condition. In the case of an interaction both the individual agent that participate in this interaction and the interaction are understood as autonomous entities, and all are understood to be in a precarious condition.

Maintaining boundaries is one of the key goals of any given system, when understood from an autopoietic perspective. This is the case both on the level of the individual agent and on the level of the interaction. It is important to say something about the relation between individual agents and the interaction. The coupling between two or more individuals as interacting agents is not something that happens accidentally. De Jaegher and Di Paolo argue that co-presence is insufficient and mutual awareness is a necessary condition. They argue it is important that the coupling is "coordinated" (De Jaegher & Di Paolo, 2007, p. 490), i.e., consciously achieved and maintained by the individuals participating in the interaction. Only when the agents are mutually aware of their coupling relation the interaction itself can take on an autonomous dynamic that can prompt us to consider it as a constituent of social understanding itself, or so they argue.

Both the precarious autonomy of the individuals and that of the interaction is at play while interacting: the component processes would run down/ extinguish without the other agent's presence.[69] This idea that "the interaction process can take on a form of autonomy" (De Jaegher & Di Paolo, 2007, p. 485) need to be unpacked. This notion of autonomy, better understood as interactive autonomy, implies that organisms cast a "web of significance" on the world. The coupling and regulating the coupling is only done because the organism, or agent, has a direction that the process is aiming at. The main aim of any autonomous system within an autopoietic framework is continuity of the self-generated identity or identities that initiate the regulation. In this sense normativity is the counterpart of the agent being a center of activity in the world (Di Paolo, Rohde, & De Jaegher, 2010; Thompson, 2007; Varela, 1997). In case of interactions the autonomous system *is* the interaction, and it is the interaction's continuity that is at stake. The interaction aims to sustain itself. It remains unclear whether De Jaegher and Di Paolo are committed to this idea as a metaphor, or more than that.

---

69 According to some accounts, social cognition is achieved not by a single individual who is directed at someone else's mental states, but by the joint (or collaborative) effort of two or more agents. De Jaegher & Di Paolo (2007) call this process "participatory sense-making" since understanding is the emergent result of the autonomous interaction process between two or more agents. This account of social cognition is intended to replace the more traditional theory- and simulation accounts. Instead of looking for the cognitive achievement of social understanding within the participating individuals (or their brain mechanisms for that matter), these authors suggest that the communication loop between the individuals literally (partly) constitutes understanding. This is called "participatory sense-making" since the agents jointly bring about the meaning of their mental acts, via interaction (De Jaegher & Di Paolo, 2007; De Jaegher, Di Paolo & Gallagher, 2010).

Like Tollefsen and Dale (2012, see section 6.1) They use concepts from dynamical systems theory. De Jaegher and Di Paolo argue that only at the relational level of collective dynamics the rich structures of interactions as processes extended in time become visible. Dynamical systems theory explains the phenomenon of coordination between coupled systems. De Jaegher and Di Paolo understand coordination as:

> *non-accidental* correlation between the behaviours of two or more systems that are in sustained coupling, or have been coupled in the past, or have been coupled to another, common, system. (De Jaegher & Di Paolo, 2007, p. 490)

In this context they define a correlation as a coherence in the behavior of two or more systems. This correlation should be *over and above* what we would expect. When is something sufficient to count as more than the correlation that would be expected? The example they give is a crowd that is walking in the same area. When they are all walking, but without a specific direction, there is no correlation. When the crowd is walking in the same direction, this *could be* a correlation, and "if we suspect that this is not by accident, we can hypothesize the presence of a coordinating factor" (De Jaegher & Di Paolo, 2007, p. 490). They include the types of coupling that we find in dynamic system approaches and refer to Schmidt and O'Brien's (1997) research on subjects swinging pendulums, where subjects are asked to avoid synchronization, yet cannot avoid coordinating. I would like to point out that this appears to be problematic in combination with the claim that the correlation should be over and above what is expected, rather than by accident. Research on emergent coordination which draws on dynamic system theory too (as discussed in section 1 of this chapter) shows that these processes are highly automatic and almost, if not completely, impossible for the agents to control. How can we distinguish what synchronizes "by accident" and what not? How can we guarantee or even understand the autonomy of the individuals that participate in the interaction? There are no such "driving factors" as they describe in their example. Emergent coordination is a mechanic description, not so much an agentic description which includes a purpose. What does it mean to say that the interaction should not arise by accident? It seems that they want this to be understood as "not by accident" on the level of the individuals participating in the interaction. This seems to imply that on two levels there is a push towards the maintenance of the precarious autonomy of the interaction-level: both on the individual level and on the interaction level this seems to be the aim.

A closer inspection of the examples provided might help us here. De Jaegher and Di Paolo argue for the distinction between couplings that are and those that are not *social* interactions. They start with the example of people who are waiting next to each other and that transfer body heat. This is not to be understood as a social interaction, because there is no active relation by the agents that are involved. Their next example is two people bumping into each other. At first, they argue, this is not a social interaction, but it can become a social interaction once one or both agents start to *regulate* the ensuing coupling. This example probably serves two functions. Firstly, it shows that a social situation can become an interaction. Secondly, the need for regulation seems an important factor for the coupling. They end with an example that should be integrally understood as a social interaction:

> . . . A conversation about a sponge is a social interaction, because the participants decide upon the topic together, regulate beginning, course and ending of the dialogue, and their autonomy (neither as living beings, nor as conversation partners) is not destroyed in the process. (De Jaegher & Di Paolo, 2007, p. 493)

De Jaegher and Di Paolo argue that the coordination of coupled individuals allows us to understand their claim that "social interaction constitutes a proper level of analysis in itself" (2007. p. 491). A distinctive difference between purely physical coupling and coupling in the social domain is the direction of the influence of the coupling. De Jaegher and Di Paolo argue that:

> patterns of coordination can directly influence the continuing disposition of the individuals involved to sustain or modify their encounter. In this way, what arises in the process of coordination (e.g. gestures, utterances and changes in intonation that are sometimes labelled as back-channeling or turn-repair, etc.) can have the consequence of steering the encounter or facilitating (or not) its continuation. (De Jaegher & Di Paolo, 2007, p. 492)

They continue by noticing that:

> The interaction process emerges as an entity when social encounters acquire this operationally closed organization. It constitutes a level of analysis not reducible, in general, to individual behaviours. This perspective bypasses the circularity that arises from preconceiving individuals as ready-made interactors. Individuals co-emerge as interactors with the interaction. This brings us to the further requirement for calling an interaction properly social. Not only must the process itself enjoy a temporary form of autonomy, but the autonomy of the individuals as interactors must also not be broken (even though the interaction may enhance or diminish the scope of individual autonomy). If this were not so, if the autonomy of one of the interactors were destroyed, the process would reduce to the cognitive engagement of the remaining agent with his non-social world. The 'other' would simply become a tool, an object, or a problem for his individual cognition.
> (De Jaegher & Di Paolo, 2007, p. 492)

A lot is going on in this quote, so let's unpack it. De Jaegher and Di Paolo write about both the structure of the interaction process that emerges as an entity, and about the individuals and their transformations due to the interaction.

Regarding the individuals they note that they emerge as interactors in, or through, the interaction. The autonomy of the individuals remains intact. This can probably be best understood as the fragile stability at the level of the individual to remain stable throughout interactions. They also claim that as soon as the autonomy of one individual is lost, it would be the end of the *social* interaction. About the level of the interaction they note the following two things. First of all, it is dependent on the autonomy of the individuals participating in the interaction. Secondly, it should be thought of as an autonomous level on its own. An autonomous system is defined as a system composed of several processes that actively generate and sustain an identity. This means that De Jaegher and Di Paolo take it that this level tries to stabilize itself. Stated differently, the interaction tries to keep itself going.

To recap, autonomy is found both on the level of the individuals and at the level of the interaction. (1) There is a coupling, which is regulated so as to generate and maintain an identity in the relational domain. The resulting relational dynamics are autonomous in the strict sense of precarious operational closure given in this paper. The dynamics allow us to define events and processes as either internal or external to the interaction. (2) The individuals involved are and remain autonomous as interactors (De Jaegher & Di Paolo, 2007).

Only the two layers, or levels, of autonomy together make it possible to talk about *social* interaction. The autonomy of the *agents* makes it *social* coupling in the interaction. If there were only autonomy on the interaction level it would not be a social engagement. They illustrate this with dancing together. Both agents of the dance couple move each other, making each other move, and are being moved by each other. This goes for both leader and follower. Following, De Jaegher and Di Paolo argue, is part of an agreement and does not equate with being shifted into position by the other. If the follower were to give up her autonomy, the couple dancing would end there, and it would look more like "a doll being carried around the dance floor" (De Jaegher & Di Paolo, 2007, p. 494). The same holds for conversations: each partner must engage from an autonomous standpoint. If conversational autonomy were given up, neither partner would be able to influence the other.

Why the autonomy of both agents is insufficient to explain this point remains unclear. To rephrase, these examples do not show the autonomy of the interaction, they only show that the interaction has an influence on the autonomy of the individuals, especially from a diachronic perspective. In socially interactive situations, coordination affects individual sense-making. It seems absurd, however, that the sense-making is *for* the interaction, it is maybe sense-making *through* the interaction. That such a coherence is only possibly when the significance of the physical manifestation is also takin into account by both interacting agents is not a radical claim. It tells us something about the directedness of agents (see also Martens & Schlicht, 2018). When the claim is truly that there is a new autonomous level, that of the interaction, more work needs to be done to spell out how the interaction, at the level of the interaction, is working to maintain its own boundaries. I.e., how it tries to remain a precarious autonomous system.

In the next section I will step away from the use of enactivism as a route to understanding social cognition and its implications for joint action. Instead I will focus on an enactive approach to skillful joint action, with a primary focus on dancing together.

6.3.3 An Enactive Approach to Dancing Together

A combination of joint action, skill and dancing is not often discussed, but Michael Kimmel (2013, 2016; Kimmel & Preuschl, 2016) forms an interesting exception, integrating these three. He targets joint embodied improvisation and suggests embodied (micro-)skills to play an important role in such joint improvisation. These embodied skills are understood using an enactivist framework. His main two issues are (1) how can two agents move as one, and (2) how is a *dynamic* structure brought about without a choreography (improvisation). Kimmel argues that there is no single capacity that allows a couple to dance together. Instead, their actions depend on well-integrated skills. In doing so he combines enactivism, including affordances, participatory sense-making and co-regulation, with a focus on skillful joint action. In line with the suggestions from enactivism Kimmel suggests that there is a super-individual, but also partial autonomy. His theoretical work builds on his empirical work where he uses different methodologies that tell us something about important elements in partner dancing and martial arts. I will portray his position below and respond to some of the suggestions in relation to the example from ballroom dancing that I provided earlier.

Compared to De Jaegher and Di Paolo, Kimmel has a more technical understanding of co-regulation, where different control laws guide the agent (and potentially guide the interaction/agents). The task and role we take on while dancing come with specific *control laws* that guide the agent. Co-regulation arises through interdependencies of different control laws. For example, a certain body-part will be moved in a certain way, but only because of (1) other related body parts and (2) the backdrop about bodily posture while dancing this particular type of dance (i.e., tango). Such interdependencies can go *beyond* phases and happen *between* agents.

Kimmel takes Argentinean tango to be an example of non-scripted interaction. This is motivated by the possibility in Argentinean tango to improvise step by step. It is important to make a distinction between the structure of a specific choreography, which is absent in the case of improvisation, and the structure that is present in the background, which will remain present when a couple is dancing completely based on improvisation. A non-scripted interaction such as dancing a tango is taking place within a scripted situation. Even when a couple is dancing together based on the smallest chunks to improvise, these chunks are made possible only because of a basic body tension, an orientation towards one another and certain rules on how to respond to the push and pull on specific muscle-groups.

Kimmel (2016, 2012) draws on findings from micro-generic interviews, think-alouds, his diary of participatory experience and motion capture studies. Based on these various research methods he lists seven skills that are involved in tango dancing (Kimmel 2016, pp. 61–66):

1. Body habits, such as the posture and the orientation of the body in relation to one's partner. These:
   a. Reduce the degrees of freedom, creating stability, and
   b. Informative the agent(s) about current possibilities.
2. Motor repertoire: dancers possess a motor repertoire of basic movements that they can combine.
3. Educated perception
   a. Dancers learn to respond to the partner's axis, partners can come to know more about one another through epistemic actions, for example dynamic touch.
   b. Dancers learn to attune to meaningful variables, perceiving do-ables (the bodily positions and history of the dance together provide "affordances").[70]
4. Communication, dancers acquire practical knowledge of how to issue signals and how to read the significance of such signals.
5. Using imagery, such as geometric and dynamic metaphors, to make or form certain shapes. This can help the dancers to focus on particular aspects around which the rest of the movement tends to organize itself.
6. Understanding solicitations that the music offers.
7. Improvisation, through combining basic movements, or clusters of movements that are adequate for the current position on the floor, the moment in the music, and so on.

---

[70] From the description it is unclear how this happens, or in which sense this is a skill.

Before turning to Kimmel's ideas on participatory sense-making, it seems worthwhile to focus on the diversity of the different skills that Kimmel lists here and their relation to skillful action as spelled out in section 4.2. First of all, Kimmel's approach to skillful joint action shares the importance of the non-scripted and not-fully-scripted situations skillful agents typically face that was also emphasized in the theories on skillful action in section 4.2. The way Kimmel spells out the different skills does also not allow for a binary approach. Secondly, it seems noteworthy to point out that Kimmel does *not* make the same appeal to a differentiation in levels of control when it comes to skillful performance (see section 4.2 on skillful action). We can understand this either as implicating that all, or at least most of, these skills involve control on the three levels that Christensen and colleagues and Fridland suggest. Or each skill that Kimmel puts forward should best be understood to play a role on (mainly) one level of the control hierarchy. Some of the specific skills that Kimmel discusses fit nicely into this idea that they play a role on one level of control. Take for example body habits, which – as their names suggest – would be rather automatized. Communication, improvisation and using imagery would more likely be better understood including also higher levels of control. Educated perception would fit well with Fridland's discussion of situational control, and Christensen and colleagues' description of situational awareness. So it might be most helpful to not try to map each skill on only one of the levels of control. Thirdly, Kimmel's list of skills is quite diverse and contains items that other authors would ordinarily not describe as skills. Take for example the understanding of the music, or the possession of a substantial motor repertoire. Kimmel does not only understand the combination of these skills to allow the agent to act skillfully, he also categorizes each sub-function or sub-characteristic as a skill in itself. With these preliminary remarks in place, I will turn to Kimmel's enactivist approach.

Dialogic Determination and Participatory Sense-Making
Dialogic determination is the idea that a couple together determines what will happen.[71] Kimmel argues that the

---

[71] Kimmel mainly focuses on a description of the leader. This might be due to his experience as a leader in dancing or it might point at a different understanding of the autonomy and decision-power that the leader and follower have. At several points he seems to suggest that the leader is determining the what, and the follower the how. At the same time, he is also committed to the idea that the couple is a super-agent. In how far this super-agent coincides with the leader-role remains unclear in his writing.

> . . . behavioral arc arises collaboratively from causal interdependencies between micro-actions of two partners. [. . .] Leaders and followers establish a resonance loop with each other through the embrace, a "mutual dynamical entanglement" of their bodies. These interdependencies are characterized as *coregulation*, a loop of constant reciprocal causation based, at each moment, on bidirectional information flow and on *participatory sense-making* of two a priori autonomous agents who, via structural coupling, produce an emergent coordination dynamic that is irreducible to the sum of its parts. (Kimmel, 2016, p. 13)

Now compare this to other parts of the same article, where Kimmel discusses the relation between the leader and follower. Based on the bodily posture of the follower, the music, and other situational constraints the leader signals invitations. The follower:

> . . . responds to "invitations" signaled by the leader with almost imperceptible delay. In between "invitations" followers remain neutrally poised in a good "axis" for immediate action readiness, stay well-grounded and calm [. . .]. Followers have some leeway for step timing or ornamentation, but without impairing the lead. In traditional tango, they shape the "how" by ensuring dynamic stability, relaxation, and precision, but not the "what", the improvised choices made. (Kimmel, 2016, p. 4)

This seems to suggest that the leader is in command of much of what is going on and the follower is "merely" offering sufficient structure to make this possible. This idea is further emphasized in the following sentence by Kimmel:

> Extensions establish a closed sensory control loop allowing the leader to "remote control" the follower's legs incrementally without ever touching or seeing them.
> (Kimmel, 2016, p. 4)

Body extensions are a way of understanding the organization of the follower which creates the opportunity for the leader to offer suggestions for moves. Kimmel refers to Clark's (2008) use of the notion. However, it is important to note that, although the follower plays an active role in offering such extensions, she is not (co-)determining what will happen next. That is, unless we accept that such offerings are sufficient to talk about co-determination. To return to the example by De Jaegher and Di Paolo (2007), the follower is not like a doll that is being carried around. But is the way Kimmel spells out the joint action interactive enough to talk about enactivist interaction? What remains of the role of the follower in dialogic determination? This question is not really answered by Kimmel. He mentions that the follower can determine the "how", but not the "what". Another possibility (although less constructive), that I can think of, is the followers' option to block a certain move by *not* providing the right extensions, co-determining through exclusion of options of sorts. Whether that is sufficient for dialogic determination and non-hierarchically structured joint action is unclear.

6.3.4 Conclusion

In this section I first discussed De Jaegher and Di Paolo's interactionist account of social cognition and then Kimmel's enactivist skillful joint action approach. I will briefly return to both topics in this conclusion.

Autopoietic Interaction
Understanding the organism as a center of activity in the world allows us to take a different perspective on interactions and joint actions that includes some form of autonomy on the level of the interaction. Through the coupling between the (autonomous) agents, another (autonomous) level is instantiated: the level of the interaction. This level is regulated so as to generate and maintain an identity in the relational domain while the individuals involved are and remain autonomous as interactors.

Only these two layers of autonomy together make it a *social* interaction. The autonomy of the *agents* makes it *social* coupling in the interaction. Each partner must engage from an autonomous standpoint. If there were only autonomy on the interaction level it would not be a social engagement. Why the autonomy of both agents is insufficient to explain this point remains unclear. De Jaegher and Di Paolo only shows that the interaction has an influence on the autonomy of the individuals, especially from a diachronic perspective, but not that we need to accept another autonomous layer. As long as the importance of the autonomy of the interaction-level remains unclear, what remains of this radical proposal is a relatively moderate idea about the importance of diachronicity in our understanding of interactions and joint actions.

Enactivist Skillful Joint Action
Kimmel takes Argentinean tango to be an example of non-scripted interaction, which can be best explained by an enactivist skillful account of joint action. This is motivated by the possibility in Argentinean tango to improvise step by step. Based on these various research methods he lists seven skills that are involved in tango dancing.

The different skills that Kimmel proposes do not nicely map onto the proposals for skillful action (e.g., Fridland, 2014; and Christensen, Sutton, & McIlwain, 2016; Christensen, Sutton, & Bicknell, 2019). Neither are they contradictory. If anything, Kimmel's analysis shows that the involved (sub-)skills or the extent to which they are needed might change depending on what it is that the agent is skillfully doing. His studies reveal that many different levels of control have to function in cohesion to allow for tango Argentina and that the proposal does not fit into a binary approach. The enactivist part of Kimmel's proposal lies in the co-determination of what is danced. As with autopoietic enactivism, also in Kimmel's proposal it remains unclear what the autonomy of the couple amounts to. Problematic for Kimmel's account is the apparent semi-autonomousness of the follower (especially when compared to the leader). In chapter seven I will give reasons to conceptualize skillful joint action differently from Kimmel. This will fit better with the active role of the follower, as I described in chapter one. Before I turn to this proposal, I will use the final section of this chapter on lower-level cognitive functions that allow agents to act jointly, to delve deeper into the sense of agency, the sense of us, and diachronicity.

6.4 A Sense of Control and a Sense of Agency in Joint Action

In this last section the focus will be on the sense of us and sense of agency that agents get from different ways of cooperating and interacting.[72] In that sense it is different from the three previous subsections which focused on coordination. The path to a sense of us will partially be explained through the phenomenology that follows from motor mechanisms involved in control, allowing us to nicely tie together some of the main lines of this book. The feeling of togetherness, and the primacy of it, has also a rich history in phenomenology (Carr, 1986; Husserl, 1989; Schutz, 1967). Recently, Schmid (2014) and Zahavi (2015) have published on the matter, relating to Searle's notion of the sense of us. In Searle's seminal 1990 article "Collective Intentions and Actions", Searle argued for the possibility of individuals having we-intentions. He introduces the sense of the other and the sense of us as conditions for we-intentions. The sense of the other and the sense of us are part of what he calls the *Background*, a set of capacities that make collective intentions possible. Although both concepts play an important role in his theoretical framework, Searle has never provided a clear account of them and they remain notoriously vague (Martens & Schlicht, 2018; Schmid, 2014; Tollefsen & Dale, 2012; Zahavi, 2015). Meanwhile, several authors have written about Searle's ideas on the background capacities that are presupposed for collective intentions, trying to clarify and work out parts of his background assumptions (Bacharach, 2006; Schmid, 2014; Tollefsen & Dale, 2012; Zahavi, 2015).[73] Not all of them come from a phenomenological background.

---

[72] This section contains parts from published work (Martens, 2018).
[73] These authors discuss either the sense of the other or the sense of us, and relate one of them to we-intentions, ignoring or neglecting the other sense of (x). As of yet, scholars have not focused on the relation between these two "senses" of our relatedness to one another.

In this section I will argue that the sense of the other is different from, and a necessary condition for, a sense of us. The other step that I want to emphasize is the role a sense of we-agency can play in the intentions that we form. My aim in this section is to introduce a picture of how the notion of a sense of *us* can (1) contribute to our understanding of the perception of possibilities for joint action, (2) how individuals can come to experience them as shared, even if they lack common knowledge, and (3) how this relates to control through a sense of we-agency. I will start with an analysis of Searle's account of these notions. This will be followed by some attempts to their phenomenological description and an exploration of theories in psychology that might be of help to understand the sense of us. I take the sense of us to provide us with further means to understand why and when agents are willing to engage with one another and are willing to invest energy and time in the interaction.

The Sense of Us
Searle's theory of collective intentionality proposes a version of the mode-account of collective intentionality. A mode-account is one in which the individual subject has a we-attitude (is in a we-mode) towards the object: "I *we-intend* to X".[74] There are several Background capacities that have to be in place in order to form such we-intentions. The Background is a set of nonrepresentational capacities that enable representing to take place. It includes biological and cultural capacities, such as skills, stances, assumptions, and presuppositions (Searle, 1983, pp. 143–144). One of these Background capacities is the sense of us. Collective intention implies seeing the other as someone to cooperate with. Searle argues that Background skills are necessary for "[t]he manifestation of any particular form of collective intentionality" (Searle, 1990, p. 41). The Background is a set of nonrepresentational capacities that enable representing to take place. It includes biological and cultural capacities, such as skills, stances, assumptions, and presuppositions. The Background is divided into the Deep Background and Local Background (Searle, 1983, pp. 143–144). The Deep Background is composed of biological skills and universal human capacities, such as eating, walking, and seeing given patterns as discrete objects. The Local Background is not universal, but culturally bound, and includes knowing what culturally-specific objects are for, recognizing culture-specific

---

74 See section 1.2 for an overview of the different accounts of collective intentionality.

situations, and the types of behavior that are appropriate in these situations (Searle, 1983).[75]

Searle thinks there are "general or pervasive" – deep – Background features for collective behavior, which he characterizes in the following two passages:

> In addition to the biological capacity to recognize other people as importantly like us, in a way that waterfalls, trees, and stones, are not like us, it seems to me that the capacity to engage in collective behavior requires something like a pre-intentional sense of "the other" as an actual or potential agent like oneself in cooperative activities.
>
> (Searle, 1990, p. 413)

And:

> that they have a similar awarencess [sic] of you as an agent like themselves, and that these awarenesses coalesce into a sense of *us* as possible or actual collective agents.
>
> (Searle, 1990, p. 414)

Upon closer analysis, Searle's indications of the "sense of the other" and the "sense of us" entail the following seven aspects:

A. Regarding the sense of the other:
 1. The sense of the other is a pre-intentional awareness.
 2. One component is biological: recognize "it" as an intentional agent, an entity capable of action.
 3. A second component is an awareness of the agent's capacity to engage in cooperative activity.
 4. The awareness of this capacity involves the supposition that the other can have a similar awareness of me as a potential cooperative agent.

B. Regarding the sense of us:
 5. The sense of us is a pre-intentional awareness.
 6. That in each of "us" (me and the other) the awarenesses of "me" and "the other" coalesce in a sense of us as a possible community of agents. We now have a similar awareness.

---

[75] The sheer heterogeneity of the Background has been criticized by many (e.g., Zahavi (2015, pp. 84–101); Schmid (2014); Tollefsen and Dale (2012) within the collective intentionality debate). Some capacities would be best described as habits, others seem to be entirely motoric and automatic, and a third category of capacities consists of presuppositions and (pretheoretical) commitments or stances.

C. Regarding both senses:
   7. The sense of the other and the sense of us are presupposed constitutive elements of collective activity.[76]

If this interpretation of Searle's remarks on the sense of the other and the sense of us as pre-suppositions for collective activity is accurate, we are left with the question whether there is any evidence for this set of theses. Searle admits that he has no argument in favor of this, except the consideration that this sense of the other must somehow be presupposed for collective intentionality to occur. Data from cognitive and social psychology can support the distinction between the sense of the other and the sense of us (Martens, 2018). But what kind of phenomenology goes with the sense of us? I will summarily point to discussions of Searle's intuitions about the sense of the other and the sense of us in relation to collective action. I will do so using recent papers of Zahavi and Schmid.[77]

6.4.1 Phenomenological Exploration of the Sense of Us

Zahavi and Schmid both point out that Searle's so-called Background assumptions have not been worked out in sufficient detail, neither by Searle nor by others. Schmid and Zahavi therefore try to fill this gap in the literature by elaborating on them. Their phenomenologically inspired elaborations go partly in the same direction. On crucial points, however, Schmid and Zahavi contradict each other. They agree that Searle's notions of "sense of the other" and "sense of us" should be understood as pre-reflective phenomena and that they should be taken seriously as constitutive for collective intentionality. But they have different opinions about the nature of the sense of us and the way this sense is related to awareness of oneself and others (you). A look at these differences

---

[76] "Not all social groups are engaged in goal-directed behavior all the time. Some of the time they are just, e.g., sitting around in living rooms, hanging out in bars, or riding on the train. Now the form of collectivity that exists in such cases isn't constituted by goal-directed intentionality because there isn't any. Such groups are, so to speak, ready for action but they are not yet engaged in any actions (i.e. they have no collective intentions-in-action) nor are they planning any (i.e. they have no collective prior intentions). Nonetheless they have the type of communal awareness which is the general precondition of collective intentionality" (Searle, 1990, p. 414).

[77] Both Schmid and Zahavi take issue with Searle's account, partially because of his radical internalism and the possibility of we-intentionality in a brain in a vat. But after pointing out these issues they both show sympathy for Searle's ideas on the general background capacities and phenomena that are presupposed by collective intentionality.

helps to sharpen the questions regarding the relation between a sense of us and togetherness. I start with a short exposé of Schmid's position. His proposal is a starting point for Zahavi's argumentation.

Schmid argues that the concept of plural pre-reflective self-awareness could be a way to understand Searle's Background notion of a sense of us (Schmid, 2014).[78] Schmid's central claim is that we should acknowledge a basic form of "plural pre-reflective self-awareness", analogous to individual self-awareness. In the individual case, pre-reflective self-awareness is understood as an awareness of a subject *as* subject that grounds any sense in which a subject can think about itself reflectively. Wittgenstein (1958), Shoemaker (1968), and others have provided analyses of this basic and immediate self-awareness that precedes any act of identification. Schmid argues that "selfhood does not only come in the singular, but also in the plural" (Schmid, 2014, p. 15). Just as we consider pre-reflective self-awareness as *constitutive* of being an individual self and having a first-person perspective, Schmid argues that we should consider the possibility that such a pre-reflective self-awareness can constitute a collective self and a we-perspective:

> ... plural self-awareness plays the same role *between* minds as singular self-awareness plays within individual minds.[79] (Schmid, 2014, p. 15)

A major problem with Schmid's suggestion is that it does not explain how individuals stand in relation to this plural pre-reflective self-awareness, which exists *between* the individuals. For an understanding of the sense of us as biologically primitive to the individual, the interpretation of the sense of us *between* the group members might not be the best starting point. A minimal condition for the plausibility of Schmid's interpretation is an explanation of the way individuals can relate to the sense of us that exists between minds. Only then can we understand what it is (for an individual) to have a shared we-perspective. This in turn requires the sense of us to be conceptualized in a way that allows shared experiences of it (Brinck, Reddy, & Zahavi, 2017; Schmid, 2014).

---

78 My interpretation of the sense of the other and the sense of us can still be conceptualized as pre-reflective (as Schmid does), however, arguing this is not the aim of this paper.

79 Schmid's attempt to demystify the sense of us raises several questions. As Schmid says the collective intention is between minds, and he has also talked about group minds we should understand Schmid's proposal as "we we-intend X". In an unpublished manuscript called *The subject of "we intend"* Schmid defends a subject account of collective intentionality, still coupled to the concept of plural pre-reflective self-awareness, suggesting we should read this mode as "we we-intend X" (or, as Katja Crone brought to my attention, we could see his account as a mix of a subject and mode account).

The solution to this problem is blocked by Schmid's claim that any communication between human beings presupposes the existence of a sense of us, and that looking for cognitive and affective preconditions for the sense of us is already a way of entering a kind of reductive reasoning (Schmid, 2014, pp. 10–11; Brinck, Reddy, & Zahavi, 2017, p. 4).

Zahavi, in contrast to Schmid, is oriented towards the phenomenology of us as had by the individuals. He argues that there cannot be a sense of us without a sense of me and a sense of the other already in place (Zahavi, 2015). The experience of us, in his opinion, always involves a plurality of subjects. Sharing emotions and intentions has nothing to do with a fusion, nor with a merged unity. Rather, sharing involves a plurality of subjects. What the individual feels when she acts with another depends on their relation to each other; there is co-regulation and constitutive interdependence. In Searle's terminology, Zahavi especially tries to describe how the awarenesses of me and the other coalesce into a sense of us as a potential collective agent who has we-experiences. His endeavors aim at an understanding of the sense of us as constituted by the reciprocal interrelation and co-regulation of the experiences and bodily motions of two subjects who are aware of each other. In other words, he tries to give an account of one of the crucial, yet barely elaborated, elements of Searle's intuition.

In an important matter, however, Zahavi modifies Searle. He emphasizes that the subjects whose awarenesses coalesce are not just experiencing each other as potential co-agents, but as a *you* (or as some put it, from a second-person perspective, i.e., Schilbach et al., 2013). A you is another agent with whom I am emotionally engaging and reciprocally interacting. For Zahavi, constituting a sense of us and having we-experiences is not simply a matter of there being any kind of relation between two (or more) agents, but rather of there being an I-Thou relation between me and another (or other) agent(s).

The basic and developmentally prior case of such we-awareness is an emotional awareness of the other. Using evidence from developmental psychology, Zahavi suggests that there are three ways of relating to the emotions of another person: empathy (knowing how the other feels), contagion (copying the emotion without necessarily making a connection to the other person) and shared emotions (where two agents co-constitute each other's experiences). Shared emotions are only possible through the second-person perspective, which allows two agents to co-constitute one-another's we-experience, Zahavi argues. These are important improvements on Searle's indications.[80]

---

80 We should make a distinction between I-Thou relations and relations in larger groups. In a collective of more people there are also third parties, additional players, witnesses. It might indeed be

Zahavi stresses that sharing in the case of we is not only awareness of the other agent as a "you" (rather than he or she), but also awareness of the perception of oneself by the other agent as a "you". The other is experienced as "*my you*" and – importantly – *I* experience myself as "*her* you" (Brinck, Reddy, & Zahavi, 2017). From this description of reciprocal emotional engagement and dependence Zahavi concludes (with Husserl) that under this reciprocal condition we live the social relationship itself, i.e. we have a sense of us. Zahavi argues that seeing oneself as a you involves a certain detachment of oneself (self-alienation) (Zahavi, 2015, p. 95). This self-alienation involves stepping away from all the details of being different from the other and towards the similarity between myself and the person I am interacting with.[81]

Zahavi remains unclear about whether the primitiveness of shared emotions (compared to shared intentions) also implies that shared emotions are always present when interacting with others, or whether they are only developmentally prior and can later be exchanged by other forms of sharedness, such as shared intentions. Regardless of Zahavi's thoughts on this matter, the I-Thou relation would remain important in both cases.

I will argue, based on evidence from cognitive science, that the affective relation need not be present in order for a we-experience to arise. I will also distance myself from Zahavi's claim that we need self-alienation in order to reach a we-perspective. I take this stance because I argue, with Pacherie, that we-agency and I-agency can, at least in principle, be both present at the same time, so there need not be any self-alienation in order to be able to shift to a we-perspective (this will be discussed in section 6.4.2).[82]

In sum, Zahavi's analyses suggest that, first, for a we-experience to be possible the awareness of other humans involves a second-person perspective to

---

questionable to what extent we perceive all other agents, even those that are involved in the joint action, as "*my* you". I argue that results in cognitive science point several ways in which a sense of us can evolve. This most likely has implications for larger groups, where we stand in varying relations to one another. I cannot elaborate all such possible relations in the context of this paper.

81 In a later paper, Brinck, Reddy and Zahavi (2017) point to developmental precursors of second-person perspective taking and the constitution of we-experiences. They argue that early relationships between caretakers and child develop further into a we. This suggests that the existence of a we and a sense of us could be the result of a developmental process. This raises the questions under which conditions and through which processes we are able to make an emotional difference between an agent and a you, and under which other conditions and through which processes this capacity develops into the emotional interconnectedness that is typical for a we-experience.

82 There is a further reason why I do not deem such self-alienation necessary, which has to do with a point made by Williamson and Sutton (2014) regarding the complementarity of the individuals – including their capacities, skills, and actions – during many joint actions.

be taken by both agents. In the developmentally prior case, another appears as a you, enabling emotional engagement and interaction. Secondly, the consequence of this I-Thou relationship is reciprocal interconnectedness of you and me – which could be qualified as a we – and leads to awarenesses and actions that fit together and are co-constitutive of the experiences of each agent's sense of us. These points can be seen as elaborations of Searle's account. Third, it remains unclear, however, how this could lead to a unified sense of us. Fourth, Zahavi suggests a developmental process that starts with making a difference between you and me from an affective perspective and which develops towards a sense of us and the possibility to share intentions. Fifth, the conditions under which the difference between you and me can be made and how this difference develops, via a sense of us, to a fully developed we in case of collective action (a sense of we-agency) is not yet clarified.

6.4.2 The Psychology of the Sense of Agency and the Sense of Us

In this section I discuss psychological research that supports the idea that certain processes can be helpful to build and develop a sense of us. I will look at conditions and processes that play a role in the space between recognizing another human as a potential partner for joint action and the existence of a fully developed sense of us that is involved in collective agency. I will focus on emergent coordination that is helpful for the development of a sense of us (6.4.1) and on control and prediction processes that lead to a sense of we-agency (6.4.2).[83] My suggestion is not that there is *one* missing element (such as Zahavi's emotional engagement or Schmid's direct access to plural self-awareness), but rather that there can be several different elements that help to give rise to a sense of us.

Pacherie (2014) offers a starting point for understanding the sense of us and control of joint action through her notion of a sense of we-agency.[84] She

---

83 We-agency in the sense of doing something together.
84 In earlier work, Pacherie argued it is unnecessary to refer to any Background capacities specifically designed for collective intentions and joint agency (Pacherie, 2007). Pacherie uses mutual presumption (a less demanding variation of Bratman's mutual knowledge condition) to explain the interlocking of one's intentions with the intentions of other agents. This interlocking is based on the idea that co-agents are sufficiently cognitively similar to us that their attitudes and intentions can be successfully simulated or inferred. This comes very close to Searle's idea that the sense of us coalesces out of the mutual awareness of two (or more) agents that the other is like oneself; a conscious agent with a sense of agency. Yet, I think that the sense of us could also be understood as arising from psychological attitudes that are not posited as a *sui generis* kind of psychological attitude, a we-intention. And when considering

starts from research in cognitive psychology on the sense of agency (Pacherie, 2014). Research on the sense of agency considers under which circumstances an agent feels like she "did this". The main explanatory concepts are prediction and control. She argues in favor of a sense of we-agency on the side of individuals. Her investigation starts with the difference between the questions "did I do it?" and "did we do it?" and the conditions that need to be in place in order to answer "yes" to the last question. In this way, she actually gives an answer to a specific case of the general question "what are the conditions for a sense of us?" She looks for the conditions under which the sense of us that is typical for cases of joint action develops. The sense of we-agency – as defined by Pacherie – is not equivalent with the general sense of us, insofar as the latter can also be about the general feeling that we "have *something* together", where this something can be an unspecific being together, a shared emotion, or a still to be specified activity (for example a group of friends who is going to decide what they will do this evening). The sense of we-agency, as spelled out by Pacherie, only deals with mental states that involve the feeling "we *did* it". It is more closely related to action. The sense of us is more general.

Pacherie bases her argument on recent psychological research on prediction, control, and their connection to the (individual) sense of agency. This research suggests that the strength of the sense of agency relates to, or is mirrored in, the feeling of control an agent has regarding her actions and the predictability of their outcomes. An agent can experience control through pre-reflective sensori-motor processes (which depend on the overlap of the prediction and feedback), or through reflective judgments that ascribe an action as performed by the agent (Bayne & Pacherie, 2007; Gallagher, 2007; Haggard & Tsakiris, 2009). Situational factors weight in on the development of a sense of agency, both in the individual and in the joint case. Uncertainty and/or a lack of knowledge can, especially in advance but potentially also retrospectively, obstruct a sense of agency.

Another interesting finding, in the light of this book, is the difference between the implicit and explicit sense of agency, or the pre-reflective and reflective sense of agency. The cognitive research done in this field will often use both implicit and explicit measures to investigate the sense of agency. The explicit measurements are often most straightforward, inquiring whether participants felt they were in control, or whether they thought they had produced a certain effect. A good example of the implicit measures comes from the (Joint)

---

that the sense of the other and the sense of us can be used for several purposes and not uniquely for collective intentionality.

Simon Task (discussed below). Implicit measurements look at behaviors or experiences that indicate the presence or absence of a sense of agency without explicit or direct inquiring of the studied phenomenon. The implicit and explicit measurements sometimes show diverting results, which can be understood as a difference between a pre-reflective and a reflective sense of agency.

Pacherie's thesis is that, like in the case of individual actions, the sense of agency the agent experiences in joint action, depends on prediction and control.[85] Studies of individual agency have shown that the strength of the sense of agency depends on how good the match (congruency) is between the prediction and the actual consequences at the cognitive, perceptual, and sensorimotor levels.

What happens to the sense of agency when two or more agents act together? This sense of agency emerges from a match between the predicted and the actual effects of combined individual actions, which together build the joint action. Like in the case of individual agency this concerns cognitive, perceptual, and sensorimotor levels. The same principles of congruency applied to joint actions, however, show more complex patterns, as agents must predict the consequences of their actions in three respects. Besides self-predictions, they must produce predictions for the actions of the others (other-prediction) and integrate both self- and other-predictions in predictions of joint consequences (joint prediction) (Pacherie, 2014, p. 26).

In a complex description, which I do not claim to fully represent here, Pacherie makes clear that, when it comes to joint action, (1) other-predictions and joint predictions are complicated and sensori-motor predictions impossible; (2) that the relation between prediction and control is difficult because, usually, the predicting agent cannot (fully) control the (consequences of others') actions that would be eligible for prediction. These difficulties point in the direction of a weaker potential sense of we-agency compared to the sense of I-agency. This weakened sense of agency can be boosted, however, by at least two factors: (1) situational factors and (2) emergent coordination, as discussed in section 6.2.[86]

---

85 In a second part of her analysis Pacherie discusses the differentiation between the sense of self-agency and sense of we-agency (37ff.) as a matter of merging one's agency in the agency of the group. I will not deal with this aspect of Pacherie's paper as this only deals with the amount of attribution of outcomes to a collective agent. I am interested here in the sense of we-agency as such. See Salmela & Nagatsu (2017) for a discussion of self-agency vs. we-agency.
86 The mechanisms of emergent coordination, discussed in section 6.2 could help the processes of prediction (both of the other agent's actions and the joint actions) because (1) the mechanisms of the two coordinating agents make the actions of the other better predictable and (2) the automatic alignment on our own side will also make our own actions better predictable. Following the hypothesis that better prediction leads to stronger feelings of control, this

Pacherie distinguishes four situational factors that affect the accessibility of relevant information and therefore the possibility of other- and joint-prediction. They are basic for an understanding of situations that enable or disable a sense of we-agency to arise. The four factors are: (1) the structure of the joint action, on a scale between egalitarian and highly hierarchical; (2) the scale of the action and group, from a small scale (one location) to a large scale where monitoring becomes impossible; (3) the degree of specialization of agents' roles, specified on a scale from near identical and interchangeable to specialized and highly differentiated roles; and (4) the longevity or transience of the collective, i.e. the strength and lastingness of the association among co-agents.

The sense of agency will more likely involve a sense of we-agency the more commensurate the contributions of the co-agents are and the more symmetrical the coordination relations among them are (or are perceived to be). Based on these factors, Pacherie concludes that one's experienced sense of agency can be a mix of self-agency and we-agency. It is possible that someone has a strong sense of self-agency while simultaneously experiencing a sense of we-agency. This means that in different contexts the same bodily movements can be perceived as part of something I did or as something we did. This possibility is deduced from the fact that the implicit and explicit measures of we-agency and I-agency can come apart, as illustrated by intentional binding. Intentional binding is argued to be a proxy of the pre-reflective experience of the sense of agency. It is an interesting phenomenon for two reasons. Firstly, it can show us that the pre-reflective and reflective sense of agency can come apart.[87] Secondly, this points at the possibility to experience both a sense of we-agency and I-agency simultaneously. This can be helpful in many cases, amongst which those where there is both a sense of doing something together and being in competition. For example, a boxing match or dancing competition where there is a sense of us between the competitors.

The Simon Task allows researchers to investigate the sense of (we-)agency implicitly and explicitly. It requires people to press a button and then report the location of the pointer on a clock at the moment they hear a beep that follows the button-press (Simon, 1969; Simon & Rudell, 1967). When people ascribe the

---

can explain why emergent coordination that happens between the agents can help in the development of a sense of we-agency and a sense of us.

87 Measured through implicit and explicit operationalizations of the sense of (we-)agency. The implicit operationalization works with a clock. Participants have to indicate where the pointer stood at the moment they heard the tone. The explicit operationalization requires them to answer the question whether they performed an action.

action to themselves they report the beep to be closer in time to the moment they pressed the button (intentional binding). The paradigm is also used in joint action tasks (the Joint Simon Task), where it is investigated whether two agents experience agency when they are both in charge, when the other agent is leading the actions (Engbert, Wohlschlager, & Haggard, 2008), or when under coercion (Caspar, Christensen, Cleeremans, & Haggard, 2016).[88] Sometimes people (verbally) report they did not control the act (that they did not do it), even though the implicit measurements show that they did compress the time between the action and the external sensory consequence, suggesting that pre-reflectively the agent is having a sense of agency over the action. Interestingly, intentional binding is also found in the follower, but this mainly occurs in more equal settings.

Depending on the situation in which the subject is pressing the same button as the co-agent we find intentional binding between the action and the sound that follows. The situation has an impact on the Joint Simon Effect (Caspar, Christensen, Cleeremans, & Haggard, 2016). These findings suggest that the situation can factor in on our perception of a *sense of us doing something*, versus the *sense of the other agent acting*. In both cases the two agents are engaged in the same bodily movements, and are aware of the presence of the other agent, suggesting that the activities themselves are not sufficient conditions to experience a sense of we-agency.

The Joint Simon Effect shows that an agent can be "ambivalent" about the sense of I-agency and we-agency. One can have a feeling of control, or lack thereof, which is not grounded, or justified, in the actions performed. The sense of we-agency has an impact on the way the agent acts, independent of its correctness or incorrectness. It feeds back into the loop of prediction and control and the formation of intentions and we-intentions. As long as such feedback loops do not break down and emergent coordination can play an important part in repairing failed prediction-control loops, even mistaken impressions of control could contribute to a strong sense of we-agency.

6.4.3 Conclusion

Let me start by briefly summarizing this section on the sense of agency. (1) A sense of we-agency tells us something about the experience of agency of an act.

---

[88] The first paradigm might need some further explication. In the "both are equal" case each participant can choose to initiate the joint action within a certain timeframe. Once one of the two initiates the action the other follows as quickly as possible.

(2) It is possible to specify the favorable structural conditions for a development of a sense of we-agency, these are related to the notions of control and predictability. (3) Emergent coordination and situational factors influence the experience of control and predictability and play a role in development of a sense of we-agency. (4) A sense of I-agency and a sense of we-agency are not mutually exclusive. Under certain conditions, like strong hierarchy or consensus, they can both be strong; and (5) A sense of we-agency can develop in the course of time. (6) A sense of we-agency differs from a sense of us. A sense of we-agency is more closely linked to bodily movements. A sense of us is more general and can arise without these prediction and control processes involved. Take for example the emergent coordination processes that I discussed in section 6.1.

Although this is not specified as such by Pacherie, we can surmise that the sense of we-agency can influence the behavior of the individual in a social context. Through several "rounds" of acting together, the sense of we-agency, of being in control together, can become stronger, especially as one becomes better at predicting what will happen. Through multiple loops of interactions between the agents an agent can become more certain over time that she is not mistaken, that they are sincerely acting *together*. This will also allow the agent to feel in control about future joint actions and feel more willing in general to engage with the world as a group. Such a sense of us might take a while to develop, but depending on the situation (including the situational factors mentioned above) it might also happen really quickly and gives us a good grip on how togetherness can be depending on multiple factors that each need not be necessarily present to give rise to the feeling.

The development of a sense of we-agency can have a retroactive effect on the sense of us. Remember that the sense of we-agency as defined by Pacherie is about confirmation of motor predictions, while the sense of us can also be about the general feeling that we are doing *something* together, where this something can be unspecific or still to be specified (for example a group of friends being together this evening). The sense of us can be present while *not acting together yet*. It can be described as a pre-intentional frame through which the agent perceives action possibilities as well as what has just happened. Having acted together and experiencing that others are not just possible partners, but actual partners in interconnected actions, affirms the sense of us in a pointed way. It also produces a differentiation of this general category: some others are experienced as (being able) to build, together with me, a specific us, a group agent.

On an average day, we encounter many potential partners for cooperation, that is, we could say, we experience many "others". A sense of the other is not, however, sufficient to be willing to engage with that other. For this we need a sense of us, which gives us an understanding of the willingness and likeliness of mutual engagement. Doing things together comes in many degrees. Sometimes it can be as small as walking through a door together and coordinating this, at other occasions we are much more dependent on one another, for example when we are colleagues working on a joint project. In the first case it might be sufficient to have a sense of us merely based on a short moment of eye contact. In the latter case such eye contact will be insufficient. I argue that the sense of us can arise through several routes. These routes become available only because we have an initial sense of the other. The primordiality of this self-other distinction is in line with Zahavi's phenomenological argument that the distinction between "you" and "I" remains intact while agents have we-experiences. The sense of the other that I have developed in this section, understood as a matter of core agency cognition, is, however, less rich than any of Zahavi's notions of sharing. It rather seems to be a necessary presupposition for Zahavi's descriptions of sharing and joint attention in we-experiences.

Regarding *the sense of us* I pointed at Searle's description that (5) the sense of us is a matter of pre-reflective awareness, and (6) in each of "us" the awarenesses of "me" and "the other" coalesce in a sense of us as a possible community of actors. I argued that this was not sufficient and pointed at several other cognitive functions that, together with mutual awareness, can give rise to a sense of us. The constitutive interdependence between several agents can be based on several processes. I pointed at motor prediction processes as potential processes that give rise to, respectively specify, the sense of us. The earlier discussed mechanisms underlying emergent coordination would be other potential processes. Studies on allocentric perspective and the impossibility to ignore others (even if the task one is doing is independent from the other agent) show that the presence of another agent has an impact on one's own behavior (Caspar, Christensen, Cleeremans, & Haggard, 2016). This impact can be larger or smaller depending on several contingent factors while interacting. The sense of us could also be influenced by plans and goals that we share, and the experience of we-agency, creating room for further shared agency. We could think of examples where the sense of us is not yet there, or very minimal although there is a certain plan or commitment, for example in a brand-new work force.

Regarding *both senses* I argued that (7) they are presupposed constitutive elements of collective activity. I approached the sense of us as something that arises over time, rather than something that is either present or absent. A positive aspect of approaching the sense of us as a feeling that can develop over time and through several underlying mechanisms is that on many levels – from emergent coordination to planning – interaction and reactions to one another can give us a clue whether we are acting together or might be mistaken. It is only in the interaction, and over time, that a robust sense of us will be formed and the agent can be sure that there is mutual awareness of each other's goals and possibly also mutual intentions and plans. This, then, can lead an agent to form shared intentions.[89]

---

[89] This fits with Searle's (1990) suggestion that we *could* be radically mistaken about the sharedness of our actions and intentions (although we usually are not).

7 Skillful Joint Action

7.1 Introduction

This book aims to propose a theory of skillful joint action that steps beyond a dichotomous view of acting together. I have defined skillful joint action as joint action that is dependent on multiple – interrelated – forms of coordination. I take it that most joint actions that human agents perform are cases of skillful joint action. Throughout this book I have relied on dancing together as an exemplary case that shows that emergent and planned coordination are insufficient (both independently and in combination) for an understanding of the phenomena in such cases of joint action. Something like a theory of skillful joint action is conspicuously absent in the existing literature on shared intentionality and joint action. This literature is inclined to categorize different forms of acting together either as a matter of emergent coordination or as a case of planned collective agency. I believe this is untenable in the face of the diverse phenomena that are described in accounts of acting together. I want to emphasize that we need a more complex conceptual framework. I therefore introduce a new category: besides *emergent* and *planned* coordination I introduce a broad middle category, which I call *situational* coordination. Some of the functions that traditionally fall into the category of emergent coordination will fall into the category of situational coordination. I further emphasize that these three categories are very often related and building upon each other. Such a tripartite theory is necessary to account for many of the phenomena that we consider as joint actions, including the popular example of "dancing together".

In the first part of this book I uncovered and criticized problematic assumptions in most current theories of joint action and their underlying theory of action. My focus in doing so was on several binary distinctions which prove to be problematic foundations for developing conceptual frameworks for collective intentionality and joint action. I discussed the binary distinctions of coordination and no coordination, control and no control and of jointness and no jointness. To properly do this I also discussed the dichotomy between automatic and non-automatic processes. One of the attractive results of a binary way of formulating these distinctions is the possibility to make a strict distinction between "joint action proper" and "parallel action". The problem is that although this distinction provides a good rule of thumb, it creates cases that cannot be captured by the existing conceptual framework. The result of the critiques formulated in this first part of my research is (1) a clear picture of shortcomings in the existing literature and (2) an indication of how, where, and why an alternative proposal should divert from the standard approaches.

In this chapter I present my proposal for a more complex theory of joint action. In the course of this attempt I will touch upon the most important critiques I expressed throughout the previous chapters. The set-up of the chapter is as follows. I will first deal with the dichotomy of planned coordination and emergent coordination. I will recapitulate these concepts and raise my objections to them. Then I will present a more nuanced picture of coordination, by giving attention to the different processes that are described in the literature. This involves a proposal to distinguish three kinds of coordination (section 7.2). In section 7.3, I recapitulate the conceptualization of the three levels of control as discussed in the literature on skillful action and apply this threefold distinction to three levels of coordination. In doing so I combine the discussion of the first two aspects that are central in this book: control and coordination. This section contains (a) the main lines of the proposed conceptual framework, (b) a discussion of its relation to the orthodox distinction between emergent coordination and planned coordination, and (c) an exploration of the framework in cases that go beyond fast-paced skillful joint action using literature on Naturalistic Decision Making and heuristics. Section 7.4 discusses the relations between the levels of coordination and control under the perspective of diachronicity and relates this discussion to the notion of togetherness or jointness. These discussions allow, finally, to cast a new light on the difference between parallel action and joint action proper.

7.2 Stepping Away from Binary Distinctions

The first step away from binary distinctions is to scrutinize the dichotomy between emergent coordination and planned coordination. A first reason to give up this binary distinction is that emergent coordination is too heterogeneous a category to function as the alternative to planned coordination. Emergent coordination, in itself, can vary between being highly automatic to relatively being non-automatic. Secondly, skillful action is not captured by either side of this orthodox dichotomy. Both points relate to the discussion in chapter two regarding the different features of automaticity – awareness, intention, efficiency, and control – and their relation to control and self-control. In what follows I will first briefly recap the orthodox dichotomous approaches to joint action theory and their key assumptions. I then move to a portrayal of the different mechanisms and functions that have been proposed to give us key ingredients for another theory of joint action and I indicate how they relate to several aspects of the so-called four horsemen of automaticity.

7.2.1 The Orthodox Binary Distinction

Planned Coordination

Bratman concentrates on the understanding of joint action as a matter of planned coordination. He wants a theory of shared agency that specifies the functional role of shared intentions and gives us a substantial account of what shared intentions could be. Regarding the first point Bratman stipulates that the functional role (or job) of shared intentions is (a) to coordinate activities, (b) to coordinate planning, and (c) to provide a framework that structures bargaining. I take it that Bratman's description of the functional role indeed is able to capture the ways in which we coordinate our actions in those cases where we can say that the coordination was a joint activity and not merely a case of two individuals coordinating for their own purposes. Bratman (2014) suggests five conditions, which together are sufficient to generate (all) three functions necessary for joint action: (1) the intention condition, (2) the belief condition, (3) the interdependence condition, (4) the common knowledge condition, and (5) the mutual responsiveness condition. The sufficient conditions for joint action that Bratman stipulates, however, can be supplemented by further (sets of) possible sufficient conditions that also realize one or more of the functions he deems essential for joint action.

The first thing I want to repeat is that, although Bratman's sufficient conditions can indeed be understood as accommodating all three indicated functional roles of shared intentions, the three functions themselves are not always needed in order to act jointly. Some joint action phenomena only need one or two of these functions, potentially through different means than a shared intention. Consequently, it is not only possible to spell out sufficient conditions that differ from those presented by Bratman, but also to spell out sufficient conditions that can only fulfill some of the functional roles that shared intentions play, yet give us joint action. This is a consequence of the broad range of phenomena that are typically considered to be joint actions. Most sets of sufficient conditions will not be sufficient to explain all cases of joint action. But, as argued in chapter six, many authors find it unlikely that Bratman's model fits all joint action phenomena that we observe. This critique is not so much about the impossibility to capture such phenomena with Bratman's theory. It is rather about the fact that doing so would be very cumbersome and most probably not the way human agents proceed in their joint actions (see also Williamson & Sutton, 2014). It does not dispute Bratman's theory as a how-possibly model.

In chapter one I highlighted three aspects of joint action – control, coordination, and jointness. The different conceptualizations of each of these aspects relate to many of the proposals and problems in the debate. The conceptualization of control and coordination relate to the three functional roles Bratman spells out. In section 7.3, I will spell out the three levels of coordination that give us the conceptual tools to capture the three functions that Bratman formulated. Each level of coordination can be understood as a different set of sufficient conditions. Planned coordination, which I allow to be understood in the way Bratman describes it, gives us all three functional roles. Other forms of coordination, such as those depending on emergent coordination, will only allow for specific roles such as to coordinate action, but not to coordinate planning.

Although I accept Bratman's specification of the functional roles, I claim that his sufficient conditions are sufficient only for some, not all, joint actions. Indeed, they are not even sufficient for all of the examples of joint action that Bratman relies on, such as dancing together. Bratman's sufficient conditions may indeed capture phenomena that are typically dealt with under the category of emergent coordination, and can in that sense be described as sufficient in such cases. But this would be a rather unconventional, cumbersome, and cognitively demanding understanding of these types of processes. This implies that his sufficient conditions can be accepted, but also that they do not produce a descriptively adequate picture of how human agents coordinate and act together. Lastly, once we accept that other ("lower-level" and "intermediate-level ") levels of coordination also play a major role in human joint action, we have to look at the integration of these different levels of coordination as they pose problems for the holistic planning picture that Bratman provides. I will say more about this in section 7.4.1 where I turn to diachronicity.

Emergent Coordination
In chapter six I discussed the main theories of joint action which start from the insights obtained in cognitive science. These accounts spell out ways in which human agents coordinate their activities with other means than planning and bargaining. In general, such theories concern a less demanding, more minimal, notion of joint action. I discussed three accounts that specify factors which allow coordination through "lower-level" mechanisms: emergent coordination by means of *alignment and synchronization*; the *minimal architecture model*, that supposedly fills the gap between emergent coordination and planned coordination; and an *enactivist account of interaction and joint action*, that focuses on the autonomy of the interaction.

First of all, each of these theories argues that it puts forward a set of functions that allow human agents to act jointly. Tollefsen and Dale (2012) argue that emergent coordination can be sufficient to account for joint action, without necessary involvement of planned coordination. Knoblich et al. (2011) distinguish between planned and emergent coordination. The minimal architecture model (Vesper, Butterfill, Knoblich, & Sebanz, 2010) develops an "in-between" layer of monitoring, predicting, and goals, and the coordination smoother. This results in a (minimal) model of processes that allow agents to act together, without the "higher" and "lower" levels of coordination that surround the minimal architecture model. I take it that all these processes indeed contribute to an understanding of how human agents coordinate and act jointly. The diversity of these theories and the functions they point at, make it clear that we need to step away from the twofold distinction between planned and emergent coordination. The minimal architecture model, which steps away from the dichotomy by adding a third – in between – layer, still makes rigid distinctions between the levels. I have two objections to this approach. It (i) argues there is a gap between emergent coordination and planned coordination and tries to show how minimal aspects, or building blocks, allow us to fill this gap and yield a better understanding of the nature of joint actions. I agree that there is a gap, but think the gap is partially a matter of conceptualization. In that sense, I disagree with how they fill the gap. First of all, I think that a re-evaluation of emergent coordination and all the different processes that are understood to be part of emergent coordination will allow us to "fill the gap" that the minimal architecture model points at. Secondly, the generality of the processes captured in the minimal architecture model leaves undecided whether there is a gap in the explanation, or a problem in the way we conceptualize the processes. A simple acceptance of the distinction between emergent coordination and planned coordination seems problematic, and it seems that a lot of the processes described in the minimal architecture model are low-level and inaccessible to the agent(s). Together with the heterogeneity of the processes established in emergent coordination approaches, these observations about the minimal architecture model give reasons to look for a more adequate conceptualization.

I have equal objections to the third theory (enactivism). The skillful enactivist account of dancing together, as put forward by Michael Kimmel, recognizes a wide variety of functions – or skills in his terminology – that allow the agents to act jointly. Although this model does not abide by the strict division between emergent and planned coordination, the different skills that are distinguished fall across the spectrum from highly automatic emergent coordination functions to full planned coordination functions. My objection to this account is that it does not provide a convincing conceptualization. The main problem, as I pointed out in section 6.3, is that his conceptualization should be improved by more conceptual clarity. For starters, he categorizes all the functions he distinguishes as skills. This is problematic, especially since the skills he distinguishes are most diverse. Calling all these functions that we have at hand when dancing together "skills" is confusing at best, especially if we want to say that dancing together is also a skill.

In sum, the sheer heterogeneity of the different processes and functions that are put forward by the discussed theories give good reasons to argue that a distinction of two strictly separate concepts of coordination, planned and emergent, is insufficient. I will turn to this point now.

7.2.2 Mapping the Different Types of Coordination

In this section I will look at different ways of grouping the rich variety of joint action functions that the different theories bring forward. In doing so, I will show why we have to step away from the binary distinction between higher-level and lower-level processes that is often directly mapped on the distinction between planned coordination and emergent coordination. As Williamson and Sutton note:

> collaborative cognition in teams, we argue, is driven by the complex interplay of what, *for convenience rather than metapsychological accuracy*, we will call higher-level and lower-level processes. (Williamson & Sutton, 2014, pp. 111–112; italics mine)

On their account higher-level processes are the kinds of things that team or group members can talk about: the kinds of processes that can be rendered explicit in writing or talking, or in deliberate, iconic bodily cueing like pointing or hand waving. The information that is communicated can be communicated before or during the action. The change of focus of a team member, through a hand wave for example, is also categorized as a higher-level process. By contrast, lower-level processes are mainly characterized as those that cannot immediately, easily or perhaps ever be "tapped by talk". They include bodily and movement-based forms of information-sharing and cueing, often driven by skillful and honed perceptual and attentional processes. These processes are often thought of as implicit and non-deliberative.

Williamson and Sutton (2014) stress "the dense and complex interplay" between higher- and lower-level processes. Furthermore, they are more flexible than most philosophers of collective intentionality in what they consider a "higher-level process". I want to follow this lead. I argue that we can pick different features of the different functions that allow us to act jointly. Each feature will lead to a (slightly) different division of the functions. This shows that a clear dichotomy can only be made when we specify in relation to what we make such a dichotomy. The common dichotomy that we find is the following (Table 4):

Table 4: Dichotomous division of types of coordination.

Coordination by means of higher-level cognitive functions	Coordination by means of lower-level cognitive function
– Shared Intention or Goal – Joint Commitment – Common Knowledge	– Alignment/Entrainment – Affordances – Perception-Action Matching – Minimal Architecture Model (MAM)

On the side of planned coordination, I not only mention shared intention, which has been the main focus in this book, but I also added Gilbert's notion of joint commitment and the often-induced notion of common knowledge that many philosophers stipulate to be necessary for there to be collective intentionality and joint action. I did so simply to make clear that the problems of a binary understanding extend beyond Bratman's proposal.

The distinction between emergent coordination and planned coordination is highly related to, or dependent on, the features that define the automaticity/non-automaticity distinction. In what follows I will position the different coordinating functions on an axis based on some of the features of the automatic/non-automatic divide – awareness, intention, efficiency, and control. This shows that a different division of functions appears depending on which feature of the automaticity/non-automaticity distinction one focuses on. We get a different conceptual field based on the underlying features that we pick.

I will begin my move towards a less binary understanding of joint action with a graphical depiction of the table I just introduced. Lower-level coordination (broadly understood as realized by automatic processes) and higher-level coordination (broadly understood as non-automatic processes that can be "tapped by talk") are situated on the X-axis (Figure 5). It should be noted that the placement of the different capacities that function in our joint actions is not meant to be exact. It might be impossible to make an exact placement. It is also not necessary for the point I am trying to convey. In some of the graphs that will follow below the width of the different bubbles differs. Although imprecise, it remains an approximate indication of the variety of ways in which the phenomenon of joint action may occur.

If, instead of making the division between (highly automatic) lower-level and (non-automatic) higher-level processes, we look up-close at different features of this division, the different coordinating functions spread differently over the X-axis. In Figure 6 the functions are displayed in relation to awareness. Consider the case of shared goals in Figure 5; these can be picked up very unconsciously,

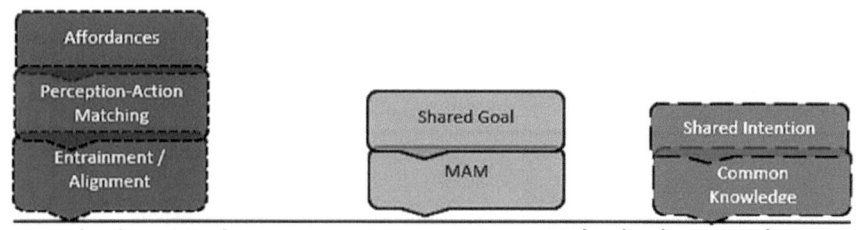

Figure 5: Breaking the dichotomy: higher- and lower- level cognitive functions.

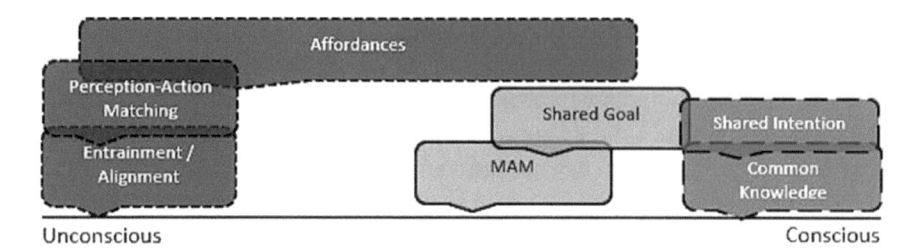

Figure 6: Breaking the dichotomy: consciousness.

but they can also be a starting point for communication. What follows is a plotting of the different functions that have been introduced above, following different features of the traditional automatic/non-automatic distinction. I start with the notion of consciousness.

Some of the functions, such as alignment and entrainment, are hardly ever (if at all) noticed by the agents. Not only do these functions and their structuring effects go unnoticed, the agent will often be incapable of stopping them or of noticing their effect, even when she focuses on it. Other aspects that usually are understood as part and parcel of emergent coordination, such as affordances, might be picked up by the agents, or even generated willfully by one agent so that another can respond to them. Compared to Figure 1 we see a wide spread of the different phenomena.

When we take a different aspect, for example the way in which Fujita and colleagues (2014) discuss the difference between "out of control" and "under control", we get a rather different spread (Figure 7). All of these functions provide structure to the interaction and joint action. The type of governance and purpose will be different for each of these functions, yet this applies to alignment and entrainment up to shared intentions and common knowledge. All contribute to structuring our coordination and do so following certain principles.

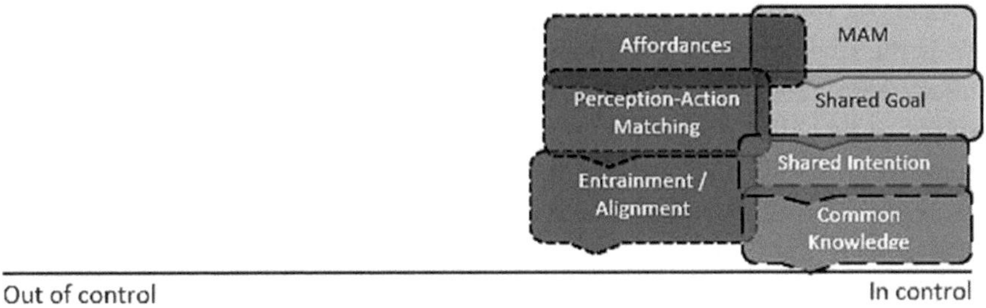

7.2 Stepping Away from Binary Distinctions

Figure 7: Breaking the dichotomy: control.

Although all these coordinating functions can be said to be *under control*, they are not all *under agentic control*. Some of these functions contribute to joint action because the agent intends them to, and others sometimes despite the agent not intending them to. In order to better capture this distinction, it is useful to present the different mechanisms on a scale assumes them all to be "under control", but not all of them to stand under self-control (see chapter three for a discussion). Such a graph would look more or less as follows (Figure 8).

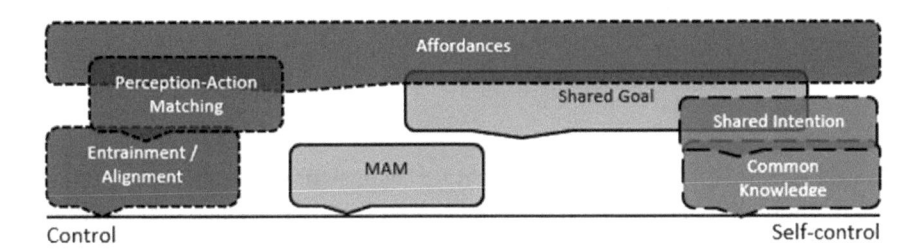

Figure 8: Breaking the dichotomy: self-control.

The aim of these graphs is not to show exactly how all the different aspects of automaticity relate to the different coordination capacities and their role in joint action, or vice versa. Rather, the point is that different ways of grouping the different ways we coordinate give us different results in how the grouping is best conceptualized. I believe the presented pictures show this point to a sufficient measure.

Although I want to step away from the binary distinction between emergent coordination and planned coordination because they cause conceptual trouble, I realize that there are good reasons for grouping certain coordinating functions together. The features of the traditional four-fold way of describing the automatic/non-automatic distinction often *are* related. Many processes are, for example, unconscious and effortless. I am not trying to deny these links. That this is the rule, however, should not make us blind for the (many) exceptions. The same goes for the way we categorize different functions that help agents coordinate. I take it that it makes sense to make the distinction between emergent coordination and planned coordination. However, I think that one should be aware of the ensuing problems and I think that a threefold distinction can dissolve some of the problems that arise when making the binary distinction. The three levels of coordination that I will introduce are intimately related to different levels of control. I will turn to these two topics now.

7.3 Three Levels of Control and Coordination

Throughout this book, I have highlighted and discussed three aspects of joint action that are prominent in the current literature: *control, coordination, and jointness*. Discussions of the treatment of these aspects in several approaches to joint action gave me many reasons to be critical of binary stances towards dividing up theories. In this section I will propose a model that makes a distinction of three levels of control and coordination. In section four I will then turn to the importance of these distinctions for our understanding of jointness.

7.3.1 Control

Control is often introduced as a problem for theories of joint action and collective intentionality. Especially theories of shared intention assume that (individual) self-control is threatened by the assumption that the "we" (collective) also has some form of intention and autonomy (see Schmid, 2009, for a discussion). If an intention is shared it appears that the individual loses her autonomy. I argue that this problem is not unique to joint action by pointing at the fact that descriptions of individual agency often also do not fit well with theories of autonomous agency in philosophy of action. We ascribe "too much" autonomy to agents while they live their everyday life.

Joint action theories, as compared to shared intentionality theories, take a looser stance on the relation between control and joint action. This allows them to picture control as the result of many different, often highly inaccessible and unconscious, processes that structure coordination. The core of my argument in chapter three on self-control was that the threats to self-control that are posed by joint action are not *joint* action specific. Rather, they belong to a group of threats surrounding (more or less) inaccessible processes that influence our actions both in the individual and the joint case. Such processes can take up different forms in the joint case, but the threat to self-control does not radically change because of this.

Furthermore, I emphasized the importance of a diachronic understanding when we think about control over what we are doing. Referring to Baier (1997) I noted that a lot of our intentional doings could be better understood as intentional "continuings". Often an agent finds herself in the middle of a bodily movement and continues, or adjusts, what she is doing, rather than starting the action intentionally. This carries over to the case of joint actions, where agents can pick up on movements, actions, and plans of others and participate in them (continuing rather than starting the joint action). Voluntary shared activities may turn out to be parasitic on non-voluntary ones, and planned shared activities parasitic on naturally coordinated ones. The plans and intentions, or the higher level of control that the agent can exert, can then only be understood in relation to the lower levels. These other levels of control, however, are not mere slaves of the higher level. They structure coordination in their own, different, ways and can – and often do – function independently of self-control.

Purpose, Control, and Self-Control

Before I turn to the different levels of coordination and control that I distinguish, I want to present some considerations why I draw the particular threefold distinction I propose. I will also point at the relation between my proposal and the threefold distinction in control in Fridland (2014) and in Christensen and colleagues (2016, 2019) in their analyses of skillful action.

As discussed in chapter three, I take control to be the more general notion and self-control the more demanding, specific notion. I follow Fujita et al. (2014) in their definition of control through governance and purpose (direction). Governance is only possible in the light of a purpose and a structure that provides a way to reach such a purpose. A function, however, can be described as having a purpose while this might not be an agentic purpose. Agentic purpose and self-control require some form of (potential) reflectivity on one's own attitudes. I find it useful to make a distinction between three features of purposes, that can be combined with the three levels of control as distinguished in the theory of skillful action. On all three levels there is governance, but the structuring is understood differently. This different understanding of the structuring relates to the notions of control and self-control. The first level allows for structure on a bodily and rhythmic level that facilitates and coordinates many movements. As has been pointed out by researchers and theorists on emergent coordination, this coordination and facilitation has similarities in the cases of one individual body coordinating limbs and of two or more bodies coordinating limbs. Alignment of the arms swinging will follow a very similar pattern in one individual swinging both arms and two individuals swinging their arms together (see the discussion on degrees of freedom in section 4.3, and the discussion on alignment in section 6.1). We could describe these mechanisms as having a certain purpose, such as making it possible to make smooth movements, or coordinated movements. When doing so, it is of great importance to make sure that the involved notion of purpose is not confused with agentic purpose, or self-control. Purpose is not dependent on the capacity of language or deliberation and an agent can often not direct or stop these processes. I take it that in Frankfurt's (1978) example the spider that walks across the table in a purposive manner coordinates its limbs and that we can distinguish between the purpose of crossing the table and the purposive way in which its legs move and coordinate. The crossing of the table is agentic, the coordination of the limbs most likely not. Although I take it that we are usually not aware of such functions that allow emergent coordination, we (a) can be aware of the social glue effects they have (such as liking someone more with whom we coordinate well) and we (b) can become aware of these functions from a third person perspective and then focus on them (with agentic purpose) to adjust, change, or undo them (to some extend).

Within the domain of *agentic* purpose (or direction) I take it that we can make a further distinction between purposive agency and deliberative agency. Purposive agency concerns agents who move themselves towards goals they have some awareness of. They adjust their behavior in light of the perception of the environment. There is no need for the capacity to assess reasons in the case of purposive agency. This is what distinguishes the actions that can be described as purposive from those that are deliberative. All deliberative agency is also purposive agency, but the reverse is not the case.

This discussion of three levels of control and agentic control can be summarized in the following table (Table 5), where I already introduce the terminology that I will discuss in the next section.

Table 5: Agentic Control, Governance, and Purpose.

	Governance	Purpose/Direction (Agency)	Deliberative Agency
Emergent Coordination/ Implementation Control	✔		
Situational Coordination/ Situation Control	✔	✔	
Planned Coordination/ Strategic Control	✔	✔	✔

The distinctions regarding governance and purpose provide a ground for making a *threefold* distinction of levels of coordination and control, to which I will turn now for a more detailed discussion.

7.3.2 Three Levels of Coordination and Control

My proposal focuses on (a) distinguishing three levels of coordination and control, and (b) the interdependence of these levels. I argue that most joint actions that we know in everyday experience and are described in scientific and philosophical accounts cannot be understood by the use of one level without the others. To illustrate this, I will turn to some examples, also outside the domain of fast-paced skillful joint action, at the end of this section. At the same time, however, I want to follow Bratman in his suggestion that human agents have the capacity of planning, which has important consequences for the way we act and interact. The core idea, that human agency is directed at and structured by future plans, a cohesive self-image, and social embeddedness, is key to my understanding of integrating the different levels. On Bratman's view a planning agent is, as discussed above, distinguished from a purposive agent through several extra constraints on the choices she makes. My interest here is in understanding the relation between such planning capacities and other capacities human agents are endowed with. The better we understand the different layers, the better we can also understand the possibilities and limits of collective planning.

Throughout my analysis I focus on the difference of, and interplay between, planning capacities and other purposive and agentive (but not planning) capacities. I try to highlight the coupling of the different processes. The following attempt to distinguish and couple three levels of coordination and control takes its point of departure in the discussion on skillful action and particularly in the conception of three levels of control that is developed in this context.

We know for certain that there is at least one domain in which we need three levels of control: (team) sports. Sports teams are often involved in fast-paced, high-stakes tasks. Athletes act on the fly and in the moment. They must act decisively, precisely and this with often hardly any time for (careful) deliberation. It would be surprising if these findings of athletes in individual sports would not also be highly needed in team sports. Athletes in teams are required to coordinate their actions, complementing and assisting each other, in the pursuit of a shared goal or aim. Many of these processes are unreportable, non-verbal processes. Athletes are guided mostly by fast processes governed by their direct, present engagement with and attunement to aspects of the task at hand, while *at the same time* the planning or strategic processes also constrain and influence a team's behavior. Ideas and plans of the team's performance have to be general, to allow for the details to be filled in in the specific situations that arise through the dynamics of a particular game. So on some level the shared intentions that the team members have will guide their joint actions. These shared intentions alone, however, will not be sufficient to understand how the team comes to on the spot decisions that fit the overall (shared) goal.

Many of our collaborative activities involve spontaneous responses to unpredictable circumstances (Preston, 2012). In such cases, coordination is often not only or primarily a matter of planning and verbally communicating those plans. The recent debate on skillful action creates room for actions that are neither automatic nor non-automatic and provides a good starting point to step away from the binary distinction between higher-level and lower-level processes that contribute to joint action (through a combination of emergent and planned coordination). The *three levels of control* that Pacherie (2008), Fridland (2014) and Christensen et al. (2016, 2019) introduce allow us to give a coherent conception of the relations between *three levels of control* and *three levels of coordination.* I briefly recap them:

A. *Strategic control*: Governance of an extended course of action in order to achieve one or more goals.
B. *Situation control*: Determining what actions need to be performed in the immediate situation in order to achieve the overarching goal. This level depends strongly on, or can be understood through, a notion of situational awareness/attention.
C. *Implementation control*: Governance of the execution of the actions specified by situation control.

A short remark with regard to this scheme: I am not committed to *one* type of process on any of these levels, nor to a strict division of three levels for that matter. I only follow these theories in recognizing another category besides lower-level and higher-level cognitive processes. The different levels are thought to have a collection of heterogeneous processes that allow their functionality. It might turn out that four levels, or a truly separate understanding of situational awareness/attention from the intermediate level allows for an even better understanding of levels of control and ways to coordinate joint action. If one opts for a continuum view then one might even be forced to give up any talk of levels. That would not undermine my main claim that two levels are insufficient and conceptually confusing.

The three levels of control can be related to three levels of interpersonal coordination. To illustrate the functions, I provide ballroom dancing examples for each level of control and coordination.

A. *Strategic Control/Planned Coordination.* The dancing couple will have long-term plans, including the choreography right before dancing and while dancing, and possibly a plan for the upcoming competitions. These all fall under strategic control.
B. *Situation Control/Situational Coordination.* Ballroom dancers will often have to adjust their plans because of contingencies, such as other couples on the floor, the size of the floor, etc. What a couple will do will depend on several skills and a rapid assessment of the situation. Such adjustments and on-the-spot improvisations need situation control and attention to the right situational factors.
C. *Implementation Control/Emergent Coordination.* At all times the couple will adjust and perfect the coordination of their movements through alignment and synchronization mechanisms.

Whether a token of an action type (making a spin-turn in a slow waltz, to volley a soccer ball) falls under strategic control or situation control can depend upon several factors, such as the accessibility of the information, and the ability to communicate this information in a way that can guarantee common knowledge. The main difference between situation control and implementation control is the amount of flexibility that the agent has while acting. This is shown in the following short descriptions of ballroom dancing and playing soccer.

Two Examples of Skillful Joint Action
Both Kimmel's analysis and my own analysis of dancing together show how dancing together involves (a) planned coordination, including strategies and the overall plan to dance together, (b) the improvisation and adjustment of specific figures, directions and speed of the steps, etc., on the level of situational coordination, and (c) alignment and synchronization on the implementation level (see sections 1.3 and 6.3.3 for the full descriptions). Kimmel's description of the seven skills that are involved in tango dancing show a similar mix of different types of coordination. Several of the individual skills that Kimmel mentions are a mix of types of control and coordination. My analysis focused on the on-the-spot decision making that couples face, something they can only successfully do when using all three levels of coordination. The dancers rely on prepared choreographies or synthesis of steps and moves in combination with improvisation and responses to contingencies.

Williamson and Sutton (2014) describe how a corner kick in soccer depends on multiple heterogeneous processes. They consider the corner kick a "microcosm" of the wider complexity found in a football match, where teams balance the demands between reliance on pre-prepared strategies and moves and responses to contingencies. (a) Both the attacking team and the defending team have overarching goals, such as "keep the ball out of the goalmouth". Based on these overarching goals they might be able to make some predictions, but these predictions will be strongly dependent on (b) contingencies and on-the-spot decision-making. The players will shift their attention between the ball and the position of their own and the other team's players. At many points they will have the opportunity to use and adapt pre-arranged, shared routines. The football example displays the many ways in which team players coordinate. The movements are (c) perfected and adjusted to, for example, the irregularity in the grass through highly automatic implementation control. Both examples not only show the three levels of coordination and control, but also the interdependence of the different coordination strategies used.

7.3.3 Expanding Beyond Fast-Paced Skillful Action: NDM and Heuristics

Although sports give us good reasons to give up the binary distinctions and the idea that skills are merely a matter of automation, it might seem that skillful action conceived as such does not have much in common with most everyday activities. The type of skillful actions that form the basis for the three levels of control are tightly coupled to fast-paced skillful bodily movement. However, not all forms of expertise (broadly understood as extended experience with the types of actions required and the circumstances under which different variations of the action are required) are so strongly related to bodily control and to speed. The hierarchical division of different tasks that has been proposed in motor cognition theories in general, and applied to theories of skill acquisition and skillful action more specifically, allows a translation to less speed and motor-control related skills and expert decisions. For example, it has also been suggested to be a good conceptual framework for describing chess (DeGroot, 1965), and Christensen and colleagues have connected Naturalistic Decision Making with the notion of three levels of control (Christensen, Sutton, & McIlwain, 2016; Christensen, Sutton, & Bicknell, 2019). In the following short discussion, I will focus on NDM and highlight some links to bounded rationality and heuristics. This discussion is only meant to give some plausibility to the thesis that the integration of three levels of coordination is important in many joint actions besides sports.

Naturalistic Decision Making
Naturalistic Decision Making (NDM) is a field of literature on decision making that focuses on experts in the field. NDM research has defined itself in contrast to formal decision-theoretic approaches to decision-making, and NDM researchers hold the view that experts don't typically make decisions by generating and analyzing an extended list of options (Klein, 1993). In that sense they divert from the traditional picture of practical deliberation where "all things" are considered in order to determine what should be done and share some elements with research on bounded rationality (Gigerenzer & Todd, 1999; Hertwig & Herzog, 2009; Kahneman, Slovic, & Tversky, 1982; H. Simon, 1983). At the same time, NDM does not assume a process that is fully automated either, which is in line with the literature on skillful action and my discussion of the non-binary distinction between automatic and non-automatic processes. NDM research has arrived at a picture of expert performance, finding that experts often engage in quite extensive cognitive processes (Christensen, Sutton, & McIlwain, 2016).

The general gist of this field of research is that experts often do not seem to evaluate *all possible action options* in order to determine which is best.[90] Rather, they look for an *action option that is good enough*. This suits well with Simon's (1983) idea of bounded rationality. NDM differs from traditional ideas about rationality as it assumes that agents decide through recognition and simulation, rather than decision-trees and practical deliberation. This fits well with the idea of situational awareness/attention as developed in the skillful action theories by Fridland (2014) and Christensen and colleagues (2016). There is also no evidence that in such expert situations the agents generate extensive amounts of options. Often, they do not even generate and compare two options (Klein, 1993). In that sense their strategy is better described as *satisficing* rather than optimizing (Simon, 1956). Satisficing stands in contrast to finding "the best possible option". It consists in looking for an option that is "good enough" for current purposes.

An often-cited example that illustrates these principles nicely is that of a fireman who has to decide on the spot in the case of a fire. Research suggests that in such situations, firemen check whether an action option *satisfies* the desired end-state and, if so, they will pick it (Klein, 1998). The fireman wants to safe someone from a house that is on fire and to do so they go through the first scenario that comes to mind; if it is a good-enough plan (not necessarily the

---

90 This research is interesting but also hard to compare with typical (lab) studies because it often involves field studies. It gives us ecological validity, but since the situational factors are less controlled, it is also less clear which cognitive components can be distinguished in the process (Klein, 1993).

best), they will act and not look further for other possible solutions. To decide whether the first idea is good enough they report a stage where they go through the scenario in their head and see if they would encounter any problems while performing the steps required for this plan. In total we can distinguish three steps: formulating an (intuitive) plan, check for the adequacy of this plan, and perform the required actions (or rerun steps one and two looking for a new approach if the plan is not adequate).

NDM and skillful action as specified above share the idea that we can act highly flexible, intelligible, and coherent, while simultaneously being efficient and fast and not following the type of practical reasoning as spelled out by Bratman, or by perfect rationality models. The decision-making process of NDM seems to fit into the level of situation control, including the characteristic aspect of situational awareness, where experts have trained their attention.

Heuristics

Research in social psychology suggests that there are many moments a day where the situation triggers a usually functional response in a way best described in terms of heuristics (Cialdini, 1984; Gigerenzer & Todd, 1999; Hertwig & Herzog, 2009; Kahneman, Slovic, & Tversky, 1982). Everyday expertise is typically acquired and appears to us as "second nature" (Bartlett & Collins, 2011; Ryle, 2009). The way in which it is usually acquired is not through constant focused and deliberate training. Our heuristics are – most of the time – satisfying, although they might not be the best possible response to a situation. In that sense they are similar to the responses in NDM. As in NDM cases, the responses are highly situation dependent and require trained attention in the way Fridland (2014) and Christensen et al. (2016) describe it.

A problem with describing heuristics and how they function is that, unlike proposals of skillful action or NDM (or planning agency for that matter), bounded rationality and heuristics are not accounted for by one coherent overarching theory. A first, rough definition of bounded rationality is that it is defined by decisions and actions that lead to success in the external world, rather than by internal coherence of knowledge and inferences. In that sense it is less about omniscient minds and coherence and agglomeration but more about being able to act quickly and reliably in a specific environment. Heuristics, which can be seen as specific thought processes that help us to be rational in such bounded ways, are understood as building blocks (or sets of building blocks) that can be combined to make accurate inferences despite being bounded by limited time, knowledge, and computation (Gigerenzer & Todd, 1999; Hertwig & Herzog, 2009; Kahneman, 2011). These building blocks, which show some level of coherence and are somewhat rational, are often incongruent when combined. This heterogeneity is, in itself, not a problem for my proposal of several layers of control and coordination.[91]

Heuristics, like NDM and skillful action, are readily available, quick and effortlessly used, and flexibly applied.[92] They cannot be fully categorized as automatic, nor do they fit into the type of planning agency that Bratman conceptualizes, mainly because it is impossible to know about agglomeration and coherence of decisions that come about through the usage of heuristics and bounded rationality. They furthermore seem to share some characteristics with situation control and situational awareness/attention in the sense that the expert (which might also be someone performing an every-day practical action) picks out important cues. These cues will often also be cues about the social domain. Heuristics mainly give us an idea of how we might understand certain functions at the situation control level. Although it would be too much of a stretch to suggest how this works in joint action cases, the general functionality of these heuristics is communicated by parents, educators, and friends, and will be general in that sense. Those that share the same heuristics can also coordinate based on such heuristics. There might be common knowledge of the heuristics, or at least mutual presumption what they are and/or what the outcome of certain heuristics will be.

7.4 Diachronicity, Jointness and the Difference Between Parallel Action and Joint Action

In this concluding last section, I will relate my proposal for three levels of coordination to the diachronic character of agency and joint agency. I will first relate diachronicity to the three levels of coordination that I just spelled out. Different coordinating functions play a role over different timescales. Understanding jointness or togetherness also has a diachronic aspect. With the discussion of diachronicity and jointness in place, I will end this section with a comment on the

---

91 It does, however, create a problem regarding how we can understand (a) the relation between different heuristics, (b) the selection mechanisms applied to select which heuristic is used, and (c) how we can understand the overall coherence between the different levels of control. This problem, however, is a generic problem, and not one that can or must be solved in this book.
92 Heuristics and bounded rationality are often coupled to the idea of *irrationality*. Especially the work by Kahneman and Tversky fits into this line of understanding. Showing where and when heuristics fail is an excellent way to show that they do not function following principles such as lined out by normative theories of rationality. Such failures, however, usually only occur because agents are "lured" into applying a heuristic in an inappropriate situation, where they usually apply the heuristic successfully and in the appropriate situation.

seemingly lost distinction between parallel and joint action, arguing that we still have some means to conceptualize the distinction.

7.4.1 Diachronicity

Up to this point diachronicity has mainly been discussed in relation to Bratman's work on planning agency. Planning agency and diachronicity of (coherence in) plans, intentions, beliefs, and desires go hand in hand. In this section I focus on diachronicity and the three levels of control and coordination. I believe that the notion of diachronicity is helpful for an understanding of the relation of different cognitive capacities and of their relation to joint action. One example that has been discussed already is how we can set up our surroundings now so that we act in accordance with our plans later on. In such a case the agent's goals help to remain autonomous in situations where the agent knows she might have trouble without setting up the situation for success (i.e., implementation intentions, and the discussion of Horstkötter's (2015) work in section 3.1 and 3.4). Preston (2012) points at spontaneous actions and how they create structure. This structure, which does not come about through planning agency, then has an impact on possible planning.

Not all different structuring functions that help us coordinate develop over the same timescale. Bietti and Sutton (2015) distinguish four different timescales that can help us understand the interaction and relations, including the coherence within and between the different levels. The four timescales (t) they propose are immediately linked to cooperation in teams. t^1 is about faster, lower-level coordination processes of behavioral matching in interactional synchrony, t^2 concerns mid-range collaborative processes which re-evoke past experiences in groups, t^3 is about cooperative processes involved in the transmission of memories over longer periods, and t^4 concerns cultural processes and practices operating within distributed socio-cognitive networks over evolutionary and historical timeframes. Their idea is that the different timescales interact with and complement each other. Each timescale potentially alters what happens on the other timescales.

On each timescale participants of the joint action in question can structure what they are doing together in different ways, supported by different principles. Some of the principles or processes mainly used on one level can also provide useful support for the understanding of other levels. However, it seems to make sense to say that specific processes are typically connected to longer or shorter periods of time. Plans and goals for the longer term, synchronization for the here and now. In order to understand the relation between such different structuring functions, we have to assume them to stand in relationships. The most obvious, and relatively minimal, relationship, is that of being a constraining factor on the other levels. On those levels where reflection is possible and where the agent knows about the functions that structure our behavior, there might be a back and forth between the constraining structures and changes in such structures for future encounters. Think, for example, about experts that try to train and alter (bits of) their highly automatic responses.

In section 5.5, I discussed policies and shared policies. Two concepts that Bratman introduces to conceptualize more generally applicable plans. I also expressed the worry that shared policies are 1) either not very helpful in many circumstances, or 2) might be less strictly distinguishable from shared practices than Bratman wants them to be. I argued for this second option, according to which the difference between shared practices and shared policies is fluid. Considering the idea of different timescales just presented, t^4 could give us many shared practices that can be used as, and later on explicated as, shared policies in the way spelled out by Bratman. A diachronic understanding would allow for the transition of social values into shared policies. Groups can coordinate with reliance on social values. Sometimes these values are implicit. They can also be made explicit and adjusted in order to further coordination. When this happens they become the shared policies that Bratman emphasizes. Such shared policies can trickle back to the social value and alter it over time. I take it that most of the time we do not need to be able to spell out such shared policies for them to play the role Bratman wants them to play. Presumably such social values are often assumed in longer existing groups, and only implicitly reinforced. In that sense it seems that many social values can be incorporated as shared policies, and often implicitly so. Such a more flexible understanding also allows us to give shared policies and shared values a role in cases where agents act together spontaneously. In those cases, however, shared values (in combination with assumptions about how these shared values feature in the (joint) "deliberation" about what to do on the spot, seem to fulfill a rather similar role. In this case social practices, which are better understood on timescale t^4, are turned into shared policies. Shared practices will often be ingrained in agents as heuristics, and might be reflected upon, showing how the different timescales stand in relation to one another.

7.4.2 Jointness

Jointness, the last aspect of the three aspects of joint action that I focused on in this book, is in a certain sense more encompassing than, but also interrelated with, the three levels of coordination. There are many ways in which we do things together, and they give rise to different layers (and feelings) of jointness or togetherness.

Jointness, i.e. the presence of a "we", is usually understood as something that must be in place before we can act together, although it can also be a result of acting together. In the first case, in which the presence of a "we" is taken to be a precondition for acting together, a more minimal understanding of "we" is usually introduced. In the second case, in which a "we" results from acting together, a more encompassing understanding of "we" is introduced. In both understandings, the "we" is thought to be either present or absent. That is, both understandings are dichotomous.

The different ways of togetherness can be understood through the different ways in which agents coordinate their actions. The resulting feeling of these different types of coordination, a sense of us doing something together, can give rise to further plans, changes in our actions, etc. In section 6.4, I focused on this relation between different layers of coordination and their role in the sense of us. I also argued that there are cases where this sense of us is immediately there, and there are cases where it develops over time. Experience with similar situations, although with different agents, can set us up for a sense of us. Studies on the "social glue effect" and "liking heuristic" show us the importance of emergent coordination for understanding more complex notions such as the sense of us and joint action (Knoblich, Butterfill, & Sebanz, 2011). The bidirectional influence of synchronization and pro-social attitudes (Chartrand & Bargh, 1999; Valdesolo, Ouyang, & DeSteno, 2010) is of specific importance when there is no specific goal or shared intention in place.

I argued that the sense of we-agency can influence the behavior of the individual in a social context. Through several "rounds" of acting together, the sense of we-agency, i.e. of being in control together, can become stronger, especially as one becomes better at predicting what will happen. Through multiple loops of interactions between the agents an agent can become more certain over time that she is not mistaken, that they are sincerely acting *together*. This will also allow the agent to feel in control about future joint actions, and feel more willing in general to engage with the world as a group. Such a sense of us might take a while to develop, but depending on the situation it might also happen really quickly and gives us a good grip on how togetherness can be depending on multiple factors that each need not be necessarily present to give rise to the feeling.

On an average day, we encounter many potential partners for cooperation, that is, we could say, we experience many "others". A sense of the other is not, however, sufficient to be willing to engage with that other. For this we need a sense of us, which gives us an understanding of the willingness and likeliness of mutual engagement. Doing things together comes in many degrees. Sometimes it can be as small as walking through a door together and coordinating this, at other occasions we are much more dependent on one another, for example when we are colleagues working on a joint project. In the first case it might be sufficient to have a sense of us merely based on a short moment of eye contact. In the latter case such eye contact will most likely be insufficient. I argue that the sense of us can arise through several routes.

The sense of us could also be influenced by plans and goals that we share, and the experience of we-agency, creating room for further shared agency. We could also think of examples where the sense of us is not yet there, or very minimal although there is a certain plan or commitment, for example in a brand-new work force.

I approached the sense of us as something that arises and can get more intense over time, rather than something that is either present or absent. A positive aspect of approaching the sense of us as a feeling that can develop over time and through several underlying mechanisms is that on many levels – from emergent coordination to planning – interaction and reactions to one another can give us a clue whether we are acting together, will be acting together, or might be mistaken. I take it that usually it is only in the interaction, and over time, that a robust sense of us will be formed and the agent can be sure that there is mutual awareness of each other's goals and possibly also mutual intentions and plans. This, then, can lead an agent to form shared intentions.

7.4.3 Parallel Action and Joint Action

The main goal of this book was to break up certain orthodox dichotomies because they prevent us from properly fitting conceptualizations. The main binary distinctions I wanted to give up were those between action and mere bodily movement, and joint action and parallel action. In order to do so I also discussed the problematic binary distinction between automatic and non-automatic. Although changing some of the problematic binary distinctions into more gradual, heterogeneous, multi-dimensional distinctions gives us conceptual tools to describe a wider set of joint action phenomena, it also causes a potential problem. The problem is this: Can we still distinguish between acting jointly and acting in parallel? When are we genuinely collaborating, acting and thinking together? Can we identify some fundamental properties and processes of joint action? The answers we give to these questions also have consequences for the way we can conceptualize autonomy, reason responsiveness, and accountability, both on the individual and group level.

My answer, although very tentative, is yes, we can still distinguish between acting jointly and acting in parallel. However, making this distinction is much more complicated than is traditionally thought. It cannot be based on a single feature or condition, for example the presence of a shared intention as in Bratman. Joint action is a multi-dimensional phenomenon. A joint action takes shape in a constellation of a particular situation, time, and various interacting forms of coordination. If we want to distinguish between joint action and parallel action, we must take into account this constellation.

References

Ainslie, G. (1992). *Picoeconomics: The Strategic Interaction of Successive Motivational States within the Person*. New York, NY: Cambridge University Press.
Alvarez, M. (2010). Kinds of Reasons: An Essay in the Philosophy of Action. Oxford University Press.
Amazeen, P. G., Amazeen, E. L., & Turvey, M. T. (1998). Breaking the Reflectional Symmetry of Interlimb Coordination Dynamics. *Journal of Motor Behavior*, 30(3), 199–216.
Anderson, J. R. (1982). Acquisition of Cognitive Skill. *Psychological Review*, 89(4), 369–406.
Anscombe, G. E. M. (1957). *Intention*. Oxford: Blackwell.
Aristotle (2011). Nicomachean Ethics. Bartlett, R.C. & Collins, S.D. (Eds.) University of Chicago Press.
Arutyunyan, G. H., Gurfinkel, V. S., & Mirskii, M. L. (1968). Investigation of Aiming at a Target. *Biophysics*, 13, 536–538.
Atmaca, S., Sebanz, N., Prinz, W., & Knoblich, G. (2008). Action Co-representation: The Joint SNARC Effect. *Social Neuroscience*, 3(3–4), 410–420.
Bach, K. (2010). Refraining, Omitting, and Negative Acts. In T. O'Connor & C. Sandis (Eds.), *Companion to the Philosophy of Action* (pp. 50–57). Oxford: Wiley-Blackwell.
Bacharach, M. (2006). *Beyond Individual Choice: Teams and Frames in Game Theory*. Princeton, NJ: Princeton University Press.
Baier, A. (1997). Doing Things with Others: The Mental Commons. In L. Alanen, S. Heinämaa, & T. Wallgren (Eds.), *Commonality and Particularity in Ethics* (pp. 15–44). New York: St. Martin's Press.
Bargh, J. A. (1994). The Four Horsemen of Automaticity: Awareness, Intention, Efficiency, and Control in Social Cognition. In R. Wyer & T. Srull (Eds.), *Handbook of Social Cognition*, pp. 1–40. Hillsdale, NJ: Lawrence Erlbaum.
Bargh, J. A., & Chartrand, T. L. (1999). The Unbearable Automaticity of Being. *American Psychologist*, 54(7), 462–479.
Bargh, J. A., & Gollwitzer, P. M. (1994). Environmental Control of Goal-Directed Action: Automatic and Strategic Contingencies between Situations and Behavior. In *Nebraska Symposium on Motivation*, Vol. 41. Integrative Views of Motivation, Cognition, and Emotion (pp. 71–124). Lincoln, NE: University of Nebraska Press.
Bartlett, R., C., & Collins, S., D. (Eds.). (2011). *Aristotle's Nicomachean Ethics*. Chicago: University of Chicago Press.
Baumeister, R. F., Heatherton, T. F., & Tice, D. M. (1994). *Losing Control: How and Why People Fail at Self-Regulation*. San Diego, CA: Academic Press.
Baumeister, R. F., Tice, D. M., & Vohs, K. D. (2018). The Strength Model of Self-Regulation: Conclusions from the Second Decade of Willpower Research. *Perspectives on Psychological Science*, 13(2), 141–145.
Bayne, T., & Pacherie, E. (2007). Narrators and Comparators: The Architecture of Agentive Self-Awareness. *Synthese*, 159(3), 475–491.
Benson, P. (2005). Taking Ownership: Authority and Voice in Autonomous Agency. In A. Joel & C. John (Eds.), *Autonomy and the Challenges to Liberalism* (pp. 101–126). Cambridge: Cambridge University Press.
Bermúdez, J. P. (2017). Do We Reflect while Performing Skillful Actions? Automaticity, Control, and the Perils of Distraction. *Philosophical Psychology*, 30(7), 896–924.

Bernstein, N. A. (1967). *The Co-ordination and Regulation of Movements*. New York: Pergamon Press.

Bertenthal, B. I., Longo, M. R., & Kosobud, A. (2006). Imitative Response Tendencies Following Observation of Intransitive Actions. *Journal of Experimental Psychology: Human Perception and Performance*, 32(2), 210–225.

Bicknell, K. (2010). Feeling Them Ride: Corporeal Exchange in Cross-Country Mountain Bike Racing. *About Performance*, 10, 81–91.

Bietti, L. M., & Sutton, J. (2015). Interacting to Remember at Multiple Timescales: Coordination, Collaboration, Cooperation and Culture in Joint Remembering. *Interaction Studies*, 16(3), 419–450.

Bizzi, E., & Mussa-Ivaldi, F. A. (1989). Geometrical and Mechanical Issues in Movement Planning and Control. In M.I. Posner (Ed.) *Foundations of Cognitive Science* (pp. 769–792). Cambridge, MA: MIT Press.

Branigan, H. P., Pickering, M. J., & Cleland, A. A. (2000). Syntactic Co-ordination in Dialogue. *Cognition*, 75(2), B13–B25.

Brass, M., Bekkering, H., & Prinz, W. (2001). Movement Observation Affects Movement Execution in a Simple Response Task. *Acta Psychologica*, 106(1), 3–22.

Bratman, M., E. (1984). Two Faces of Intention. *Philosophical Review*, 93(3), 375–405.

Bratman, M. E. (1987). *Intention, Plans, and Practical Reason*. Cambridge, MA: Harvard University Press.

Bratman, M. E. (1993). Shared Intention. *Ethics*, 104(1), 97–113.

Bratman, M. E. (1999). *Faces of Intention: Selected Essays on Intention and Agency*. Cambridge: Cambridge University Press.

Bratman, M. E. (2000). Valuing and the Will. *Noûs*, 34(s14), 249–265.

Bratman, M. E. (2007). *Structures of Agency: Essays*. Oxford: Oxford University Press.

Bratman, M. E. (2014). *Shared Agency: A Planning Theory of Acting Together*. Oxford: Oxford University Press.

Brewer, M. B. (1988). A Dual Process Model of Impression Formation. In T. R. Srull, & R. S. Wyer, *Advances in Social Cognition*, Vol. 1. (pp. 1–36). Hillsdale, NJ: Lawrence Erlbaum Associates, Inc.

Brinck, I., Reddy, V., & Zahavi, D. (2017). The Primacy of the "We"? In C. Durt, T. Fuchs, & C. Tewes (Eds.), *Embodiment, Enaction, and Culture: Investiagting the Constitution of the Shared World* (pp. 131–148). Cambridge, MA: MIT Press.

Brownstein, M. (2017, Spring). Implicit Bias. In E. N. Zalta (Ed.), *The Stanford Encyclopedia of Philosophy*. Retrieved November 10, 2017, from https://plato.stanford.edu/archives/spr2017/entries/implicit-bias/.

Bruner, J. S. (1957). On Perceptual Readiness. *Psychological Review*, 64(2), 123–152.

Burger, J. M. (2007). Fleeting Attraction and Compliance with Requests. In A. R. Pratkanis (Ed.), *The Science of Social Influence, Advances and Future Progress* (pp. 155–166). New York: Psychology Press.

Burger, J. M., Soroka, S., Gonzago, K., Murphy, E., & Somervell, E. (2001). The Effect of Fleeting Attraction on Compliance to Requests. *Personality and Social Psychology Bulletin*, 27(12), 1578–1586.

Butterfill, S. A. (2007). What Are Modules and What is Their Role in Development? *Mind and Language*, 22(4), 450–473.

Butterfill, S. A. (2012). Joint Action and Development. Philosophical Quarterly, 61(246), 23–47.

Butterfill, S. A. (2015). Planning for Collective Agency. In C. Misselhorn (Ed.), *Collective Agency and Cooperation in Natural and Artificial Systems*, pp. 149–168. Springer.

Butterfill, S. A., & Sinigaglia, C. (2014). Intention and Motor Representation in Purposive Action. *Philosophy and Phenomenological Research*, 88(1), 119–145.

Byrne, D. (1997). An Overview (and Underview) of Research and Theory within the Attraction Paradigm. *Journal of Social and Personal Relationships*, 14(3), 417–431.

Calvo-Merino, B., Glaser, D. E., Grèzes, J., Passingham, R. E., & Haggard, P. (2005). Action Observation and Acquired Motor Skills: An FMRI Study with Expert Dancers. *Cerebral Cortex*, 15(8), 1243–1249.

Carr, D. (1986). Cogitamus Ergo Sumus. *The Monist*, 69(4), 521–533.

Caspar, E. A., Christensen, J. F., Cleeremans, A., & Haggard, P. (2016). Coercion Changes the Sense of Agency in the Human Brain. *Current Biology*, 26(5), 585–592.

Chaiken, S. (1987). The Heuristic Model of Persuasion. In M. P. Zanna, *Social Influence: The Ontario Symposium*, Vol. 5 (pp. 3–39). Hillsdale, NJ: Lawrence Erlbaum Associates, Inc.

Chaiken, S., & Stangor, C. (1987). Attitudes and Attitude Change. *Annual Review of Psychology*, 38, 575–630.

Chan, D. K. (1995). Non-Intentional Actions. *American Philosophical Quarterly*, 32(2), 139–151.

Chant, S. R. (2007). Unintentional Collective Action. *Philosophical Explorations*, 10(3), 245–256.

Chant, S. R., Hindriks, F., & Preyer, G. (2014). Introduction: Beyond the Big Four and the Big Five. In S. R. Chant, F. Hindriks, & G. Preyer (Eds.), *From Individual to Collective Intentionality: New Essays* (pp. 1–9). Oxford: Oxford University Press.

Chartrand, T. L., & Bargh, J. A. (1999). The Chameleon Effect: The Perception-Behavior Link and Social Interaction. *Journal of Personality and Social Psychology*, 76(6), 893–910.

Christensen, W., Sutton, J., & Bicknell, K. (2019). Memory Systems and the Control of Skilled Action. *Philosophical Psychology*, 32(5), 693–719.

Christensen, W., Sutton, J., & McIlwain, D. J. F. (2016). Cognition in Skilled Action: Meshed Control and the Varieties of Skill Experience. *Mind & Language*, 31(1), 37–66.

Christman, J. P., & Anderson, J. (2005). *Autonomy and the Challenges of Liberalism: New Essays*. Cambridge University Press.

Cialdini, R. B. (1984). *Influence: The Psychology of Persuasion*, Revised Edition. New York: Harper Collins.

Clark, A. (1997). *Being There: Putting Brain, Body, and World Together Again*. Cambridge, MA: MIT Press.

Constantini, M., & Sinigaglia, C. (2011). Grasping Affordance: A Window onto Social Cognition. In A. Seemann (Ed.), *Joint Attention: New Developments in Psychology, Philosophy of Mind, and Social Neuroscience* (pp. 431–460). Cambridge, MA: MIT Press.

Craver, C. F. (2006). When Mechanistic Models Explain. *Synthese*, 153(3), 355–376.

Cross, E. S., Hamilton, A. F., & Grafton, S. T. (2006). Building a Motor Simulation de novo: Observation of Dance by Dancers. *NeuroImage*, 31(3), 1257–1267.

Davidson, D. (1967). The Logical Form of Action Statements. In N. Rescher & A. R. Anderson (Eds.), *The Logic of Decision and Action* (pp. 81–120). Pittsburgh: University of Pittsburgh Press.

Davidson, D. (1971). Agent, Action, and Reason. In R. Binkley, R. Bronaugh, & A. Marras (Eds.), *Agent, Action, and Reason* (pp. 3–37). Toronto: University of Toronto Press.

Davidson, D. (1980). *Essays on Actions and Events*. Oxford: Oxford University Press.

Davis, W. A. (2010). The Causal Theory of Action. In T. O'Conner and C. Sandis (Eds.), *A Companion to the Philosophy of Action* (pp. 32–39). Oxford: Wiley-Blackwell.

De Bruijn, E. R. A., de Lange, F. P., von Cramon, D. Y., & Ullsperger, M. (2009). When Errors Are Rewarding. *The Journal of Neuroscience*, 29(39), 12183–12186.

Deakin, J. M., & Cobley, S. (2003). An Examination of the Practice Environments in Figure Skating and Volleyball: A Search for Deliberate Practice. In J. Starkes & K. A. Ericsson (Eds.), *Expert Performance in Sports: Advances in Research on Sport Expertise* (pp. 9–113). Campaign, IL: Human Kinetics.

DeGroot, A. D. (1965). *Thought and Choice in Chess*. The Hague: Mouton.

Di Paolo, P. E. A., Rohde, M., & De Jaegher, H. (2010). Horizons for the Enactive Mind: Values, Social Interaction, and Play. In J. Stewart, O. Gapenne, & P. E. A. Di Paolo (Eds.), *Enaction: Towards a New Paradigm for Cognitive Science* (pp. 33–88). Cambridge, MA: MIT Press.

Douskos, C. (2019). The Spontaneousness of Skill and the Impulsivity of Habit. *Synthese*, 196(10), 4305–4328.

Doyen, S., Klein, O., Pichon, C.-L., & Cleeremans, A. (2012). Behavioral Priming: It's All in the Mind, But Whose Mind? *PloS One*, 7(1), e29081.

Dretske, F. (1986). Misrepresentation. In R. Bogdan (Ed.), *Belief: Form, Content, and Function* (pp. 17–36). Oxford: Oxford University Press.

Dreyfus, H. L., & Dreyfus, S. E. (1986). *Mind over Machine: The Power of Human Intuition and Expertise in the Era of the Computer*. New York: Free Press.

Ekstrom, L. W. (1993). A Coherence Theory of Autonomy. *Philosophy and Phenomenological Research*, 53(3), 599–616.

Engbert, K., Wohlschlager, A., & Haggard, P. (2008). Who Is Causing What? The Sense of Agency Is Relational and Efferent-Triggered. *Cognition*, 107(2), 693–704.

Ericsson, K. A. (2006). The Influence of Experience and Deliberate Practice on the Development of Superior Expert Performance. In K. A. Ericsson, N. Charness, P. J. Feltovich, & R. R. Hoffman (Eds.), *The Cambridge Handbook of Expertise and Expert Performance* (pp. 683–704). Cambridge: Cambridge University Press.

Ericsson, K. A., Krampe, R. T., & Tesch-Römer, C. (1993). The Role of Deliberate Practice in the Acquisition of Expert Performance. *Psychological Review*, 100(3), 363–406.

Evans, J. S. B. T., & Stanovich, K. E. (2013). Dual-Process Theories of Higher Cognition: Advancing the Debate. *Perspectives on Psychological Science*, 8(3), 223–241.

Fazio, R. H. (1990). Multiple Processes by which Attitudes Guide Behavior: The Mode Model as an Integrative Framework. *Advances in Experimental Social Psychology*, 23, 75–109.

Fiske, S. T., & Neuberg, S. L. (1990). A Continuum of Impression Formation, from Category-Based to Individuating Processes: Influences of Information and Motivation on Attention and Interpretation. In M. P. Zanna (Ed.), *Advances in Experimental Social Psychology* (Vol. 23, pp. 1–74). New York: Academic Press.

Fitts, P. M. (1964). Perceptual-Motor Skill Learning. In A. W. Melton (Ed.), *Categories of Human Learning* (pp. 243–285). Cambridge, MA: Academic Press.

Fitts, P. M., & Posner, M. I. (1967). *Human Performance*. Oxford: Brooks/Cole.

Frankfurt, H. (1971). Freedom of the Will and the Concept of a Person. *Journal of Philosophy*, 68, 5–20.

Frankfurt, H. G. (1978). The Problem of Action. *American Philosophical Quarterly*, 15(2), 157–162.

Frankfurt, H. G. (1988). *The Importance of What We Care About: Philosophical Essays*. Cambridge: Cambridge University Press.

Frankish, K. (2016). Playing Double: Implicit Bias, Dual Levels, and Self-Control. In M. Brownstein & J. Saul (Eds.), *Implicit Bias and Philosophy*, Vol. 1: *Metaphysics and Epistemology* (pp. 23–46). Oxford: Oxford University Press.

Fridland, E. (2014). They've Lost Control: Reflections on Skill. *Synthese*, 191(12), 2729–2750.

Fridland, E. (2017). Automatically minded. *Synthese*, 194(11), 4337–4363.

Fromkin, V. A. (Ed.). (1980). *Errors in Linguistic Performance*. New York: Academic Press.

Fujita, K. (2011). On Conceptualizing Self-Control as More than the Effortful Inhibition of Impulses. *Personality and Social Psychology Review*, 15(4), 352–366.

Fujita, K., Trope, Y., Cunningham, W. A., & Liberman, N. (2014). What is Control?: A Conceptual Analysis. In J. W. Sherman, B. Gawronski, & Y. Trope (Eds.), *Dual-Process Theories of the Social Mind* (pp. 50–65). New York: Guilford Press.

Gallagher, S. (2007). The Natural Philosophy of Agency. *Philosophy Compass*, 2(2), 347–357.

Galton, F. (1979). *Hereditary Genius: An Inquiry into Its Laws and Consequences*. London: Julian Friedman (Originally published in 1869).

Gawronski, B., & Bodenhausen, G. V. (2014). The Associative-Propositional Evaluation Model: Operating Principles and Operating Conditions of Evaluation. In J. W. Sherman, B. Gawronski, & Y. Trope (Eds.), *Dual-Process Theories of the Social Mind* (pp. 188–203). New York: Guilford Press.

Gawronski, B., Sherman, J. W., & Trope, Y. (2014). Two of What?: A Conceptual Analysis of Dual-Process Theories. In J. W. Sherman, B. Gawronski, & Y. Trope (Eds.), *Dual-Process Theories of the Social Mind* (pp. 3–19). New York: Guilford Press.

Gendler, T. S. (2008). Alief and Belief. *Journal of Philosophy*, 105(10), 634–663.

Gibson, J. J. (1979). *The Ecological Approach to Visual Perception*. Boston: Houghton Mifflin.

Gigerenzer, G., & Todd, P. M. (1999). Fast and Frugal Heuristics: The Adaptive Toolbox. In G. Gigerenzer, P. M. Todd, & The ABC Research Group, *Evolution and cognition. Simple heuristics that make us smart* (pp. 3–34). New York: Oxford University Press.

Gilbert, M. (1987). Modelling Collective Belief. *Synthese*, 73(1), 185–204.

Gilbert, M. (1989). *On Social Facts*. London: Routledge.

Gilbert, M. (1990). Walking Together: A Paradigmatic Social Phenomenon. *Midwest Studies in Philosophy*, 15(1), 1–14.

Gilbert, M. (2006). *A Theory of Political Obligation: Membership, Commitment, and the Bonds of Society*. Oxford: Oxford University Press.

Gilbert, M. (2009). Shared Intention and Personal Intentions. *Philosophical Studies*, 144(1), 167–187.

Goldman, A. (2006). *Simulating Minds: The Philosophy, Psychology, and Neuroscience of Mindreading*. Oxford: Oxford University Press.

Gollwitzer, P. M., Bayer, U. C., & McCulloch, K. C. (2005). The Control of the Unwanted. In R. R. Hassin, J. Uleman, & J. A. Bargh (Eds.), The New Unconscious. Oxford University Press.

Graf, M., Reitzner, B., Corves, C., Casile, A., Giese, M., & Prinz, W. (2007). Predicting Point-Light Actions in Real-Time. *NeuroImage*, 36, T22–T32.

Grice, P. (1975). Method in Philosophical Psychology (From the Banal to the Bizarre). *Proceedings and Addresses of the American Philosophical Association*, 48, 23–53.

Haddock, A. (2010). Bodily Movements. In T. O'Conner and C. Sandis (Eds.), *A Companion to the Philosophy of Action* (pp. 26–31). Oxford: Wiley-Blackwell.

Haggard, P., & Tsakiris, M. (2009). The Experience of Agency: Feelings, Judgments, and Responsibility. *Current Directions in Psychological Science*, 18(4), 242–246.

Hassin, R. R., Bargh, J. A., Engell, A. D., & McCulloch, K. C. (2009). Implicit Working Memory. *Consciousness and Cognition*, 18(3), 665–678.
Hassin, R. R., Uleman, J., & Bargh, J. A. (Eds.). (2005). *The New Unconscious*. Oxford: Oxford University Press.
Hertwig, R., & Herzog, S. M. (2009). Fast and Frugal Heuristics: Tools of Social Rationality. *Social Cognition*, 27(5), 661–698.
Hornsby, J. (1980). *Actions*. London: Routledge and Kegan Paul.
Hornsby, J. (2004). Agency and Action. In J. Hyman and H. Steward (Eds.), *Agency and Action* (pp. 1–23). Cambridge: Cambridge University Press.
Horstkötter, D. (2015). Self-Control and Normativity: Theories in Social Psychology Revisited. *Theory & Psychology*, 25(1), 25–44.
Hove, M. J., & Risen, J. L. (2009). It's All in the Timing: Interpersonal Synchrony Increases Affiliation. *Social Cognition*, 27(6), 949–961.
Hursthouse, R. (1991). Arational Actions. *Journal of Philosophy*, 88(2), 57–68.
Husserl, E. (1989). *Ideas Pertaining to a Pure Phenomenology and to a Phenomenological Philosophy* [1912–1914] (R. Rojcewicz & A. Schuwer, Trans.). Dordrecht: Kluwer.
Insko, C. A., & Wilson, M. (1977). Interpersonal Attraction as a Function of Social Interaction. *Journal of Personality and Social Psychology*, 35(12), 903–911.
Jaegher, H. D., & Paolo, E. D. (2007). Participatory Sense-Making. *Phenomenology and the Cognitive Sciences*, 6(4), 485–507.
Jaegher, H. de, Paolo, E. di, & Gallagher, S. (2010). Can Social Interaction Constitute Social Cognition? *Trends in Cognitive Sciences*, 14(10), 441–447.
James, W. (1890). *Principles of Psychology*. New York: Holt.
Johnson, P. (1984). The Acquisition of Skill. In M. M. Smyth & A. M. Wing (Eds.), *The Psychology of Human Movement* (pp. 215–240). London: Academic Press.
Johnston-Laird, P. N. (1983). *Mental Models: Towards a Cognitive Science of Language, Inference, and Consciousness*. Cambridge, MA: Harvard University Press.
Jordan, M. I. (1986). *Serial Order: A Parallel Distributed Processing Approach*. Technical report of the U.S. Department of Energy, Office of Scientific and Technical Information, June 1985–March 1986.
Kahneman, D. (2011). *Thinking, Fast and Slow*. New York: Farrar, Straus and Giroux.
Kahneman, D., Slovic, P., & Tversky, A. (1982). *Judgment Under Uncertainty: Heuristics and Biases*. Cambridge: Cambridge University Press.
Kahneman, D., & Tversky, A. (1979). Prospect Theory: An Analysis of Decision Under Risk. *Econometrica*, 47(2), 263–291.
Kennett, J., & Smith, M. (1994). Philosophy and commonsense: The case of weakness of will. In M. Michael & J. O'Leary-Hawthorne (Eds.), Philosophy in mind: The place of philosophy in the study of mind (pp. 141–157). Dordrecht, the Netherlands: Kluwer Academic.
Kimmel, M. (2013). Intersubjectivity at Close Quarters: How Dancers of Tango Argentino Use Imagery for Interaction and Improvisation. *Cognitive Semiotics*, 4(1), 76–124.
Kimmel, M. (2016). Embodied "micro-"skills in tango improvisation – How a collaborative behavioral arc comes about, In F. Engel & S. Marienberg (eds.): Out for a walk. Das Entgegenkommende Denken, Actus et Imago. Berliner Schriften für Bildaktforschung und Verkörperungsphilosophie 15, Berlin, 57–74.
Kimmel, M., & Preuschl, E. (2016). Dynamic Coordination Patterns in Tango Argentino: A Cross-Fertilization of Subjective Explication Methods and Motion Capture. In J.-P.

Laumond & N. Abe (Eds.), *Dance Notations and Robot Motion* (pp. 209–235). Cham: Springer International Publishing.

Klein, G. (1993). A Recognition-Primed Decision (RPD) Model of Rapid Decision Making. In G. Klein, J. E. Orasanu, & R. E. Calderwood (Eds.), *Decision Making in Action: Models and Methods* (pp. 138–146). Norwood, NJ: Ablex.

Klein, G. (1998). Sources of Power: How People Make Decisions. MIT Press.

Knoblich, G., Butterfill, S. A., & Sebanz, N. (2011). Psychological Research on Joint Action: Theory and Data. In B. H. Ross (Ed.), *The psychology of learning and motivation*: Vol. 54. The psychology of learning and motivation: Advances in research and theory (p. 59–101). Elsevier Academic Press.

Knoblich, G., & Sebanz, N. (2008). Evolving Intentions for Social Interaction: From Entrainment to Joint Action. *Philosophical Transactions of the Royal Society B: Biological Sciences*, 363(1499), 2021–2031.

Koskinen, K. U. (2010). *Autopoietic Knowledge Systems in Project-Based Companies*. Palgrave Macmillan UK.

Kosslyn, S. M., Ganis, G., & Thompson, W. L. (2001). Neural Foundations of Imagery. *Nature Reviews Neuroscience*, 2(9), 635–642.

Krasnow, D., & Wilmerding-Pett, M. V. (2015). *Motor Learning and Control for Dance: Principles and Practices for Performers and Teachers*. Leeds: Human Kinetics.

Lakin, J. L., Jefferis, V. E., Cheng, C. M., & Chartrand, T. L. (2003). The Chameleon Effect as Social Glue: Evidence for the Evolutionary Significance of Nonconscious Mimicry. *Journal of Nonverbal Behavior*, 27(3), 145–162.

Lashley, K. S. (1951). The Problem of Serial Order in Behavior. In L. A. Jeffress (Ed.), *Cerebral Mechanisms in Behavior* (pp. 112–131). New York: Wiley.

Lieberman, M. D., Gaunt, R., Gilbert, D. T., & Trope, Y. (2002). Reflexion and Reflection: A Social Cognitive Neuroscience Approach to Attributional Inference. *Advances in Experimental Social Psychology*, 34, 199–249.

List, C., & Pettit, P. (2011). *Group Agency: The Possibility, Design and Status of Corporate Agents*. Oxford: Oxford University Press.

Locke, J. (1975). *An Essay Concerning Human Understanding* [1690], edited by P. H. Nidditch. Oxford: Oxford University Press.

Logan, G. D. (1985). Executive Control of Thought and Action. *Acta Psychologica*, 60(2), 193–210.

Malfait, N., Valyear, K. F., Culham, J. C., Anton, J.-L., Brown, L. E., & Gribble, P. L. (2010). FMRI Activation during Observation of Others' Reach Errors. *Journal of Cognitive Neuroscience*, 22(7), 1493–1503.

Marsh, K. L., Richardson, M. J., & Schmidt, R. C. (2009). Social Connection Through Joint Action and Interpersonal Coordination. *Topics in Cognitive Science*, 1(2), 320–339.

Martens, J. (2018). Exploring the Relation between the Sense of Other and the Sense of Us: Core Agency Cognition, Emergent Coordination, and the Sense of Agency. *Journal of Social Philosophy*, 49(1), 38–60.

Martens, J. H. & Roelofs, L. (2018). Implicit Coordination: Acting Quasi-Jointly on Implicit Shared Intentions. Journal of Social Ontology, 4(2), 93–120.

Martens, J., & Schlicht, T. (2018). Individualism versus Interactionism about Social Understanding. *Phenomenology and the Cognitive Sciences*, 17(2), 245–266.

Maturana, H. R., & Varela, F. G. (1980). *Autopoiesis and Cognition the Realization of the Living*. Springer Netherlands.

Mechsner, F., & Knoblich, G. (2004). Do Muscles Matter for Coordinated Action? *Journal of Experimental Psychology: Human Perception and Performance*, 30(3), 490–503.

Mele, A. R. (1995). *Autonomous Agents: From Self-Control to Autonomy*. New York: Oxford University Press.

Merleau-Ponty, M. (2002). *Phenomenology and Perception* [1945]. London and New York: Routledge.

Metzinger, T. (2004). Being No One: The Self-Model Theory of Subjectivity. *Mind*, 113(450), 369–372.

Miles, L. K., Nind, L. K., & Macrae, C. N. (2009). The Rhythm of Rapport: Interpersonal Synchrony and Social Perception. *Journal of Experimental Social Psychology*, 45(3), 585–589.

Miller, G. A. (1956). The Magical Number Seven, Plus or Minus Two: Some Limits on our Capacity for Processing Information. *Psychological Review*, 63(2), 81–97.

Millikan, R. G. (1989). Biosemantics. *Journal of Philosophy*, 86(7), 281–297.

Millikan, R. G. (1989). In Defense of Proper Functions. *Philosophy of Science*, 56(6), 288–302.

Mischel, W., Cantor, N., & Feldman, S. (1996). Principles of Self-Regulation: The Nature of Willpower and Self-Control. In A. W. Kruglanski and E. T. Higgins (Eds.), *Social Psychology: Handbook of Basic Principles* (pp. 329–360). New York, NY: Guilford Press.

Moore, A. (2002). *Ballroom Dancing* (10th ed.). Bloomsbury.

Moors, A. (2014). Examining the Mapping Problem in Dual-Process Models. In J. W. Sherman, B. Gawronski, & Y. Trope (Eds.), *Dual-Process Theories of the Social Mind* (pp. 20–34). New York: Guilford Press.

Moors, A., & De Houwer, J. D. (2006). Automaticity: A Theoretical and Conceptual Analysis. *Psychological Bulletin*, 132(2), 297–326.

Moors, A., & De Houwer, J. D. (2007). What is Automaticity? An Analysis of Its Component Features and Their Interrelations. In J. A. Bargh (Ed.), *Social Psychology and the Unconscious: The Automaticity of Higher Mental Processes* (pp. 11–50). New York, NY: Psychology Press.

Mottet, D. G., Ferrand, Y., Bootsma, T., & Reinoud, J. (2001). Two-Handed Performance of a Rhythmical Fitts Task by Individuals and Dyads. *Journal of Experimental Psychology: Human Perception and Performance*, 27(6), 1275–1286.

Mylopoulos, M., & Pacherie, E. (2017). Intentions and Motor Representations: The Interface Challenge. *Review of Philosophy and Psychology*, 8(2), 317–336.

Mylopoulos, M., & Pacherie, E. (2019). Intentions: The Dynamic Hierarchical Model Revisited. *Wiley Interdisciplinary Reviews: Cognitive Science*, 10(2), e1481.

Newman-Norlund, R. D., Ganesh, S., van Schie, H. T., De Bruijn, E. R. A., & Bekkering, H. (2009). Self-Identification and Empathy Modulate Error-Related Brain Activity during the Observation of Penalty Shots between Friend and Foe. *Social Cognitive and Affective Neuroscience*, 4(1), 10–22.

Nisbett, R. E., & Wilson, T. D. (1977). Telling More than We Can Know: Verbal Reports on Mental Processes. *Psychological Review*, 84(3), 231.

Noë, A. (2004). *Action in Perception*. Cambridge, MA: MIT Press.

Norman, D. A. (1981). Categorization of Action Slips. *Psychological Review*, 88(1), 1–15.

O'Brien, L. (2015). *Philosophy of Action*. Palgrave Macmillan UK.

Oshana, M. A. L. (2005). Autonomy and Free Agency. In J. S. Taylor (Ed.), *Personal Autonomy: New Essays on Personal Autonomy and Its Role in Contemporary Moral Philosophy* (pp. 183–204). Cambridge: Cambridge University Press.

O'Shaughnessy, B. (1980). *The Will: A Dual Aspect Theory*. Vol. 2. Cambridge: Cambridge University Press.
O'Shaughnessy, B. (2008). *The Will: A Dual Aspect Theory*. Vol. 2. Cambridge: Cambridge University Press.
Oullier, O., Guzman, G. C. de, Jantzen, K. J., Lagarde, J., & Kelso, J. A. S. (2008). Social Coordination Dynamics: Measuring Human Bonding. *Social Neuroscience*, 3(2), 178–192.
Pacherie, E. (2007). Is Collective Intentionality Really Primitive? In M. Beaney, C. Penco, & M. Vignolo, *Mental Processes: Representing and Inferring* (pp. 153–175). Cambridge: Cambridge Scholars Press.
Pacherie, E. (2008). The Phenomenology of Action: A Conceptual Framework. *Cognition*, 107(1), 179–217.
Pacherie, E. (2013). Intentional Joint Agency: Shared Intention Lite. *Synthese*, 190(10), 1817–1839.
Pacherie, E. (2014). How Does It Feel to Act Together? *Phenomenology and the Cognitive Sciences*, 13(1), 25–46.
Papineau, D. (2013). In the Zone. *Royal Institute of Philosophy Supplements*, 73, 175–196.
Pashler, H., Coburn, N., & Harris, C. R. (2012). Priming of Social Distance? Failure to Replicate Effects on Social and Food Judgments. *PloS One*, 7(8), e42510.
Petty, R. E., & Cacioppo, J. T. (1986). The Elaboration Likelihood Model of Persuasion. In R. E. Petty & J. T. Cacioppo (Eds.), *Communication and Persuasion: Central and Peripheral Routes to Attitude Change* (pp. 1–24). New York, NY: Springer.
Pew, R. W. (1966). Acquisition of Hierarchical Control over the Temporal Organization of a Skill. *Journal of Experimental Psychology*, 71(5), 764–771.
Pollard, B. (2006). Explaining Actions with Habits. *American Philosophical Quarterly*, 43(1), 57–69.
Pollard, B. (2008). Habits in Action: A Corrective to the Neglect of Habits in Contemporary Philosophy of Action. VDM Verlag Dr. Müller Aktiengesellschaft & Co.
Pollard, B. (2010). Habitual Actions. In T. O'Conner & C. Sandis (Eds.), *A Companion to the Philosophy of Action* (pp. 74–81). Oxford: Wiley-Blackwell.
Postman, L., Bruner, J. S., & McGinnies, E. (1948). Personal Values as Selective Factors in Perception. *The Journal of Abnormal and Social Psychology*, 43(2), 142–154.
Preston, B. (2012). *A Philosophy of Material Culture: Action, Function, and Mind*. Routledge.
Pylyshyn, D. (2003). *Seeing and Visualizing*. Cambridge, MA: MIT Press.
Richardson, D. C., & Dale, R. (2005). Looking to Understand: The Coupling between Speakers' and Listeners' Eye Movements and Its Relationship to Discourse Comprehension. *Cognitive Science*, 29(6), 1045–1060.
Richardson, M. J., Marsh, K. L., & Baron, R. M. (2007). Judging and Actualizing Intrapersonal and Interpersonal Affordances. *Journal of Experimental Psychology: Human Perception and Performance*, 33(4), 845–859.
Richardson, M. J., Marsh, K. L., Isenhower, R. W., Goodman, J. R. L., & Schmidt, R. C. (2007). Rocking Together: Dynamics of Intentional and Unintentional Interpersonal Coordination. *Human Movement Science*, 26(6), 867–891.
Rizzolatti, G., & Sinigaglia, C. (2010). The Functional Role of the Parieto-Frontal Mirror Circuit: Interpretations and Misinterpretations. *Nature Reviews Neuroscience*, 11, 264–274.
Rosenbaum, D. A. (1985). Motor programming: A review and scheduling theory. In H. Heuer, U. Kleinbeck, & K.-M. Schmidt (Eds.), Motor behavior: Programming, control, and acquisition (pp. 1–33). Berlin: Springer-Verlag.

Rosenbaum, D. A. (2009). *Human Motor Control*. Cambridge, Massachusetts: Academic Press.
Ryle, G. (2009). *The Concept of Mind*. London and New York: Routledge.
Salmela, M., & Nagatsu, M. (2017). How Does It Really Feel to Act Together? Shared Emotions and the Phenomenology of We-Agency. *Phenomenology and the Cognitive Sciences*, 16(3), 449–470.
Sartre, J.-P. (1975). Existentialism Is a Humanism. In W. Kaufmann (Ed.), *Existentialism from Dostoevsky to Sartre* (pp. 287–311). New York: Meridan/Penguin.
Schack, T., & Mechsner, F. (2006). Representation of Motor Skills in Human Long-Term Memory. *Neuroscience Letters*, 391(3), 77–81.
Schilbach, L., Timmermans, B., Reddy, V., Costall, A., Bente, G., Schlicht, T., & Vogeley, K. (2013). Toward a Second-Person Neuroscience. *Behavioral and Brain Sciences*, 36(4), 393–414.
Schmid, H. B. (2009). *Plural Action: Essays in Philosophy and Social Science*. Dordrecht: Springer.
Schmid, H. B. (2014). Plural Self-Awareness. *Phenomenology and the Cognitive Sciences*, 13(1), 7–24.
Schmidt, R. A., & Wrisberg, C. A. (2008). *Motor Learning and Performance: A Situation-Based Learning Approach*. Leeds: Human Kinetics.
Schmidt, R. C., Carello, C., & Turvey, M. T. (1990). Phase Transitions and Critical Fluctuations in the Visual Coordination of Rhythmic Movements between People. *Journal of Experimental Psychology. Human Perception and Performance*, 16, 227–247.
Schmidt, R. C., & O'Brien, B. (1997). Evaluating the Dynamics of Unintended Interpersonal Coordination. *Ecological Psychology*, 9(3), 189–206.
Schmidt, R. C., & Richardson, M. J. (2008). Dynamics of Interpersonal Coordination. In A. Fuchs & V. K. Jirsa (Eds.), *Coordination: Neural, Behavioral and Social Dynamics* (pp. 281–308). Berlin and Heidelberg: Springer.
Schuch, S., & Tipper, S. P. (2007). On Observing Another Person's Actions: Influences of Observed Inhibition and Errors. *Perception & Psychophysics*, 69(5), 828–837.
Schutz, A. (1967). *The Phenomenology of the Social World*. Evanston, IL: Northwestern University Press.
Schweikard, D. P., & Schmid, H. B. (2013). Collective Intentionality. In E. N. Zalta (Ed.), *The Stanford Encyclopedia of Philosophy* (Summer 2013). Retrieved from http://plato.stanford.edu/archives/sum2013/entries/collective-intentionality/.
Searle, J. R. (1983). *Intentionality: An Essay in the Philosophy of Mind*. Cambridge: Cambridge University Press.
Searle, J. R. (1990). Collective Intentions and Actions. In P. R. C. J. Morgan & M. Pollack (Eds.), *Intentions in Communication* (pp. 401–415). Cambridge, MA: MIT Press.
Searle, J. R. (2001). *Rationality in Action*. Cambridge, MA: MIT Press.
Sebanz, N., Bekkering, H., & Knoblich, G. (2006). Joint action: Bodies and minds moving together. *Trends in Cognitive Sciences*, 10(2), 70–76. https://doi.org/10.1016/j.tics.2005.12.009
Semin, G. R., & Cacioppo, J. T. (Eds.). (2008). *Embodied Grounding: Social, Cognitive, Affective, and Neuroscientific Approaches*. New York: Cambridge University Press.
Shaffer, L. H. (1975). Multiple Attention in Continuous Verbal Tasks. In P. M. Rabbitt & S. Dornic (Eds.), *Attention and Performance V* (pp. 157–167). London: Academic Press.
Sherman, J. W., Gawronski, B., & Trope, Y. (2014). *Dual-Process Theories of the Social Mind*. New York: Guilford Press.

Shiffrin, R. M. (1988). Attention. In R. J. Hernsteinq, G. Lindzey, & R. D. Luce (Eds.), *Stevens' Handbook of Experimental Psychology* (Vol. 2, pp. 739–811). New York: Wiley.

Shiffrin, R. M., & Schneider, W. (1977). Controlled and Automatic Human Information Processing: II. Perceptual Learning, Automatic Attending and a General Theory. *Psychological Review*, 84(2), 127–190.

Shockley, K., Baker, A. A., Richardson, M. J., & Fowler, C. A. (2007). Articulatory Constraints on Interpersonal Postural Coordination. *Journal of Experimental Psychology*, 33(1), 201–208.

Shockley, K., Santana, M.-V., & Fowler, C. A. (2003). Mutual Interpersonal Postural Constraints Are Involved in Cooperative Conversation. *Journal of Experimental Psychology*, 29(2), 326–332.

Shoemaker, S. S. (1968). Self-Reference and Self-Awareness. *The Journal of Philosophy*, 65(19), 555–567.

Simon, H. A. (1956). Rational Choice and the Structure of the Environment. *Psychological Review*, 63(2).

Simon, H. (1983). *Reason in Human Affairs*. Cambridge, MA: Stanford University Press.

Simon, J. R. (1969). Reactions toward the Source of Stimulation. *Journal of Experimental Psychology*, 81(1), 174–176.

Simon, J. R., & Rudell, A. P. (1967). Auditory S-R Compatibility: The Effect of an Irrelevant Cue on Information Processing. *The Journal of Applied Psychology*, 51(3), 300–304.

Smith, E. R., & DeCoster, J. (2000). Dual-Process Models in Social and Cognitive Psychology: Conceptual Integration and Links to Underlying Memory Systems. *Personality and Social Psychology Review*, 4(2), 108–131.

Smith, M. 1998. The Possibility of Philosophy of Action. In J. Bransen and S. Cuypers (Eds.), *Human Action, Deliberation and Causation* (pp. 17–41). Dordrecht, Kluwer.

Spelke, E., Hirst, W., & Neisser, U. (1976). Skills of Divided Attention. *Cognition*, 4(3), 215–230.

Squire, L. R. (1987). *Memory and brain*. New York: Oxford University Press.

Squire, L. R. (2009). Memory and Brain Systems: 1969–2009. *Journal of Neuroscience*, 29(41), 12711–12716.

Stoutland, F. (1997). Why Are Philosophers of Action so Anti-Social? In L. Alanen, S. Heinämaa, & T. Wallgren (Eds.), *Commonality and Particularity in Ethics* (pp. 45–74). New York: St. Martin's Press.

Strack, F., & Deutsch, R. (2004). Reflective and Impulsive Determinants of Social Behavior. *Personality and Social Psychology Review*, 8(3), 220–247.

Strayer, D. L., & Drews, F. A. (2007). Cell-Phone-Induced Driver Distraction. *Current Directions in Psychological Science*, 16(3), 128–131.

Swinnen, S. P., Massion, J., Heuer, H., & Casaer, P. (2013). *Interlimb Coordination: Neural, Dynamical, and Cognitive Constraints*. San Diego: Academic Press.

Thompson, E. (2007). *Mind in Life: Biology, Phenomenology, and the Sciences of Mind*. Cambridge, MA: Harvard University Press.

Thompson, E., & Varela, F. J. (2001). Radical Embodiment: Neural Dynamics and Consciousness. *Trends in Cognitive Sciences*, 5(10), 418–425.

Tollefsen, D. (2005). Let's Pretend!: Children and Joint Action. *Philosophy of the Social Sciences*, 35(1), 75–97.

Tollefsen, D. (2015). *Groups as Agents*. Cambridge UK: Polity.

Tollefsen, D., & Dale, R. (2012). Naturalizing Joint Action: A Process-Based Approach. *Philosophical Psychology*, 25(3), 385–407.

Tomasello, M., Carpenter, M., Call, J., Behne, T., & Moll, H. (2005). Understanding and Sharing Intentions: The Origins of Cultural Cognition. *Behavioral and Brain Sciences*, 28(5), 675–691.
Trope, Y. (1986). Identification and Inferential Processes in Dispositional Attribution. *Psychological Review*, 93(3), 239–257.
Tuomela, R. (1999). Philosophical Foundations of the Social Sciences. *Philosophy and Phenomenological Research*, 59(4), 1086–1090.
Tuomela, R. (2007). *The Philosophy of Sociality: The Shared Point of View*. New York: Oxford University Press.
Tuomela, R., & Miller, K. (1988). We-Intentions. *Philosophical Studies*, (53), 367–389.
Tversky, A., & Kahneman, D. (1981). The Framing of Decisions and the Psychology of Choice. *Science*, 211(4481), 453–458.
Valdesolo, P., Ouyang, J., & DeSteno, D. (2010). The Rhythm of Joint Action: Synchrony Promotes Cooperative Ability. *Journal of Experimental Social Psychology*, 46(4), 693–695.
Vallacher, R. R., & Wegner, D. M. (1987). What Do People Think They're Doing? Action Identification and Human Behavior. *Psychological Review*, 94(1), 3–15.
Van Schie, H. T., Mars, R. B., Coles, M. G. H., & Bekkering, H. (2004). Modulation of Activity in Medial Frontal and Motor Cortices during Error Observation. *Nature Neuroscience*, 7(5), 549–554.
Varela, F. G., Maturana, H. R., & Uribe, R. (1974). Autopoiesis: The organization of living systems, its characterization and a model. *Currents in Modern Biology*, 5(4), 187–196.
Varela, F. J. (1997). Patterns of life: Intertwining identity and cognition. *Brain and Cognition*, 34, 72–87.
Varela, F., Thompson, E., & Rosch, E. (1991). *The Embodied Mind: Cognitive Science and Human Experience*. Cambridge, MA: MIT Press.
Vargas, M., & Yaffe, G. (2014). Introduction. In M. Vargas & G. Yaffe (Eds.), *Rational and Social Agency: The Philosophy of Michael Bratman* (pp. 1–11). Oxford: Oxford University Press.
Velleman, J. D. (1992). What Happens When Someone Acts? *Mind*, 101, 461–481.
Velleman, J. D. (1997). How to Share an Intention. *Philosophy and Phenomenological Research*, 57(1), 29–50.
Velleman, J. D. (2000). *The Possibility of Practical Reason*. Michigan: Michigan Publishing.
Vesper, C., Butterfill, S., Knoblich, G., & Sebanz, N. (2010). A Minimal Architecture for Joint Action. *Neural Networks*, 23(8–9), 998–1003.
Waroquier, L., Marchiori, D., Klein, O., & Cleeremans, A. (2010). Is It Better to Think Unconsciously or to Trust Your First Impression?: A Reassessment of Unconscious Thought Theory. *Social Psychological and Personality Science*, 1(2), 111–118.
Watson, G. (1975). Free Agency. *Journal of Philosophy*, 72, 205–220.
Wegner, D. M. (2004). Précis of The Illusion of Conscious Will. *Behavioral and Brain Sciences*, 27(5), 649–659.
Wegner, D. M., & Wheatley, T. (1999). Apparent Mental Causation: Sources of the Experience of Will. *American Psychologist*, 54(7), 480–492.
William, L. B., & Harter, N. (1899). Studies on the Telegraphic Language: The Acquisition of a Hierarchy of Habits. *Psychological Review*, 6(4), 345–375.
Wilson, M., & Knoblich, G. (2005). The Case for Motor Involvement in Perceiving Conspecifics. *Psychological Bulletin*, 131(3), 460–473.
Wiltermuth, S. S., & Heath, C. (2009). Synchrony and Cooperation. *Psychological Science*, 20(1), 1–5.

Williamson, K., & Sutton, J. (2014). Embodied Collaboration in Small Groups. In C. T. Wolfe (Ed.), Brain Theory (pp. 107–133). Springer.
Wittgenstein, L. (1953). *Philosophical Investigations*. Oxford: Wiley-Blackwell.
Wittgenstein, L. (1958). *The Blue and Brown Books*. New York: Harper & Row.
Wu, W. (2011). Confronting Many-Many Problems: Attention and Agentive Control. *Noûs*, 45(1), 50–76.
Wu, W. (2014). *Attention*. London: Routledge.
Zahavi, D. (2014). *Self and Other: Exploring Subjectivity, Empathy, and Shame*. Oxford: Oxford University Press.
Zahavi, D. (2015). You, Me, and We: The Sharing of Emotional Experiences. *Journal of Consciousness Studies*, 22(1–2), 84–101.

Subject Index

Acting Together 3, 7, 9, 90, 128, 158, 159, 161, 182, 183
Action Execution Complexity Argument 57
Action Simulation 125
Activity 6, 35–41, 63, 119, 133, 154
Adjustment 12, 125, 175
Affordances 124, 134, 142, 168
Agency 33, 45, 46, 48, 69–119, 136, 146, 155, 157, 173, 179
Agential Authority 46, 47, 112
Agential Control 33, 109, 112
Agential Direction 43, 46, 114
Agential Governance 43, 46, 47
Aggregate Action 18
Akrasia 34
Alignment 11, 17, 125, 126, 164, 168, 171, 175
Ascription 8, 128
Associative 27, 28, 56
Associative Phase 56
Automatic 2–5, 15, 20, 21–24, 26, 27, 29, 48, 51, 57, 67, 126, 161
Automatic Phase 56
Automatic Processes 2, 4, 15, 20, 21–23, 26, 61, 91, 122, 161, 177
Automaticity 4, 5, 16, 20, 21, 24–26, 29, 30, 33, 34, 55, 59, 65, 67, 107, 162, 167. See also four horsemen of automaticity
Autonomous Action 43, 114
Autonomous Agency 41–45, 110, 112–114, 170
Autonomous Phase 56
Autonomy 41–43, 45, 47, 49, 71, 93, 109–113, 134, 136–140, 145, 146, 170, 183
Autonomy-Hierarchy thesis 43, 113
Autopoiesis 134–136
Autopoietic Interaction 136–141
Awareness 3, 24–25, 37, 39, 41, 153, 167

Background
 – Deep Background 147
 – Local Background 147
Ballet 65
Ballroom Dancing 9–12, 60, 65, 67, 141, 175

Behavior 3, 16, 22, 30, 34, 38, 41, 52–54, 61, 75, 78, 80, 88, 91, 94, 96, 97, 102, 106, 115, 119, 123, 126, 129, 132, 135, 138, 147, 158, 172, 181
Behavioral Space 61
Belief Condition 88, 163
Binary 143, 161, 167
Binary Distinction 1, 2, 4, 20–22, 48, 161, 162–170, 176, 183
Bodily Action 33, 35, 54
Bounded Rationality 66, 74, 104–107, 108, 119, 176–178
Brain in a Vat 8

Children 71, 83–85, 90, 95, 121, 123
Choreography 10, 11, 13, 60, 142, 175
Chunk 53, 142
Circularity 9, 135
Cognition 77, 124, 133, 134
Cognitive Capacities 77, 83, 90, 93, 99, 105, 106, 180
Cognitive Limitations 78, 103–109
Cognitive Phase 55
Cognitive Process 26, 66, 124, 134, 174, 177
Cognitive Science 20, 21, 45, 54, 72, 78, 121, 122, 124, 152, 164
Coherence 32, 45–47, 73, 82, 92–97, 118, 138, 178, 180
Coherentist Accounts of Autonomy 110
Collective Acceptance 7
Collective Agency 18, 96, 108, 153, 161
Collective Emotion 7
Collective Goals 6
Collective Intentionality 5, 7–9, 14, 16, 19, 69, 71, 82, 85, 87, 90, 110, 112, 115, 116, 121, 122, 124, 125, 147, 149, 161, 166, 167, 170
Collective Intentions 7, 8, 19, 86, 124, 146
Collective Mind 8
Collectivity 7
Common Knowledge 8, 17, 19, 89, 90, 100, 117, 147, 167, 168, 175, 179
Common Knowledge Condition 88, 118, 163

https://doi.org/10.1515/9783110671315-009

Conative Attitudes 43, 46, 94, 113
Consistency 47, 70, 74, 82, 91, 93, 98, 100
Constraints 39, 64, 65, 70, 78, 82, 87, 93, 118, 144, 173
Content Account 8, 9
Context 1, 18, 34, 52, 57, 96, 97, 98, 107, 116, 117, 134, 138, 156, 173
Control
- Agential control 33, 109, 112
- Diachronic control 47
- Implementation control 175
- Motor control 20, 49, 51, 54, 63
- Online control 59
- Self-control 16, 20–22, 33, 34, 41, 42, 45, 47–49, 67, 70, 91, 109, 118, 162, 169, 170–172
- Sense of control 26, 146–160
- Situational control 59, 61, 91, 143
- Strategic control 58–60, 62, 174, 175
- Synchronic control 47–49
- Three levels of control 2, 5, 17, 18, 20, 52, 58–62, 67, 170–179
Controllability 25, 26
Controlled Processes 2, 23, 30, 57
Cooperation 6, 129, 180, 182
Coordination
- Emergent coordination 1, 2, 5, 9–12, 15, 17, 18, 20, 60, 69, 74, 90, 118, 122–128, 138, 144, 153, 155, 157, 159, 161, 162, 164–166, 167–169, 171, 182, 183
- Intermediate coordination 18
- Interpersonal coordination 17, 128, 129, 174
- Planned coordination 1, 2, 5, 9, 10, 12, 15, 20, 60, 74, 119, 122–124, 128, 161–166, 169, 174, 175
- Situational coordination 69, 161, 175
Coordination Smoother 129, 132, 133, 165
Coupling 11, 93, 123, 125, 134, 136–138, 140, 145, 173
Creature Construction 73–75, 85, 98, 108, 114
Cueing 17, 166

Dancing 13, 65, 130, 140–142. *See also* ballet and ballroom
- Dancing Together 6, 9–14, 59, 86, 122, 140–144, 161, 164, 165, 175
Decision-making 3, 12, 62, 107, 176, 178

Degrees of freedom 51, 52, 62–66
Demystification 73, 75–78
Desires
- First-order desires 79, 98, 110
- Guiding desires 94–95
- Higher-order desires 42, 46, 79, 98, 111
Diachronic Control 47
Diachronicity 46–47
Dialogic Determination 143–144
Dichotomies 23, 29, 183
Dichotomous 2, 4, 20, 23, 36, 38, 128, 161, 162, 182
Dichotomy 2, 4, 21, 22, 29, 30, 36, 40, 67, 119, 161, 162, 165, 166
Direction of Fit 76
Disjunctive conceptualizations 28. *See also* non-disjunctivist
Dual Mode View 23, 24
Dualism 1, 4, 6, 17, 22, 34
Dual-Process Theory 27
Dynamic Systems Theory 125

Efficiency 26, 64, 162, 167
Efficient 3, 23, 28, 57, 178
Emergent Coordination 2, 5, 9–12, 15, 17, 18, 20, 69, 74, 90, 91, 118, 119, 122–128, 133, 138, 144, 153, 155, 157–159, 161, 162, 164–169, 171, 182, 183
Enabling 153
Enabling Conditions 11, 17, 123
Enactivism 133–146, 165
Enactivist Account of Interaction and Joint Action 122, 164
Entrainment 12, 124–127, 168
Environment 15, 22, 61, 70, 101, 117, 134, 172, 178
Experience 1, 6, 9, 18, 19, 25, 57, 64, 131, 142, 151, 153, 154, 156, 159, 173, 176, 180, 182

Fast 27, 178
First-Order Desires 79, 98, 110
Four Features of Automaticity 24–26
Four Horsemen of Automaticity 3, 22–24, 162
Full-blown Intentionality/full-blown intentional action 1, 17, 20, 31, 34, 38. *See also* intentional action

Goal-directed 30, 31, 70, 118
Goals 6, 17, 19, 30, 31, 41, 43, 45, 48, 59, 64, 74, 89, 124, 126, 129, 131, 133, 136, 159, 160, 165, 167, 172, 173, 176, 180, 182, 183
Governance 30, 31, 43, 58, 136, 168, 171, 173
Gradual Distinction 2, 4, 22, 26–29, 34, 57
Guiding Desires 94–95

Habit 15, 31, 36–38, 56, 94, 106, 142, 143
Habitual 15, 34, 37–38, 41, 61
Heuristics 72, 74, 93, 105, 106, 162, 176, 178–179, 182
Hierarchical Accounts of Autonomy 110
Higher-Level Processes 166, 167
Higher-Order Desires 42, 46, 79, 80, 98, 111
Holism 30

I Intend That We J 8, 89, 90–92, 115, 116
I We-intend X 8
I-Agency 152, 155–158
Identity 46, 111, 113, 133, 136, 137, 140, 145
If-then Plans. *See* implementation intentions
Implementation Control 58, 174–176
Implementation Intentions 30, 48
Implicit 17, 67, 97, 98, 109, 154–156, 181
Implicit Coordination 18, 19
Improvisation 10–13, 141–143, 175
Individual Agency 9, 20, 69, 74, 85, 88, 99, 101, 116, 119, 155, 170
Individual Autonomy 110
Individual Ownership Claim 42
Individualistic 8, 86
Intend That 86, 115–117
Intend To 115–117
Intention
– Intention Condition 88, 163
– Two faces of intention 36
Intentional
– intentional action 1, 2, 14, 20, 33–41, 48, 67, 94, 107, 117. *See also* full-blown intentional action
– Intentional Under a Description 40
Intentionality 9, 24, 25, 33, 170
Intentions in Action 71

Interaction 6, 17, 59, 63, 80, 107, 109, 118, 121–160, 168, 182, 183
Interdependence 6, 18, 63, 84, 88, 115, 159, 173
Interdependence Condition 88, 118, 163
Interdependencies 63, 124, 141, 143
Intermediate 4
Intermediate Coordination 18
Interpersonal Coordination 17
Interrelatedness 2, 29
Introspectable 16, 27. *See also* non-introspectable
Introspection 17, 111
I-Thou 151, 152

Joint Action 1, 2, 4–7, 9, 14, 15–19, 20, 21, 33, 51, 52, 60, 62, 65, 67, 69, 71, 84, 87, 91, 100, 102, 107, 109, 117, 121–160, 161–184
Joint Agency 179
Joint Attention 7, 159
Joint commitment 6, 9, 109, 167
Joint Habit 15
Joint Simon Task (Joint Simon Effect) 157
Joint Skills 15
Jointness 13, 18, 161, 163, 170, 179, 181–183

Knowledge 15, 41, 54, 87, 154, 178

Language Processing 3
Lower-level Processes 17, 107, 166, 174

Memory Capacity 26
Mere Activity 35–41, 48, 67
Mere Bodily Movement 1, 16, 34, 36, 38–40, 48, 183
Meshing Intentions 8
Methodological 7, 73
Methodology 69, 71, 75–78
Minimal Architecture Model 122, 128–133, 164, 165
Mirroring 6, 10
Mode Account 8
Modest Sociality 7, 84
Monitoring 129, 130, 156

Motivation 31, 43, 74, 92, 93, 99, 102, 111, 113
Motor Cognition 51, 52, 63, 132, 176
Motor Control 20, 49
Motor Intentions 36, 51, 129
Multidimensional Space 2, 4, 20
Mutual Adjustment 12
Mutual Alignment 12
Mutual Responsiveness Condition 88, 163

Naturalistic Decision Making (NDM) 60, 66, 67, 162, 176, 178
Naturalizing 71, 72
Necessary Conditions 41, 88, 115, 137, 147
Neuroscience 15
Nicomachean Ethics 34
Non-agential 18
Non-automatic 2–4, 20, 21–32, 57, 161, 162, 174, 183
Non-deliberative 17, 166
Non-disjunctivist conception 35
Non-introspectable 16, 27
Non-Summative Account 8
Normativity 16, 34, 36, 39, 105, 137

Online Control 59, 60
Orthogonal 23, 34
Ownership 111

Parallel Action 2, 5, 161, 183
Participatory Sense-Making 141, 143, 144
Passivity 39
Perception-action Matching 124, 126
Phenomenology 19, 146, 149
Planned Coordination 1, 2, 5, 9, 10, 12, 15, 20, 60, 74, 119, 122, 123, 128, 161–166, 169, 174, 175
Planning Agency 9, 36, 46, 69–119, 123, 178, 180
Planning Structures 70, 80, 81, 83, 91, 93, 96
Plans 17, 42, 45, 46, 53, 54, 60, 62, 70, 76, 77, 79, 80, 87, 92, 93, 96, 98, 107, 114, 118, 159, 171, 173, 175, 180, 183
Plural Pre-Reflective Self-Awareness 150
Plural Subject 9, 116

Policies 45, 74, 76, 80, 92, 97–102, 104, 106, 115, 119, 181
Practice 55, 56, 65, 86, 131, 180, 181
Prediction 122, 129, 131, 153–155, 157, 159, 176
Processes
– automatic 2, 4, 15, 20, 21, 23, 26, 29, 30, 57, 61, 67, 91, 122, 161, 177
– cognitive 26, 66, 124, 134, 174, 177
– controlled 1, 2, 23, 29, 30, 57
– dual-process theory 27
– higher-level 166, 167, 174
– language 3
– lower-level 17, 107, 166, 174
Propositional Attitude 7, 8, 38, 40, 111, 128, 133
Purpose 30, 31, 39, 44, 168, 171, 172
Purposeful Action 39
Purposive Agency 38, 71, 83, 96–98, 107–110, 172
Purposive Agents 70, 82, 107, 118, 173
Purposive Shared Agency 83, 84, 107, 109

Rational Limitations 106
Reason-Responsiveness 42
Reflection 43, 55, 93, 119, 181
Reflective 5, 27, 42, 79, 110
Reflexive 27, 36
Representation 25, 53, 54, 57, 123, 126, 129
Responsibility 15, 47, 110
Rules 7, 11, 21, 53, 54, 98, 99, 129, 142

Satisficing 177. *See also* heuristics
Selective Attention 62
Self-Control 16, 20–22, 33, 34, 41–45, 47, 48, 67, 70, 91, 109, 118, 169–172
Sense of Agency 146–160
Sense of Control 146–160
Sense of the Other 19, 146, 148, 149, 151, 158, 159, 182
Sense of Us 147–149
Sequencing 52, 54
Shared Agency 9, 36, 119, 121
Shared Belief 7
Shared Commitments 99–101
Shared Cooperative Activity 85, 87, 88
Shared Intentionality 33, 84, 161, 170

Shared Policies 99–102
Situation 14, 33, 57, 60, 94, 98, 99, 106, 117, 142, 177, 182
Situational 3, 6, 13, 59, 60, 66, 69, 117, 143, 154, 158, 161
Situational Awareness 59, 60, 61, 174, 177, 178, 179
Situational Control 59, 61, 91, 143
Situational Coordination 69, 175
Situational Factors 12, 117, 154, 155, 158, 175
Skill 28, 31, 36, 37, 49, 56, 57, 59, 60, 61, 65, 66, 127, 134, 142, 143, 145, 147, 165, 175, 176. *See also* joint skill
Skill Acquisition 4, 17, 51, 52, 54–57, 60, 64
Skillful 52, 57, 105, 166
Skillful Action 4, 16, 20, 34, 38, 41, 51–67, 74, 78, 107, 162, 171, 173, 174, 176–179
Skillful Joint Action 15, 21, 67, 69, 109, 141, 143, 145, 146, 161–184
Slow 27
Social Cognition 3, 27, 84, 109, 135, 136, 141, 145
Social Psychology 21, 23, 34, 47, 72, 78, 149, 178
Social Rules 100
Spectrum 2, 5, 16, 49, 165
Speech 17, 54
Stimuli 25
Stimulus 25
Strategic Control 58–60, 62, 174, 175
Structure 30, 31, 45
Subject Account 150
Subliminal 25
Sub-Personal 16
Sufficiency Conditions 86, 89, 113, 115, 117

Summative Account 8. *See also* non-summative account
Supraliminal 25
Synchronic Control 47–49
Synchronicity 47, 48, 70, 92
Synchronization 17, 127, 132, 138, 164, 175, 180, 182
Synchrony 11, 17, 125–127, 180
Synergies 63, 65, 124
System 1 27
System 2 27

Teleology 31, 39
Temporal Extendedness 46, 70, 71, 113. *See also* diachronicity
Temptation 34
The Will 40
Three Levels of Control 2, 5, 17, 18, 20, 52, 58–62, 67, 162, 170–179
Togetherness 3, 15, 18, 19, 116, 122, 146, 150, 158, 162, 179, 182
Traditional View 3
Training 13, 15, 28, 56, 178
Trigger 25, 178
Triple Mode View 28
Two faces of intentions 36

Unaware 24, 25, 40, 74
Unintentional 3, 4, 25, 28, 61
Unwilling addict 41

Value Judgment 42, 92, 101, 114
Values 7, 111

We-Agency 19, 147, 152–159, 182, 183

Index of Names

Ainslie 79
Amazeen 63
Anderson 55, 111, 112
Anscombe 37, 71, 75
Aristotle 34
Arutyunyan 64
Atmaca 126

Bacharach 19, 146
Baier 7, 14, 91, 115, 171
Baker 17
Bargh 3, 15, 21, 22, 24–26, 28–31, 127, 182
Baron 65
Bartlett 178
Baumeister 22
Bayne 154
Behne 71
Bekkering 122, 126, 131
Benson 111, 112
Bermudez 61, 62
Bernstein 62–64
Bertenthal 126
Bicknell 2, 5, 38, 58–60, 145, 176
Bizzi 63
Bodenhausen 28
Bootsma 65
Branigan 123
Brass 126
Bratman 5, 6, 8, 9, 11, 14, 16–18, 20, 32, 34–36, 40, 42–49, 59, 69–80, 82–119, 121, 122, 163, 164, 167, 173, 178–181, 184
Brinck 150–152
Brownstein 27
Bruner 23
Burger 127
Butterfill 9, 17, 18, 51, 69, 71, 83, 86, 91, 95, 109, 121–124, 126–128, 130, 132, 164, 182
Byrne 127

Cacioppo 124
Call 71
Calvo-Merino 126

Cantor 22
Carello 124
Carpenter 71
Carr 146
Casaer 63
Caspar 157, 159
Chaiken 27
Chan 35
Chant 18, 71
Chartrand 15, 18, 22, 127, 182
Cheng 18, 127
Christensen 2, 5, 38, 51, 52, 57–61, 64, 66, 143, 145, 157, 159, 171, 174, 176–178
Cialdini 106, 178
Clark 134, 144
Cleeremans 22, 157, 159
Cleland 123
Cobley 56
Coburn 22
Collins 178
Constantini 125
Craver 72
Cross 126
Cunningham 30, 31, 44

Dale 9, 17, 19, 62, 65, 71, 121–125, 138, 146, 164
Davidson 37, 40, 70, 71
Davis 36, 42
De Bruijn 131
De Houwer 3, 21, 26–28
De Jaegher 134–141, 144, 145
De Lange 131
Deakin 56
DeCoster 27
DeGroot 176
DeSteno 127, 182
Deutsch 27
Di Paolo 134–141, 144, 145
Douskos 39
Doyen 22
Drews 57
Dreyfus, H.L. 55
Dreyfus, S.E. 55

https://doi.org/10.1515/9783110671315-010

Ekstrom 110
Engbert 157
Engell 28
Ericsson 55, 56, 58
Evans 27

Fazio 27
Feldman 22
Ferrand 65
Fiske 27
Fitts 55, 56, 57
Fowler 17, 123
Frankfurt 16, 36, 38, 39, 41, 42, 46, 79, 80, 110, 111, 113, 172
Frankish 27
Fridland 2, 5, 30, 34, 38, 51, 52, 55, 58–62, 64, 66, 143, 145, 171, 174, 177, 178
Fromkin 54
Fujita 16, 22, 28, 30, 31, 44, 45, 47, 48, 136, 168, 171

Gallagher 154
Galton 55
Ganesh 131
Ganis 59
Gaunt 27
Gawronski 23, 27, 28
Gendler 36
Gibson 134
Gigerenzer 177, 178
Gilbert, D.T. 27
Gilbert, M. 5, 6, 8, 9, 14, 18, 27, 42, 75, 84, 109, 112, 122, 167
Glaser 126
Goldman 71
Gollwitzer 24, 30
Gonzago 127
Goodman 123, 125
Graf 131
Grafton 126
Grice 73–76
Gurfinkel 64
Guzman 17

Haddock 35
Haggard 126, 154, 157, 159

Hamilton 126
Harris 22
Hassin 15, 22, 28
Heatherton 22
Hertwig 177, 178
Herzog 177, 178
Heuer 63
Hirst 56
Hornsby 35, 42
Horstkötter 15, 16, 21, 22, 30, 34, 35, 44, 48, 180
Hove 127
Hursthouse 36
Husserl 146, 152

Insko 127
Isenhower 123, 125

James 52
Jantzen 17
Jefferis 18, 127
Johnston-Laird 59
Jordan 54

Kahneman 27, 103, 104, 107, 177, 178
Kelso 17
Kimmel 141, 142–146, 165, 175
Klein 22, 66, 177
Knoblich 9
Kosobud 126
Kosslyn 59
Krasnow 65

Lagarde 17
Lakin 18, 127
Lashley 54
Liberman 30, 31, 44
Lieberman 27
List 18
Locke 113
Logan 28
Longo 126

Macrae 17, 126
Malfait 131
Marchiori 22

Marsh 65, 123–125
Martens 18, 19, 141, 146, 149
Massion 63
McCulloch 28, 30
McGinnies 23
McIlwain 2, 5, 51, 57–59, 61, 66, 145, 176, 177
Mechsner 57, 59
Mele 34
Merleau-Ponty 38
Metzinger 72
Miles 17, 126
Miller 8, 54
Mirskii 64
Mischel 22
Moll 71
Moore 10
Moors 3, 21, 23, 26–29
Mottet 65
Murphy 127
Mussa-Ivaldi 63
Mylopoulos 51, 52, 58

Neisser 56
Newman-Norlund 131
Nind 17, 126
Nisbett 25
Noë 134

O'Brien 17, 34–36, 38, 95, 125, 138
Oshana 111
O'Shaughnessy 40, 41
Oullier 17, 125
Ouyang 127, 182

Pacherie 5, 18, 38, 51, 52, 58, 83, 91, 109, 152–156, 158, 174
Papineau 57, 58
Pashler 22
Passingham 126
Pettit 18, 112
Petty 27
Pew 56
Pichon 22
Pickering 123
Pollard 37, 38

Postman 23
Preston 95, 96, 174, 180
Preuschl 141
Prinz 126
Pylyshyn 61, 62

Reddy 150–152
Reinoud 65
Richardson 17, 65, 123–125
Risen 127
Rizzolatti 126
Roelofs 18
Rohde 134, 137
Rosch 133
Rosenbaum 52, 53, 55, 59, 63, 64
Rudell 156
Ryle 75, 178

Santana 123
Sartre 114
Schack 52, 57, 59
Schilbach 151
Schlicht 19, 141, 146
Schmid 19, 112, 115, 146, 149–151, 153, 170
Schmidt 17, 58, 123–125, 138
Schneider 55
Schuch 131
Schutz 146
Schweikard 112
Searle 5, 6, 8, 9, 14, 15, 19, 24, 40, 84, 89, 109, 112, 122, 146, 147, 148, 149, 150, 151, 153, 159
Sebanz 9, 17, 18, 86, 95, 121–124, 126–128, 130, 132, 165, 182
Semin 124
Shaffer 56
Sherman 23, 27, 28
Shiffrin 28, 55
Shockley 17, 123
Simon 66, 103–105, 107, 154, 156, 157, 177
Sinigaglia 51, 126
Slovic 103, 177, 178
Smith 27, 35
Somervell 127
Soroka 127
Spelke 56

Squire 55, 56
Stoutland 7, 91, 115
Strack 27
Strayer 57
Sutton 2, 5, 38, 51, 57–59, 61, 66, 145, 163, 166, 175–177, 180
Swinnen 63

Thompson 133, 134, 137
Tice 22
Tipper 131
Todd 177, 178
Tollefsen 7–9, 17, 19, 62, 65, 69, 71, 90, 91, 121–125, 138, 146, 164
Tomasello 69, 71
Trope 23, 27, 28, 30, 31, 44
Tuomela 8, 112, 122
Turvey 63, 124
Tversky 103, 104, 107, 177, 178

Uleman 15, 22
Ullsperger 131

Valdesolo 127, 182

Vallacher 58
Van Schie 131
Varela 133–135, 137
Vargas 95, 103, 104
Velleman 7, 14, 16, 35, 42, 91, 95
Vesper 9, 121, 123, 128–132, 164
Vohs 22
Von Cramon 131

Waroquier 22
Watson 42
Wegner 15, 22, 58
Wheatley 16, 22
William 58
Wilmerding-Pett 65
Wilson 25, 127, 131
Wiltermuth 17, 127
Wittgenstein 35, 39, 108, 150
Wohlschlager 157
Wu 61, 62

Yaffe 95, 103, 104

Zahavi 17, 19, 146, 149–153, 159